Crisis Reporters, Emotions, and Technology

Johana Kotišová

Crisis Reporters, Emotions, and Technology

An Ethnography

palgrave
macmillan

Johana Kotišová
Faculty of Arts
Charles University
Prague, Czech Republic

The author of the fictional news report in the Postscript is Koen Vidal.
The author of the drawings is Peter Van Goethem.

ISBN 978-3-030-21427-2   ISBN 978-3-030-21428-9 (eBook)
https://doi.org/10.1007/978-3-030-21428-9

© The Editor(s) (if applicable) and The Author(s) 2019, corrected publication 2022. This book is an open access publication
Open Access This book is licensed under the terms of the Creative Commons Attribution 4.0 International License (http://creativecommons.org/licenses/by/4.0/), which permits use, sharing, adaptation, distribution and reproduction in any medium or format, as long as you give appropriate credit to the original author(s) and the source, provide a link to the Creative Commons licence and indicate if changes were made.
The images or other third party material in this book are included in the book's Creative Commons licence, unless indicated otherwise in a credit line to the material. If material is not included in the book's Creative Commons licence and your intended use is not permitted by statutory regulation or exceeds the permitted use, you will need to obtain permission directly from the copyright holder.
The use of general descriptive names, registered names, trademarks, service marks, etc. in this publication does not imply, even in the absence of a specific statement, that such names are exempt from the relevant protective laws and regulations and therefore free for general use.
The publisher, the authors and the editors are safe to assume that the advice and information in this book are believed to be true and accurate at the date of publication. Neither the publisher nor the authors or the editors give a warranty, express or implied, with respect to the material contained herein or for any errors or omissions that may have been made. The publisher remains neutral with regard to jurisdictional claims in published maps and institutional affiliations.

Cover image: © Jung Ho Kim / EyeEm//Getty; all rights reserved, used with permission.
Cover design: eStudioCalamar

This Palgrave Macmillan imprint is published by the registered company Springer Nature Switzerland AG
The registered company address is: Gewerbestrasse 11, 6330 Cham, Switzerland

The original version of this book was revised. A correction to this book can be found at https://doi.org/10.1007/978-3-030-21428-9_7

To all cynics

Preface

What follows is a research monograph based on in-depth interviews with real people—47 European "crisis reporters"—and ethnographic fieldwork conducted at real places—in three different newsrooms at Czech media organizations—between June 2015 and January 2019.

It takes a form of a novel about James, a fictional journalist, taking off for an unpredictable business trip. In other words, the ethnographic data and analysis are framed by a fictional, albeit minimalist, story. As such, the monograph combines factual and fictional narratives, the latter being illustrative—or, to put it in literary terms, serving as an allegory—of the story told and the arguments put forward within the factual narrative.

The interrelations between the factual and the fictional narratives, together with their functions, are explained in detail in the section called "Creative Nonfiction and the Research Method" at the near end of the text. It is important to stress at the beginning, however, that the fictional narrative, first, does not in any way diminish or relativize the authenticity of the data, and, second, is not an end in itself. Furthermore, to anticipate the inevitable question "who speaks?" it needs to be said that the interpretations of the data and the work with the scholarly literature are almost entirely a product of my mind (which, in turn, is a product of diverse authors and factors).

The word "almost" means that the research participants were included in all stages of the research process including the writing phase, and thus actively refined both the fictional and the factual narratives, particularly the endings, based on their sense of the accuracy of my provisional analysis.

Most obviously, the result of this research process is an account of journalists' emotions and crisis reporting—it reconstructs the journalists' emotional labor and development under crisis conditions and within their professional, organizational, and technological milieu. On this plane, the book attempts to describe the complex interplay between journalists, media organizations, technologies, journalists' professional ideology, and crisis events.

Simultaneously, the study attempts to provide an empirically grounded reflection on absolute rationalism and contemporary forms of power over life and bodies circulating in organizations—in this case, the media—intertwined with the spreading of cynical ideology and leading to the "forgetting of being as such."

Last but not least, the monograph points to an immediate problem, specific forms of precarity of certain groups of journalists, and suggests some modest and partial solutions.

The fictional narrative is, among other things, a rhetorical strategy that attempts to bring the three planes together by illustrating—in a subtle, intimate way—how media professionals learn to think and act within crisis situations.

The "Creative Nonfiction and the Research Method" section explains in detail how the research was conducted and how the book was written. Although the order of the chapters invites the reader to first read about the journey, and to consult the method only afterward, it is possible to start with the "Creative Nonfiction and the Research Method" and read it as a standard methodological chapter.

Prague, Czech Republic   Johana Kotišová

To freeze: to become hardened into ice or into a solid body.
to become hard or stiffened because of loss of heat.
to suffer the effects or sensation of intense cold.
to lose warmth of feeling.
to become speechless or immobilized.
to stop suddenly and remain motionless.
to become obstructed by the formation of ice.
to die or be injured because of frost or cold.
to become fixed to something by or as if by the action of frost.
to become unfriendly, secretive, or aloof (often fol. by *up*).
to become temporarily inoperable; cease to function (often fol. by *up*).

Acknowledgments

I would like to thank primarily all the interviewees and research participants. I cannot stress enough how enriching it was to meet all these interesting, intelligent, reflexive, and devoted people. Many thanks also to those who kindly granted me access to their media, newsrooms, and teams, and those who helped me to gain the access or to arrange the interviews. Special thanks to those research participants who took the time to read the draft and helped me to make the story more accurate.

Many thanks to Lucy Batrouney and the three anonymous reviewers for their invaluable comments and suggestions.

Many thanks to Christophe Dubois, Csaba Szaló, Eva Šlesingerová, Ondřej Kaleta, Petr Mezihorák, and Simon Smith for all the discussions, for the time they spent with various phases of the draft, for their inspiring thoughts and remarks, and for their unshakeable support.

Thanks to Peter van Goethem for the drawings of the frozen city, and for inspiration; to Koen Vidal for his refreshing ideas, his spirit, and for the Postscript; to Benjamin Vail for his sensitive proofreading and his helpfulness; and to Vojtěch Kolman and Ivan David for their effort to make the book better accessible.

Thank you to my colleagues Petr Szczepanik and Pavel Zahrádka for their support; to Frédéric Schoenaers and all my colleagues at CRIS, primarily Sophie Thunus, and to Česká televize and Lidové noviny. Thank you to Charles University, Prague, for funding this open-access book.

Thank you to my father Jan for his will to life.

A warm thank you to Ondřej for his supernatural love.

Funding

This work was supported by the European Regional Development Fund project "Creativity and Adaptability as Conditions of the Success of Europe in an Interrelated World" (reg. no.: CZ.02.1.01/0.0/0.0/16_01 9/0000734) implemented at Charles University, Faculty of Arts. The project is carried out under the ERDF Call "Excellent Research" and its output is aimed at employees of research organizations and Ph.D. students.

The book is partly based on a Ph.D. dissertation thesis entitled "Freezing: An Ethnography of Crisis Reporters," defended in January 2018 at the University of Liège in Belgium and Masaryk University in Czechia. Some of the data that the book is based on had been published in Journalism and European Journal of Communication as a part of the Ph.D. curriculum.

EUROPEAN UNION
European Structural and Investment Funds
Operational Programme Research,
Development and Education

MINISTRY OF EDUCATION,
YOUTH AND SPORTS

Contents

1 An Introduction to Crisis Reporting: Setting Out   1

2 Defining a Crisis: Boarding   29

3 The Emotional Experience of Crisis Reporters: The Journey   69

4 Articulating Journalists' Emotional Experiences of Crisis: Touching Down   119

5 Emotions, Technology, and Crisis Reconsidered: Ending   171

6 Creative Nonfiction and the Research Method   189

Correction to: Crisis Reporters, Emotions, and Technology   C1

Postscript: Travel Slow and Light   221

Index   225

List of Figures

Image 1.1	The concepts of crisis, emotions, and technology and the current streams of research on media and crisis. Drawing (on the issue of *Le Soir* from 23 March 2016) by the author	8
Image 1.2	A frozen city. Drawing by Peter Van Goethem, 2017. Courtesy of the artist	18
Image 2.1	Demonstration on 17 November 2015, Prague, organized by Bloc Against Islam (Blok proti Islámu), to support Czech president's opinions on immigration and Islam. Picture taken by the author as a part of her fieldwork in *Czech Television*	34
Image 2.2	Demonstration on 17 November 2015, Prague, organized by Bloc Against Islam (Blok proti Islámu), to support Czech president's opinions on immigration and Islam. Picture taken by the author as a part of her fieldwork in *Czech Television*	35
Image 2.3	A frozen city. Drawing by Peter Van Goethem, 2017. Courtesy of the artist	57
Image 4.1	Albert Camus' historic lecture, "The Human Crisis," performed by actor Viggo Mortensen, New York City, 2016. Source: *YouTube*, "Albert Camus's 'The Human Crisis' read by Viggo Mortensen, 70 years later"; channel: Columbia Maison Française. Screenshot taken by the author	121
Image 4.2	A control room in *Czech Television*, Autumn 2015. Picture taken by the author	122
Image 4.3	A frozen city. Drawing by Peter Van Goethem, 2017. Courtesy of the artist	140

Image 4.4	*Czech Television*'s manual for breaking news obtained during the fieldwork, Autumn 2015, translated from Czech by the author. Screenshot of the Word document taken by the author	151
Image 5.1	A frozen city. Drawing by Peter Van Goethem, 2017. Courtesy of the artist	172
Image 6.1	The author's press credentials issued during the fieldwork in *The People's Newspaper*, Autumn 2016. Picture taken by the author	212

CHAPTER 1

An Introduction to Crisis Reporting: Setting Out

James accepted his boss' offer—or rather demand—to report on the catastrophe at the island of San Lorenzo with a sense of responsibility. Not that he naïvely believed that his individual action would matter, locally or globally. Rather, he had made the choice to enjoy the game while sticking to some journalistic principles and ideals that he maintained and even believed in.

Apart from the frozen corpses that were rumored on Twitter, James did not really know what to expect. After all, it was supposed to be his first experience with crisis reporting. He was therefore making a thorough research into anything relevant and, after that, less relevant. While waiting for his flight to San Lorenzo in the departure lounge and scrolling through the web, he eventually chanced on several personal confessions from experienced reporters.

"I never thought I'd get PTSD. I was calm, rational and decisive. I enjoyed being in charge of large editorial teams. I felt I could detach myself from tough situations when needed. (…) The flashbacks, the anxiety, my emotional numbness and poor sleep had long worried my wife, Mary," the editor Dean Yates, who had been working for *Reuters* for 23 years, wrote in a special report for the news agency (Yates 2016). In a podcast recorded for War College, he expanded upon his current emotional state: "Even crying, for example. One of the problems that I found, I just … I find it hard to really express my emotions. Because I've been emotionally numb for so many years" (*War College* 2016). His post-traumatic stress disorder (PTSD) resulted from the long-term stress he

© The Author(s) 2019
J. Kotišová, *Crisis Reporters, Emotions, and Technology*,
https://doi.org/10.1007/978-3-030-21428-9_1

had experienced as a reporter, covering, among other things, the tsunami in Indonesia's Aceh province in 2004, the Iraq War between 2003 and 2008, and the Bali bombings in 2002. In particular, Dean struggled with feelings of guilt after two Middle Eastern colleagues for whom he was responsible were shot dead by a US Apache helicopter. Also, he could not get rid of the images of thousands of corpses he saw while covering the Indonesian tsunami. Every now and then, they popped up in his head. But it was only in 2016 that Dean and his family fully felt the effects. "I had played down the symptoms, denied I had a problem. Five months later I'd be in a psychiatric ward," he wrote at *Reuters*' website.

In another *Reuters* story (Joelving 2010), former *BBC* reporter Chris Cramer, suffering from a similar problem, admitted: "The last thing you wanted to do in those days was to admit to your boss that you kind of lost your nerve. (…) Newsrooms were very macho places, you know." Cramer had been carrying his PTSD since 1980 when he, together with 25 other people, was taken hostage in Teheran by six Iranian gunmen.

"I will be honest, I … I … I reached a plane where I couldn't identify the things that were horrific. I couldn't even notice that there were things that were happening around me that were important or significant or that an international audience or Arab audience or anyone should actually see," Rami Jarrah, a Syrian reporter covering the besieged city of Aleppo at the end of 2016, said in an interview with Christiane Amanpour for her *CNN* show (*Amanpour* 2016). "You mean because you got numb to it, Rami?" Christiane asked for clarification. Rami replied, redirecting viewers' attention back to the people of Aleppo: "The people inside are totally numb. They don't see what is happening around them anymore." Rami had the "advantage" that he, as a domestic reporter, could cover the airstrikes and bombings by Assad and the Russians on the spot in the increasingly dangerous areas, since the regime had mostly stopped giving out press credentials to international media professionals.

However, not even distant reporting on Aleppo was a walk in the park. Kareem Shaheen, a Middle East reporter for *The Guardian*, based in Beirut, in an article called "Covering the last days of Aleppo: Even from afar, the heart breaks" (Shaheen 2016), ruminated: "how do you maintain a dispassionate distance when you've been, for three months, looking at the bodies of the children those doctors had to treat? Or stayed up through the night to listen in to the palpable horror in the voices of those living under the bombs? How could you not pray for their safety, and ask them to take care of themselves?"

There was a unique and deeply intimate experience behind each of the quotations. At the same time, they were all journalists' publicly shared narratives about the personal consequences of covering various crisis situations—post-traumatic stress disorder, emotional numbness, feelings of guilt, denial of emotional problems, physical risks, loss of insightfulness, neglecting one's own emotional health when face to face with the tragedies of other people, trauma caused by witnessing distant suffering, confrontation with the paradoxes of passion and detachment, and acting and observing. Obviously, the journalists' own stories accounted primarily for the emotional experiences that ultimately pervade their social and professional lives. All the stories, placing the journalists themselves at the center of the narrative, were also cases of extreme, escalated visibility of journalists' own emotions being reported in the news. It was one of the few occasions when James saw that journalists *were* the story, not just writing it.

After a short moment of empathy, he conceived a distaste for the journalists. Like some of his colleagues—Bob, Diego, but mainly Farrukh—he actually disliked when the reporters brought themselves into focus, thus overshadowing the "real" victims of crises.

Yet, based not only on what he had just read but also on his past conversations with his colleagues and friends who often, usually late and over a glass, brought up "how it felt" when they were covering this or that crisis, he had to acknowledge that the reporters' own mental well-being at work might have been a problem—both in itself for them and in affecting their reporting.

The emotional aspects of crisis reporting have been also a constantly under-researched and under-theorized issue within media and journalism studies (Beckett and Deuze 2016; Peters 2011). Apart from a few recent papers directly focused on journalists' emotional labor (e.g. Hopper and Huxford 2015), media and journalism research, including the orthodox works on crisis reporting (e.g. Cottle 2009), have not had much to say about journalists' emotions. The vast majority of research on the media in crises focuses on the coverage of crisis situations. Those studies that address journalists' practices and professionalism mention emotions only in the margins. Many—most often quantitative, and frequently normative—studies of crisis reporting deal with general framing, sourcing and gatekeeping strategies, or representation of actors in the crises (e.g. Ben-Yehuda et al. 2013; Falkheimer and Olsson 2015; Van Der Meer et al. 2016; Van Leuven et al. 2013). Second, leaving aside the relatively few works on ethnographic, new, or literary journalism that focus directly on journalists' personal engagement, immersion, and related genres (e.g. Pauly 2014), most studies addressing journalists' *practices and professional culture* still mention emotions only in the margins, stressing the complex and ambivalent relation of personal attachment/detachment to objectivity, truth, and professionalism (Andén-Papadopoulos and Pantti 2013; Tumber 2006; cf. Glück 2016). Journalists' emotions and their effect on reporting remain black boxes, elephants in the room of journalism studies. The low interest in journalists' emotions within existing research on the media is particularly noticeable when compared to the extensive research dedicated to the emotionality of other professionals—such as doctors and caretakers—within the realm of the sociology of work (e.g. Hayward and Tuckey 2011). Third, the emotional risks and well-being of journalists, mainly those who are responsible for conveying traumatic events to the public, have come under scrutiny rather from think tanks, research organizations, and professional associations such as the Dart Centre for Journalism and Trauma (DCJT) and the International News Safety Institute (INSI). The researchers attached to these institutes agree that covering crises and repeated exposure to drastic user-generated content can bring about serious psychological effects: post-traumatic stress disorder, headache, and early waking syndrome (Dubberley et al. 2015; Hight and Smyth 2003; Sambrook 2016). But since their aim is to offer evidence-based recommendations and to design individual training programs for those covering war zones, terrorism, or natural disasters, they do not attempt to put the findings into theoretical and social context. Thus, although all these research streams concern crisis reporters' emotional culture, directly or indirectly, they either fail to open the black box, or stress the structural and normative aspects of newswork at the expense of journalists' individually lived experiences, or fail to provide tools that would enable contextualized understanding and critique.

The media are limited neither to words and representations nor to sets of values and principles; they are complexes of persons, things such as technological devices and architecture, texts, meanings, and power relations (Hansen 2006; Lievrouw 2014; Packer and Crofts Wiley 2012). In particular, there are journalists' thoughts and practices—strategic actions, their unintended consequences, more or less conscious choices of words, use of practical devices—that lead to the construction of frames and other (desired) effects that, taken together, constitute media content and foreshadow its social and political biography. Thus, it is important to examine the influences of these various factors on the reporting of crises (Neumann and Fahmy 2016). In a crisis, it is profoundly important to ask *how* journalists are working within the media organization, to study their routines in a broad sense, all the more so that recent changes in media logic—the increasing importance of interpretation and speculation at the expense of description—give the journalists a more prominent position in the news (Nord and Strömbäck 2006). Since journalists' emotions are part of the media complexes of people, devices and other material artifacts, texts, and power relations, they are also vital for the processes of crisis reporting and their outcomes. As Charlie Beckett and Mark Deuze write, especially with digital, networked journalism, "emotion is becoming a much more important dynamic in how news is produced and consumed" (Beckett and Deuze 2016: 2). Likewise, Karin Wahl-Jorgensen (2016) sees emotion as a central force shaping the news agenda and enabling new forms of engagement among audience members. Finally, Mervi Pantti (2010) speaks about the normalness of emotion in television news and identifies a shift in journalists' perceptions of the use of emotion in favor of its greater acceptance.

James glanced up to the ceiling; one of the light bulbs was flickering. Then, his gaze, usually searching and radiant with interest but today rather groggy, slid down to an empty massage chair directly opposite him. The bleak space of the early morning hall, albeit situated in the heart of the "First World," was already stirring up melancholy.

Studying journalists' emotions is particularly essential in the field of research on crisis reporting. Journalists' emotions lie precisely at the core of the paradox of the traditional journalistic commitment to objectivity/detachment and witnessing other people's suffering (Andén-Papadopoulos and Pantti 2013; Richards and Rees 2011). In crisis reporting, more than in other journalistic fields, journalists' position between an involved actor and detached observer, entailing the dichotomies of engaged/non-participating, active/passive, empathic/dispassionate, or close/distant, becomes more palpable and pressing (e.g. Tumber 2011). Moreover, journalists and media easily become central to the politics of conflicts (e.g. Altheide 2004; Hoskins and O'Loughlin 2010), which imparts specific kind of importance to crisis reporters' practices, thoughts, and feelings.

How should (and can) I, James thought, live through, let in, sympathize with, work with, let out, and use for the sake of the story people's tragedies that constitute crises? (How) can I stay detached, neutral, emotionally disinterested, when I actually *am* there? And do I want to?

He looked at the departure board. The flight to San Lorenzo was 35 minutes late, so he still had almost two hours until boarding. Although he was one of those who felt more comfortable on the move, armed only with independence, and who showed little interest in the steady, calm, and homely kind of happiness, he was never able to focus on work at airports—these boundary zones, these no man's lands. Ruminating about the problem of journalists' emotions, and immersed in the questions it raised, James' thoughts kept wandering to his chaotic memories of colleagues' stories, his own college years, and his newsroom experience.

Intermingling with, at times following yet often going well beyond James' thoughts, this study seeks to enhance the existing research on the interrelations between communication media and crisis situations by focusing on crisis reporters'—James' colleagues'—emotional culture. In particular, it deals with their emotional experience at work and how it is articulated by and in their professional practices. It addresses three main research questions: What does "crisis" in "crisis reporting" mean? What is the emotional experience of crisis reporters? How does the newsmaking technology articulate journalists' emotional experience of crisis?

Each of the questions gives rise to further sub-questions, such as the following: How do reporters perceive the place and role of emotions in their news/reports? What coping mechanisms and practices do they use? How is their psychological well-being addressed by media organizations?

STATE OF THE ART

Vague Ideas of Crisis, Emotions, Technology

James, having graduated a few years before and being rather more excited about any and all knowledge than focusing on crisis reporting, had only a vague idea about the basic, sensitizing concepts that would guide this study (Blumer 1954; Bowen 2006): crisis, emotions, and technology.

He knew the original medical (and legal and theological) meaning of the word "crisis" (Vincze 2014; see the chapter "Defining a Crisis: Boarding"). But the word could be used and was being used in (m)any other context(s). He was also aware that "crisis reporting" had long ago become a classic field of both journalism and journalism research. Media scholars define the catchphrase "crisis" as a sudden, unpredictable, or challenging event that may pose a danger to society and create strong uncertainty, time pressure, and confusion that challenge journalistic practices and standards (Van Der Meer et al. 2016; Vincze 2014), and contrast "crisis" with "normal times" (McDonald and Lawrence 2004).

James experienced emotions as "thoughts somehow 'felt' in flushes, pulses, 'movements' of our livers, minds, hearts, stomachs, skin, (…) embodied thoughts, thoughts seeped with the apprehension that 'I am involved'" (Rosaldo 1984: 143). As "embodied thoughts," emotions are not only individually biological/psychological but also to a large extent culturally determined, defined, and shaped practices of feeling and thinking, lying at the intersection of political, biological, and social bodies of human beings (Scheer 2012; Scheper-Hughes and Lock 1987). Correspondingly, "emotional experience" entails both automatic responses and active doings: emotions can be mobilized, named, communicated, and regulated (see Hochschild 1983; Illouz 2007; Scheer 2012).

The third concept, technology, was initially supposed to conceptualize the link between James as a human being with his bodily sensations subjected to outside forces, and the situation of crisis that he was just about to enter—things with which he would be constitutively entangled (Orlikowski 2007) while covering a crisis situation. However, conceiving technologies as mere devices would be inaccurate, because the fact that James had a voice recorder and a camera in his backpack was indistinguishable from his position as a journalistic semi-rookie working for a particular media company. The sum of things, power vectors, processes, and signs that linked James the journalist to his context, appeared to be best conceptualized very broadly as a complex of technologies of production, technologies of sign systems, technologies of power, and technologies of the self (Foucault 1988). This "technology" would encompass material, immaterial, organic, and inorganic conditions and means of news production; the sign systems employed throughout newswork and especially for making news; embodied power relations, for example expectations from management and codified professional principles; and the ways of handling one's self, including bodily emotions (see Du Gay 1996; Greene 2012; Hay 2012; Packer and Crofts Wiley 2012).

James felt restless. Too much time for doing nothing, too little time for starting to do something. From habit, he pulled out an old issue of *Le Soir* and started aimlessly leafing through its pages.

Although, for now, the sensitizing concepts seem rather abstract, in between them there appear three concrete streams of existing research that interlink the former, each of them in one way or another related to emotions in crisis reporting (Image 1.1).

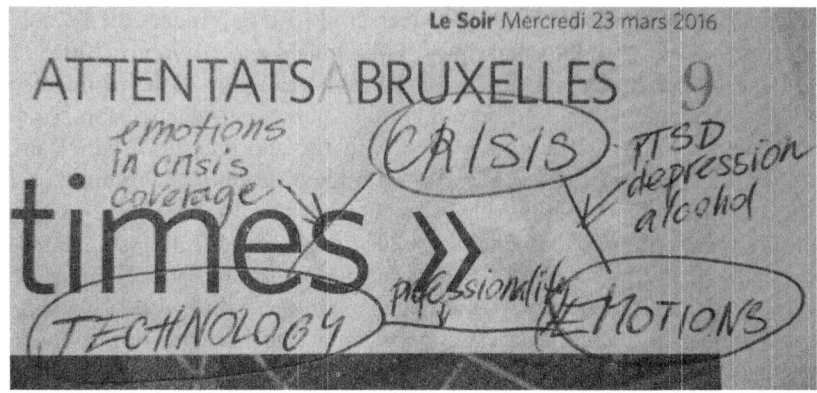

Image 1.1 The concepts of crisis, emotions, and technology and the current streams of research on media and crisis. Drawing (on the issue of *Le Soir* from 23 March 2016) by the author

The knowledge that had emerged within the three relevant streams of research, namely studies of crisis coverage; conceptualizations of emotionality, objectivity, and professionalism; and applied research of reporters' emotions, is a useful starting point. Although they put one-sided emphasis on media content or, contrarily, on principles, norms, and values, or let the description float, all the current research streams are mutually interconnected by the very practices and emotions of journalists. Moreover, they emerge at the gap sites between, and at the margins of, the concepts of crisis, technology, and emotions.

First, the research on (emotions in) crisis coverage attempts to grasp how the technology of newsmaking enters, but also constitutes a crisis event, and how the latter challenges the technology. (While focusing on outcomes of reporting, however, it cannot take into account journalists' "raw" emotions.) Second, the work on emotionality and objectivity in journalistic professionalism investigates the place and the role of emotions within the newsmaking machine. (But with a few exceptions, it does not account for a possible change in the traditional, emotionally detached professionalism that a crisis event can bring about.) Third, the applied research on journalists' mental difficulties well describes the entanglement of human beings' emotions and crisis events (but fails to establish a theoretically solid and unequivocal relation with the complex technological context of crisis reporting).

Emotions in Crisis Coverage

James got to the last page of *Le Soir*. Annoyed by the monotone frustration it radiated, he put it away.

Given the importance of the news values on negativity or "bad news" (Galtung and Ruge 1965; Harcup and O'Neill 2001), it is not surprising that crisis reports and events in general attract the public, media workers, and media researchers. The interrelations of media messages and wars, conflicts, terror attacks, natural disasters, environmental catastrophes, economic depressions, technological breakdowns, transportation disasters, and so on have been thematized by major media scholars (e.g. Allan et al. 2000; Cottle 2009; Tumber 2006; Zelizer and Allan 2011). Much of the research and theory stresses the shift toward a milieu in which the media and the news become involved in decision-making processes, and thus central to the politics of conflicts (Altheide 2004; Hjarvard 2008; Hoskins and O'Loughlin, 2010). The "CNN effect," referring to the process by which global broadcasting companies, by transmitting scenes of human suffering, prompt shifts in (trans)national foreign policies and can even stimulate humanitarian interventions backed by military forces (Cottle 2009), has also been thoroughly investigated. To mention just a few examples, Hemda Ben-Yehuda et al. (2013: 72), Toni G. L. A. Van Der Meer et al. (2016), and Rico Neumann and Shahira Fahmy (2016) have argued that by making crisis news, journalists may affect escalation processes. According to the researchers, framing transforms events through filtering and reflecting images of reality in world politics, so that, for example, chasing after ratings may bring about a rise in tensions or create panic. In short, the news media not only communicate crises to the public but also discursively and, at times, tangibly constitute them (see Van Loon 2002).

It is not unjustified, then, that the vast majority of research on the media and various kinds of crisis focuses on media coverage of the latter. The classic works on crisis reporting such as Daniel C. Hallin's *The "Uncensored War": The media in Vietnam* (1986) and Simon Cottle's *Global Crisis Reporting: Journalism in the Global Age* (2009) are based primarily on analysis of media content and media construction of crises, which provides background for speculating about the effect of media content in national or global societies.

Even James had read Hallin and Cottle—nearly all journalism students did peek into this hall of fame.

Hallin describes in great detail the history of reporting on the Vietnam War, criticizes what TV news and the papers had to say about it, while showing the apparently growing prominence of the media. He not only investigates and engagingly depicts the representation of different phases of the war, and of its main protagonists and antagonists (good American "round-eyes" and the bad guys from the Viet Cong) but also traces the mutual effects of television/press coverage of the war and military/political decisions. Indeed, one of the most important and interesting motives of his book is (the limits of) television's role in the collapse of consensus within American society. However, any claims related to this issue inevitably remain hypothetical: studying media effects is epistemologically deeply problematic, such that the debate whether empirical research can show that specific messages transmitted by television have any specific effects on their audiences remains unresolved (e.g. Livingstone 1996), and research empirically based primarily on analysis of media *content* can only speculate about media effects. Yet, Hallin very convincingly shows the ambivalence inherent to (American) journalism: the paradox that the great tales of journalistic heroism are based on reporters' feelings that they need to question the people in power and that their work is grounded in political independence, while the media have become integrated into the process of government. What a pity that the book, drawing also on interviews with journalists involved in the war, does not have much to say about the anthropological—or rather human—dimension of American journalism during the war, as if journalists were standardized executors of certain journalistic principles. The author only hints at their (emotional) experience, simultaneously acknowledging and relativizing its importance by stressing the US domestic political context of the war:

> Surely it made a difference, for instance, that many journalists were shocked both by the brutality of the war and by the gap between what they were told by top officials and what they saw and heard in the field, and were free to report all this. But it is also clear that the administration's problems with the 'fourth branch of government' resulted in large part from political divisions at home. (Hallin 1986: 213)

In short, Hallin has very little to say about how journalists themselves thought about what they did.

By comparison, Cottle does not focus on an individual crisis, but explores and theorizes processes of social construction in the mediation of various global crises. In other words, he looks into how global crises become defined, deliberated, and sensationalized—or denied, hidden, forgotten by the world's news media. While addressing "the media's role within globalization's dark side" and "how media feature within and frame particular global crises" (Cottle 2009: 26), he demonstrates how some of journalism's principles, for example, news values, fuel and shape media interest in crises of a specific scope, duration, and geographic context, and even touches upon the emotionality of reporting. In particular, while discussing the role of the media in natural disasters, the author shows how the events become ritualized and subjected to the rhetoric of national collectivity and morality. Like Hallin, Cottle deals primarily with crisis coverage, its role among audiences, and its political context, in the process rendering individual journalists invisible. In his book, "global journalism" or "foreign correspondence" is mostly approached as institutions, depersonalized systems of practices and exercises. Neither of the authors really looks *inside* journalism.

Other orthodox authors turn even more outward. For example, Robert M. Entman, together with his colleagues, studies connections between frame competition and political conflict, and identifies the weak relationship between the frames dominating the news and the facts on the ground that are essential for policymaking (Entman et al. 2009; Knüpfer and Entman 2018).

Thus, all these authors analyze media content and speculate about its effects in political contexts. None of them, however, enters the backstage of crisis reporting by taking into account journalists' experiences and perspectives. (At the same time, they all imply that how journalists experience a certain crisis is vital for what the coverage looks like, and thus how the public perceives the crisis, and thus how the coverage helps to shape globalized emotions and cosmopolitan pity, and thus bring into being people's sense of belonging to the rest of the world and their willingness to act.)

The same applies to many other studies of crisis reporting that deal not only with framing, but also with sourcing, gatekeeping strategies, and representation of perpetrators. The studies depict crisis coverage as generally less objective and factual (Nord and Strömbäck, 2006; Olsson and Nord 2015), but also less interpretive than political news (Olsson and Nord 2015); as more biased, relying heavily on official political and police sources (Falkheimer and Olsson 2015; Van Leuven et al. 2013), delayed in comparison to social media (Pang 2013); and as emotional. For example, Ian McDonald and Regina Lawrence in their research of television news after September 2011 noticed that the coverage of the terrorist attack was significantly emotional; in early September 11 coverage, emotional content even outweighed informational content (McDonald and Lawrence 2004; see also Zelizer and Allan 2011). Thus, crisis coverage is considered to be of lower quality (Olsson and Nord 2015), even though— given its centrality to the politics of conflicts—the professional incentives to produce the best possible news may be higher than in "normal times" (McDonald and Lawrence 2004). In line with the focus of the researchers on media coverage and with the tendency to investigate connections of media coverage and political decisions, diverse examples of "failures" of media performance are often criticized without looking *into* journalism: at journalists, their practices, and specific media organizations (e.g. Bennett et al. 2007).

Nevertheless, media coverage of crises is not uniform (Ben-Yehuda et al. 2013; Cottle 2009), as "crisis" is not a seamless phenomenon. There are diverse types of crises of different origins, natures, duration, and newness, that, in turn, have varied relations to media practices (Coombs 2010; Nord and Strömbäck 2003; Sellnow and Seeger 2013). Lars Nord and Jesper Strömbäck (2003) distinguish four types of crises based on their predictability (surprising character) and newness (repetition), that is, their supposed relation to media practices: "new and surprising events," "new but expected events," "surprising events that have happened before," and "expected events that have happened before" (type I-IV, Nord and Strömbäck 2003: 71).

Although these were rather ideal-typical events, James doubted there can still be something new and surprising or, conversely, a completely calculable situation. Within current geopolitical realities, "new and surprising events" and "expected events that have happened before" are becoming less relevant. On one hand, after 9/11, it would be hard to come up with something less conceivable (Falkheimer and Olsson 2015); on the other hand, long-term crises—such as the hybrid war in Ukraine—take a form which is for various reasons new, and thus pose new challenges to reporters (Hoskins and O'Loughlin 2010). The two remaining types of situations, "new but expected events" and "surprising events that have happened before," were more conceivable. For example, the so-called refugee crisis (James did not like the term "crisis" but yielded to the common usage, as in many other cases) was said to be unprecedented, but could have been expected. In contrast, terrorist attacks in nearby European cities such as Paris, Brussels, and Berlin were always shocking but had happened before.

Journalists' practices are vital for how reports and news look and, in turn, are shaped not only by the predictability and newness of the crisis but also by journalists' emotional experience (Beckett and Deuze 2016). It is therefore surprising that emotional aspects of crisis reporting have been largely overlooked by media scholars studying crisis reporting.

A non-white man of James' age arguing with a security guard who was just trying to undress him behind the metal detectors caught James' eyes. James yawned, got up, stretched like a big beast of prey, and strolled away to find another place to sit.

Objections to Objectivity: Emotionality and Professionalism

Glancing at a newspaper rack by a tobacco shop, he thought of the news-making machine beyond it. Behind each piece of news, there was at least one professional who had directly or indirectly lived the story through.

Some researchers mention that the disruptive nature of crisis poses substantial professional problems for journalists (Falkheimer and Olsson 2015); certain kinds of events even seem to shake the foundations of what it means to be a journalist (Zelizer and Allan 2011). This section thus looks at crisis reporters' emotions from a perspective that corresponds with the second research stream. What place do emotions have in the practices and outcomes of crisis newsmaking and in journalists' professional ideology?

The traditional version of journalists' professional ideology,[1] that is, a collection of shared but continuously challenged strategies and values guiding journalists' construction of their expertise and authority (Andén-Papadopoulos and Pantti 2013: 962), includes the commitment to objectivity. Objectivity—understood as detachment, impartiality, fairness, or professional distance (Deuze 2005)—remains a cornerstone of journalists' professional self-perception, an assumed source of their authority and a privileged signifier of "good journalism" (e.g. Carpentier and Trioen 2010;

---

[1] The study takes into account only the relatively current (post-World War II [WWII]) thinking of journalism, which is most relevant for today's media research and journalism practice, not least because it has been tightly linked to journalism's monitorial role within democratic societies. However, as Christians et al. (2009) show, its normative character goes back to Plato and Aristotle.

Schudson 2001). Together with some other norms and values such as autonomy and public service, objectivity represents the core normative and ethical aspect of professionalism (Andén-Papadopoulos and Pantti 2013; Deuze 2005); some scholars even argue that the objectivity norm is central to the constitution of the journalistic field and works as a privileged signifier of "good journalism" (Carpentier and Trioen 2010; Vos 2011). According to Michael Schudson (2001: 149), "the objectivity norm guides journalists to separate facts from values and to report only the facts. Objective reporting is supposed to be cool, rather than emotional, in tone." Correspondingly, the procedural notion of objectivity, that is, objectivity understood as a kind of performance and a set of practices (Blaagaard 2013; Carpentier and Trioen 2010), leads journalists to give voice to each side of a political controversy and report news in a factual, non-interpretive, "rational" style without commenting on it, distorting it, or shaping its formulation (Peters 2011; Schudson 2001), not to mention not being overwhelmed and paralyzed by their feelings. "Normally, journalists don't get struck by events. They report when events strike others. And it is this basic immunity from action that makes the whole regime of neutrality, objectivity, and detachment even thinkable, let alone practical for journalists," Jay Rosen (2011: 36) writes, while persuasively illustrating that on September 11, such a regime was unimaginable for New York reporters.

James' phone was ringing. Fred.

"Yes?" James answered. His voice sounded exceptionally husky this morning.

"2 k bits, man," his foreign editor announced rather theatrically.

Rather than keeping James updated on the number of casualties, he wanted to check if everything was alright. After all, it was James' first big journey for such a "holy-shit story" (Romano 1986 in Olsson and Nord 2015: 344), and Fred was a good manager. He even looked like and had the manners of a good manager, which at times humorously contrasted with all the hues of slight untidiness yet nobility of the intellectuals that he managed.

James had seen the number on Twitter. "I see. Thanks," he hung up and checked the piece of information once again with another source—one of those news agencies and large media companies that, as he was taught, was reliable enough.

Crisis reporting is a field in which disruptions to the professional ideology become clearly visible, as the key journalistic values of objectivity, impartiality, and detachment are constantly challenged (Olsson and Nord 2015). Journalists involved in crisis reporting face and need to deal with the paradox that they are supposed to keep in mind the traditional normative defining features of journalism while witnessing other people's suffering and tragedies, such that they may experience tension between being an involved actor and being a fly on the wall (Andén-Papadopoulos and Pantti 2013; Richards and Rees 2011). This difficult position, together with the extraordinary circumstances faced by the news organizations, might be the reasons why crisis coverage is often evaluated by media researchers as lesser quality reporting (Falkheimer and Olsson 2015; McDonald and Lawrence 2004; see also the previous section "Emotions in Crisis Coverage").[2]

The paradox of detachment/involvement (see Elias 1956) that makes crisis reporting more difficult than other journalistic fields is tightly interconnected with the ambivalence of the role of emotions (not only) in crisis reporting. Do emotions emerging from my personal experience, James thought, contaminate objectivity? Or are they an inevitable ingredient of truthful experience, information, and accounts? The journalistic professional discourse faces a profound rupture between normative and descriptive definitions of the role and place of emotions. According to Barry Richards and Gavin Rees, the belief that emotion contaminates objectivity prevails in the journalistic discourse: "Professional norms of detached objectivity are set against journalists' own awareness that they are emotionally affected by the situations they report on, and against their empathy for the individuals involved in the story" (Richards and Rees 2011: 864). However, even the hard, objective, "just the facts" journalism is not unemotional; emotionality is profoundly constitutive of journalistic narratives (Peters 2011; Wahl-Jorgensen 2013; see later in the chapter).

James was cool enough, but he considered any attempt to separate facts from interpretation or his own opinions in a text a losing battle. Also, he found the mainstream sorting of journalistic genres into the more and the less emotional to be ridiculous, obsolete, and annoying.

Likewise, journalism and journalism studies, similarly to other disciplines, have seen an "affective turn" (Richards and Rees 2011). Not only

---

[2] Moreover, media workers have been confronted with multiple interpretations of objectivity related to new media technologies (Deuze 2005); in particular, the traditional commitment to objectivity has been challenged by entanglements with citizen journalism (Andén-Papadopoulos and Pantti 2013; Blaagaard 2013; Thorsen 2008).

have media scholars started to pay attention to the fact that media is an emotionally charged environment and to suggest that personal, affective, and emotional engagement with newswork needs to be considered carefully. Also, students of journalism and media professionals have redefined the classic idea of journalistic objectivity and news itself (Beckett and Deuze 2016). Not that the news has become more emotional; rather, the acceptability of involvement has become more explicit and diverse emotional styles have emerged (Peters 2011).

Considering the contemporary forms of journalism (Christians et al. 2009), especially since the 1960s, the newly emerging trends in journalism such as ethnographic, new, or literary approaches have been advocating the acknowledgment of reporters' emotions as a legitimate part of reports (e.g. Pauly 2014), which resulted in merging the genres of "soft" and "hard" news. In the theory of journalism, (feminist) media scholars have argued that, contrary to the professional "mythology" surrounding traditional journalism, subjectivity and its various manifestations do not contradict objectivity. Both the values are constitutive and necessary elements of journalists' professional identity (Van Zoonen 1998). James knew that some of his colleagues appreciated the trend. In practice, however, very few were really going against the tide.

Furthermore, these shifts have not diminished the demanding nature of the double existence of journalists as involved actors and flies on the wall that requires them to keep their distance. "You cannot be swept away completely by your emotion," as Lotte, one of James' colleagues, said. As K. Megan Hopper and John E. Huxford (2015) in their study of newspaper journalists' engagement in emotional labor put it, journalists advisedly make the distinction between "eye" (i.e. the perspective of a detached observer) and "I" (subjective opinions of the individual reporter). The extent of one's emotional engagement must be carefully monitored—both on the input and on the output. Howard Tumber (2006) gives the example of the Balkan conflict, in which media including the *BBC* were harshly criticized for acting merely as transmission vehicles. At the same time, depicting the emotional face of war was condemned for opening the door to imprecision and moralizing. Analyzing Pulitzer Prize-winning stories, Karin Wahl-Jorgensen speaks about a "strategic ritual of emotionality" and suggests that "there is an institutionalized and systematic practice of journalists narrating and infusing their reporting with emotion" (Wahl-Jorgensen 2013: 130). The ritual, Wahl-Jorgensen writes, operates alongside the analogous strategic ritual of objectivity. Nevertheless, rather than expressing their own emotions, journalists "outsource," police, and discipline the emotional expression. Kari Andén-Papadopoulos and Mervi Pantti (2013) consider the skill to mediate and mitigate suffering in the form of meaningful compositions as one of the key differences between professional and citizen journalists; likewise, Chris Peters (2011) believes that emotion management (Hochschild 1983) is one of the crucial foundations of the job. Following Peter Stearns (1994), Peters (2011: 303) describes the emotional style of a trusted journalist as "American Cool": "To be 'cool' is not to be emotionless, nor is it to be unfeeling. Rather, this emotional posture demands finding the right balance of disengagement and nonchalance, without appearing disinterested." This implies that the right emotional posture can and must be crafted (Hochschild 1983; Illouz 2007).

Journalists' Emotional Labor and Trauma

Indeed, James recalled conversations with his colleagues regarding their emotional paths from idealistic, enthusiastic college students to tough, hardened old hands. "When you live in it, you realize that the only rescue is cynicism," Kryštof, one of his former colleagues from *Czech Television*, who was only a few years older than James, told him.

Being seated closer to his gate, James started scrolling through the web again, and chanced into a few studies of reporters' emotionality carried out by think tanks, research centers, and professional associations such as the Eyewitness Media Hub, the Dart Centre for Journalism and Trauma, and the International News Safety Institute.

Taken together, the literature turned out to be about diverse types of trauma. Before James lost interest in the studies, he managed to learn that "Professionals who work with eyewitness media watch disturbing footage from war zones, natural and manmade disasters and accidents over and over again to verify its veracity and to edit out images that are deemed too extreme for viewing by the general public" (Dubberley et al. 2015: 4). "Reporters, editors, photojournalists and news crews are involved in the coverage of many tragedies during their lifetimes. They range from wars to terrorist attacks to aeroplane crashes to natural disasters to fires to murders. All having victims. All affecting their communities. All creating lasting memories" (Hight and Smyth 2003: 2). James was among the 52 percent of journalists who view distressing user-generated content several times a week; on the other hand, he still wasn't able to say whether or not it had, similarly as for 40 percent of his colleagues,[3] a negative impact on his personal life. Nightmares, feelings of isolation, a negative view of the world, flashbacks (Dubberley et al. 2015; see also Høiby and Ottosen 2015; Marthoz 2017)? Did I ever have a positive view of the world? James was not sure. A few eyewitness graphic images from San Lorenzo that he saw on Twitter a while ago came unbidden to his mind (Image 1.2). And then older memories and sounds.[4]

The relatively few previous studies on crisis reporters' emotions showed that the practice of covering crises and conflicts is indeed significantly interwoven with journalists' emotional experience and mental well-being. The prevalence of PTSD among journalists is higher than among the general population (Aoki et al. 2012). In particular, higher rates of mental ill-health have been found in the subcategories of war reporters, journalists covering conflicts and crises, and those working with user-generated

Image 1.2 A frozen city. Drawing by Peter Van Goethem, 2017. Courtesy of the artist

---

[3] These 40 percent refer to the general sample, comprising not only journalists but also human rights and humanitarian professionals.
[4] Sound is one of the most distressing elements of eyewitness media (Dubberley et al. 2015).

content that often includes disturbing images (Feinstein et al. 2015; Reinardy 2011; Richards and Rees 2011). Frequent, repeated, cumulative, and unexpected exposure to violent images, be it direct or indirect, is emotionally distressing to such an extent that it purportedly determines depression, anxiety, post-traumatic stress disorder, alcohol abuse, headaches, and early waking syndrome (Dubberley et al. 2015; Feinstein et al. 2015).

According to a survey conducted by researchers from the International News Safety Institute, the mental health of journalists is *increasingly* at risk (Clifford 2016). Indeed, symptoms of PTSD are evident not only among on-the-spot reporters, but also among the staff working on a frontline which is no longer geographic but digital (Clifford 2016; Dubberley et al. 2015). One of the reasons might be that post-traumatic reactions are not determined solely by being on the scene and directly witnessing human suffering, but are also related to increased exposure to dilemmas, feelings of guilt, or tension between journalists' beliefs about professionalism and its practice in the field (Backholm and Idås 2015; Keats and Buchanan 2012). The potential of new media to diminish geographical distance thus applies also to emotional experience. Rather, personal closeness determines emotional experience in the sense that, for example, eyewitness content is more distressing when it depicts events to which a journalist can personally relate: through material things, settings, or through people she knows (Dubberley et al. 2015; Tumber 2011).

James implicitly sensed the need for preparations and training, but he did not know of any college that would attempt to prepare future journalists systematically to the experience of trauma. He had learned about the importance of coping mechanisms, but as far as he knew, these were much too often "unhealthy" (Dubberley et al. 2015) or did not solve the problem at all—such as the use of black humor, focusing on practical, mechanical aspects of the crisis, or controlling one's emotions (Buchanan and Keats 2011; Hopper and Huxford 2015; Kotišová 2017). Most importantly, he read about the key role played by media organizations and their support for their employees, which, however, was rarely well performed. Although awareness of PTSD and other psychological risks has increased among newsroom managers and journalists over the last ten years, very few media organizations have formal institutional systems to support their staff, and journalists who have mental problems are still afraid of stigmatization (Aoki et al. 2012; Clifford 2016; Dubberley et al. 2015; Keats and Buchanan 2012; see also Pedelty 1995). Were employers reluctant to inform journalists about potential mental health problems and help them, or did they simply lack the resources and knowledge to do so (Aoki et al. 2012)?

Still, the associations and research centers such as the Dart Centre and INSI offered not only individual training programs for those covering war zones, terrorism, and natural disasters but also evidence-based recommendations for organizations (Dubberley et al. 2015; Hight and Smyth 2003; Keats and Buchanan 2012; Sambrook 2016). On the one hand, James appreciated the attempts to de-individualize the psychological risks; he was fed up with shifting responsibility for social crisis phenomena onto the shoulders of individuals (Beck and Beck-Gernsheim 2001) and promoting biographical solutions for systematic problems (Heaphy 2007; Scheper-Hughes and Lock 1987). On the other hand, sentences like, "The practical tips in this booklet can help you become more effective in handling these vital areas" (Hight and Smyth 2003: 3) aroused his suspicions. He reckoned that such rhetoric, stressing (organizational) effectiveness, revealed the fact that the recommendations that were supposed to work as therapeutic tools actually worked also as a means of readapting human beings suffering trauma to the continuous state of potential war, reproducing them as subjects deployable within the next crisis event (Väliaho 2014). All the more so that there was no questioning of what the journalist saw or did.

Nevertheless, such an approach is consistent with the sensitizing understanding of emotions as culturally and socially shaped, determined and defined. The research clearly suggests that crisis reporting and crisis reporters' emotional experiences need to be studied not only in terms of personal psychological peculiarity and risk, but also as a social phenomenon and sociological problem.

Such a turn from psychology to the sociology of media—the acknowledgment and further exploration of the fact that it is the newsmaking logic and crisis context that together play a large part in shaping journalists' mental health—has already been carried out by some media researchers (mainly Glück 2016; Hopper and Huxford 2015; Jukes 2017; Pantti 2010; Richards 2007; Richards and Rees 2011). For example, Hopper and Huxford investigate how journalists, while fulfilling the ideals of objectivity, neutrality, and balance, are required to suppress their own feelings, and thus knowingly engage in emotional labor, that is, in "the management of emotion required of employees based on the demands of their job" (Hopper and Huxford 2015: 25; for a more thorough definition of emotional labor, see the chapter "The Emotional Experience of Crisis Reporters: The Journey"). The authors suggest that newspaper journalists both perceive the importance of keeping an emotional distance from the people and events that they cover, and experience a difficult balancing act between performing professional detachment and showing personal emotion. Correspondingly, Pantti (2010) observes that journalists reflect upon the right use of their emotions, and shift, in the course of their careers, toward greater awareness of the negative consequences of their full emotional disclosure (interestingly, while condemning the employment of "non-authentic," "artificial" emotions). In these studies, emotion management typically means developing a professional shield that brings about a specific semi-detached emotional style that has been called "autopilot," "cynicism," "right distance," or "American cool" (Backholm 2017; Hopper and Huxford 2015, 2017; Jukes 2017; Richards and Rees 2011). By comparison, Antje Glück (2016), studying British and Indian journalists, found that her interviewees unanimously consider empathy toward their sources as a central quality of their work, albeit often an invisible one. In their view, empathy can turn good journalism into great or exceptional journalism; however, the point is to know how much empathy and in which way to use it. In any case, the studies agree that journalists in general—not only crisis reporters—routinely perform emotional labor that allows them to keep the right distance from situations that they cover.

Importantly, the research suggests that the very suppression of personal, emotional identity and the reconfiguration of the self along lines of rationalism represented by journalistic objectivity (see the chapters "Articulating Journalists' Emotional Experiences of Crisis: Touching Down" and "Emotions, Technology, and Crisis Reconsidered: Ending")—doing it on autopilot, as Steven Jukes (2017) puts it—might be one factor that influences journalists' mental (ill-)health. For example, Hopper and Huxford (2015) mention that their interviewees sometimes remained troubled by incidents that happened years and even decades earlier, and were haunted by long-term guilt and even self-hatred (see also Nicolas' story from Liberia in the section "Moral Dilemmas and Guilt"). Therefore, addressing the social and sociological dimensions of crisis reporters' emotionality by dealing with the research questions listed at the beginning of this Introduction could help us understand reporters' emotions within the context of social crises and newsmaking technology. Seeing emotions as a social phenomenon and taking into account that they constitute a form of precarity (see e.g. Hesmondhalgh and Baker 2011) are vital for designing any institutionalized solutions.

James' memories of diverse snatches of conversations with his colleagues were starting to deluge his consciousness and were vying for his attention. For now, they resembled a chaotic whirl. Despite his short career, he had already worked in and for several European media—television, radio, newspapers, online platforms—both as an employee and as a freelancer. During that time, he talked about emotions with dozens of colleagues; rookies and old hands; men and women; "armchair" journalists making news on crises from their newsrooms; flying and roving "parachute reporters" covering crises on the spot; and permanent correspondents in conflict zones. The crises that they talked about included long-term and short-term negative events; more and less new and predictable events; and conflicts, wars, terror attacks, transportation disasters, natural disasters, environmental catastrophes, and social and economic crises that happened on five continents, with casualties ranging from individuals to hundreds of thousands.

He got up and went to the lavatory.

REFERENCES

Allan, S., et al. (Eds.). (2000). *Environmental Risks and the Media*. London: Routledge.

Altheide, D. (2004). Media Logic and Political Communication. *Political Communication, 21*(3), 293–296.

Amanpour. (2016). Syrian journalist: People 'are totally numb' to war. *CNN*. Retrieved from http://edition.cnn.com/videos/world/2016/11/01/intv-amanpour-rami-jarrah-syria.cnn.

Andén-Papadopoulos, K., & Pantti, M. (2013). Re-imagining Crisis Reporting: Professional Ideology of Journalists and Citizen Eyewitness Images. *Journalism, 14*(7), 960–977.

Aoki, Y., et al. (2012). Mental Illness Among Journalists: A Systematic Review. *International Journal of Social Psychiatry, 59*(4), 377–390.

Backholm, K. (2017). Distress Among Journalists Working the Incidents. In L. C. Wilson (Ed.), *The Wiley Handbook of the Psychology of Mass Shootings (Wiley Clinical Psychology Handbooks)* (pp. 247–263). Chichester: John Wiley & Sons.

Backholm, K., & Idås, T. (2015). Ethical Dilemmas, Work-related guilt, and Posttraumatic Stress Reactions of News Journalists Covering the Terror Attack in Norway in 2011. *Journal of Traumatic Stress, 28*, 142–148.

Beck, U., & Beck-Gernsheim, E. (2001). *Individualization: Institutionalized Individualism and Its Social and Political Consequences.* London: SAGE.

Beckett, C., & Deuze, M. (2016). On the Role of Emotion in the Future of Journalism. *Social Media + Society, 2016*(3), 1–6.

Bennett, W. L., et al. (2007). *When the Press Fails: Political Power and the News Media from Iraq to Katrina.* Chicago: The University of Chicago Press.

Ben-Yehuda, H., et al. (2013). When Media and World Politics Meet: Crisis Press Coverage in the Arab–Israel and East–West Conflicts. *Media, War and Conflict, 6*(1), 71–92.

Blaagaard, B. B. (2013). Shifting Boundaries: Objectivity, Citizen Journalism and Tomorrow's Journalists. *Journalism, 14*(8), 1076–1090.

Blumer, H. (1954). What Is Wrong with Social Theory? *American Sociological Review, 18*, 3–10.

Bowen, G. A. (2006). Grounded Theory and Sensitizing Concepts. *International Journal of Qualitative Methods, 5*(3), 1–8.

Buchanan, M., & Keats, P. (2011). Coping with Traumatic Stress in Journalism: A Critical Ethnographic Study. *International Journal of Psychology, 46*, 127–135. https://doi.org/10.1080/00207594.2010.532799.

Carpentier, N., & Trioen, M. (2010). The Particularity of Objectivity: A Poststructuralist and Psychoanalytical Reading of the Gap Between Objectivity-as-a-value and Objectivity-as-a- practice in the 2003 Iraqi War Coverage. *Journalism, 11*(3), 311–328.

Christians, C. G., et al. (Eds.). (2009). *Normative Theories of the Media: Journalism in Democratic Societies.* Chicago: University of Illinois Press.

Clifford, L. (2016). *Under Threat: The Changing State of Media Safety.* International News Safety Institute. Retrieved from https://newssafety.org/underthreat/index.html#.

Coombs, T. W. (2010). *Ongoing Crisis Communication.* London: SAGE.

Cottle, S. (2009). *Global Crisis Reporting: Journalism in the Global Age.* Maidenhead: Open University Press.

Deuze, M. (2005). What Is Journalism? Professional Identity and Ideology of Journalists Reconsidered. *Journalism, 6*(4), 442–464.

Du Gay, P. (1996). *Consumption and Identity at Work.* London: SAGE.

Dubberley, S. et al. (2015). *Making Secondary Trauma a Primary Issue: A Study of Eyewitness Media and Vicarious Trauma on the Digital Frontline.* Eyewitness Media Hub. Retrieved from http://eyewitnessmediahub.com/research/vicarious-trauma.

Elias, N. (1956). Problems of Involvement and Detachment. *The British Journal of Sociology, 7*(3), 226–252.

Entman, R. M., et al. (2009). Doomed to Repeat: Iraq News, 2002–2007. *American Behavioral Scientist, 52*(5), 689–708.

Falkheimer, J., & Olsson, E. K. (2015). Depoliticizing Terror: The News Framing of the Terrorist Attacks in Norway, 22 July 2011. *Media, War and Conflict,* 8(1), 70–85.

Feinstein, A., et al. (2015). Witnessing Images of Extreme Violence: A Psychological Study of Journalists in the Newsroom. *Journal of the Royal Society of Medicine,* 6(2), 1–7.

Foucault, M. (1988). Technologies of the Self. In L. H. Martin, H. Gutman, & P. H. Hutton (Eds.), *Technologies of the Self: A Seminar with Michel Foucault* (pp. 16–49). London: Tavistock Publications.

Galtung, J., & Ruge, M. B. (1965). The Structure of Foreign News. *Journal of Peace Research,* 2(1), 64–91.

Glück, A. (2016). What Makes a Good Journalist? *Journalism Studies,* 17(7), 893–903.

Greene, R. W. (2012). Lessons from the YMCA: The Material Rhetoric of Criticism, Rhetorical Interpretation and Pastoral Power. In J. Packer & S. B. Crofts Wiley (Eds.), *Communication Matters: Materialist Approaches to Media, Mobility, and Networks* (pp. 219–230). London: Routledge.

Hallin, D. C. (1986). *The "Uncensored War": The Media and Vietnam.* Berkeley: University of California Press.

Hansen, M. (2006). Media Theory. *Theory, Culture and Society,* 23(2–3), 297–306.

Harcup, T., & O'Neill, D. (2001). What Is News? Galtung and Ruge Revisited. *Journalism Studies,* 2(2), 261–280.

Hay, J. (2012). The Birth of the "Neoliberal" City and Its Media. In J. Packer & S. B. Crofts Wiley (Eds.), *Communication Matters: Materialist Approaches to Media, Mobility, and Networks* (pp. 121–140). London: Routledge.

Hayward, M. R., & Tuckey, R. M. (2011). Emotions in Uniform: How Nurses Regulate Emotion at Work Via Emotional Boundaries. *Human Relations,* 64(11), 1501–1523.

Heaphy, B. (2007). *Late Modernity and Social Change.* London: Routledge.

Hesmondhalgh, D., & Baker, S. (2011). *Creative Labour: Media Work in Three Cultural Industries.* London: Routledge.

Hight, J., & Smyth, F. (2003). *Tragedies and Journalists: A Guide for More Effective Coverage.* Dart Center for Journalism and Trauma. Retrieved from http://dartcenter.org/sites/default/files/en_tnj_0.pdf.

Hjarvard, S. (2008). The Mediatization of Society: A Theory of the Media as Agents of Social and Cultural Change. *Nordicom Review,* 29(2), 105–134.

Hochschild, A. R. (1983). *The Managed Heart.* Berkeley: University of California Press.

Høiby, M. H., & Ottosen, R. (2015). *Journalism Under Pressure: A Mapping of Editorial Policies for Journalists Covering Conflict.* Oslo: Høgskolen i Oslo og Akershus.

Hopper, K. M., & Huxford, J. (2015). Gathering Emotion: Examining Newspaper Journalists' Engagement in Emotional Labor. *Journal of Media Practice*, *16*(1), 25–41.
Hopper, K. M., & Huxford, J. (2017). Emotion Instruction in Journalism Courses: An Analysis of Introductory News Writing Textbooks. *Communication Education*, *66*(1), 90–108.
Hoskins, A., & O'Loughlin, B. (2010). *War and Media: The Emergence of Diffused War*. Cambridge: Polity Press.
Illouz, E. (2007). *Cold Intimacies: The Making of Emotional Capitalism*. Cambridge: Polity Press.
Joelving, F. (2010, December 17). When the News Breaks the Journalist: PTSD. *Reuters*. Retrieved from http://www.reuters.com/article/us-ptsd-reporter/when-the-news-breaks-the-journalist-ptsd-idUSTRE6BG3NG20101217.
Jukes, S. (2017). *Affective Journalism – Uncovering the Affective Dimension of Practice in the Coverage of Traumatic News*. PhD Thesis, Goldsmiths University, United Kingdom.
Keats, P. A., & Buchanan, M. J. (2012). Covering Trauma in Canadian Journalism: Exploring the Challenges. *Traumatology*, *19*(3), 210–222.
Knüpfer, C. B., & Entman, R. M. (2018). Framing Conflicts in Digital and Transnational Media Environments. *Media, War & Conflict*, *11*(4), 476–488.
Kotišová, J. (2017). Cynicism Ex Machina: The Emotionality of Reporting the 'Refugee Crisis' and Paris Terrorist Attacks in Czech Television. *European Journal of Communication*, *32*(3), 242–256.
Lievrouw, L. A. (2014). Materiality and Media in Communication and Technology Studies: An Unfinished Project. In T. Gillespie et al. (Eds.), *Media Technologies: Essays on Communication, Materiality and Society* (pp. 21–52). Cambridge: The MIT Press.
Livingstone, S. (1996). On the Continuing Problems of Media Effects Research. In J. Curran & M. Gurevitch (Eds.), *Mass Media and Society* (pp. 305–324). London: Edward Arnold.
Marthoz, J. P. (2017). *Terrorism and the Media: A Handbook for Journalists*. Paris: UNESCO.
McDonald, I. R., & Lawrence, R. G. (2004). Filling the 24×7 News Hole: Television News Coverage Following September 11. *American Behavioral Scientist*, *48*(3), 327–340.
Neumann, R., & Fahmy, S. (2016). Measuring Journalistic Peace/War Performance: An Exploratory Study of Crisis Reporters' Attitudes and Perceptions. *International Communication Gazette*, *78*(3), 223–246.
Nord, L. W., & Strömbäck, J. (2003). Making Sense of Different Types of Crises: A Study of the Swedish Media Coverage of the Terror Attacks Against the United States and the U.S. Attacks in Afghanistan. *Press/Politics*, *8*(4), 54–75.

Nord, L. W., & Strömbäck, J. (2006). Reporting More, Informing Less: A Comparison of the Swedish Media Coverage of September 11 and the Wars in Afghanistan and Iraq. *Journalism, 7*(1), 85–110.
Olsson, E. K., & Nord, L. W. (2015). Paving the Way for Crisis Exploitation: The Role of Journalistic Styles and Standards. *Journalism, 16*(3), 341–358.
Orlikowski, W. J. (2007). Sociomaterial Practices: Exploring Technology at Work. *Organization Studies, 28*(9), 1435–1448.
Packer, J., & Crofts Wiley, S. B. (2012). Introduction: The Materiality of Communication. In J. Packer & S. B. Crofts Wiley (Eds.), *Communication Matters: Materialist Approaches to Media, Mobility, and Networks* (pp. 3–16). London: Routledge.
Pang, A. (2013). Social Media Hype in Times of Crises: Nature Characteristics and Impact on Organizations. *Asia Pacific Media Educator, 23*(2), 309–336.
Pantti, M. (2010). The Value of Emotion: An Examination of Television Journalists' Notions on Emotionality. *European Journal of Communication, 25*(2), 168–181.
Pauly, J. J. (2014). The New Journalism and the Struggle for Interpretation. *Journalism, 15*(5), 589–604.
Pedelty, M. (1995). *War Stories: The Culture of Foreign Correspondents.* London: Routledge.
Peters, C. (2011). Emotion Aside or Emotional Side? Crafting an 'Experience of Involvement' in the News. *Journalism, 12*(3), 297–316.
Reinardy, S. (2011). Newspaper Journalism in Crisis: Burnout on the Rise, Eroding Young Journalists' Career Commitment. *Journalism, 12*(1), 33–50.
Richards, B. (2007). *Emotional Governance.* Basingstoke: Palgrave Macmillan.
Richards, B., & Rees, G. (2011). The Management of Emotion in British Journalism. *Media, Culture and Society, 33*(6), 851–867.
Romano, C. (1986). What? The Grisly Truth About Bare Facts. In R. K. Manhoff & M. Schudson (Eds.), *Reading the News: Pantheon guide to popular culture* (pp. 38–78). New York: Pantheon.
Rosaldo, M. Z. (1984). Towards an Anthropology of Self and Feeling. In R. A. Schweder & R. A. LeVine (Eds.), *Culture Theory: Essays on Mind, Self and Emotions* (pp. 137–157). Cambridge: Cambridge University Press.
Rosen, J. (2011). September 11 in the Mind of American Journalism. In B. Zelizer & S. Allan (Eds.), *Journalism after September 11* (2nd ed., pp. 35–43). London: Routledge.
Sambrook, R. (2016, April 11). Newsrooms Should Prepare to Cover Terrorist Attacks. *International News Safety Institute.* Retrieved from http://www.newssafety.org/news/insi-news/insi-news/detail/newsrooms-should-prepare-to-cover-terrorist-attacks-1722/.
Scheer, M. (2012). Are Emotions a Kind of Practice (And Is That What Makes Them Have a History)? A Bourdieuian Approach to Understanding Emotion. *History and Theory, 51,* 193–220.

Scheper-Hughes, N., & Lock, M. (1987). The Mindful Body: A Prolegomenon to Future Work in Medical Anthropology. *Medical Anthropology Quarterly*, *1*(1), 6–41.
Schudson, M. (2001). The Objectivity Norm in American Journalism. *Journalism*, *2*(2), 149–170.
Sellnow, T. L., & Seeger, M. W. (2013). *Theorizing Crisis Communication*. New Jersey: John Wiley and Sons.
Shaheen, K. (2016, December 22). Covering the Last Days of Aleppo: Even from afar, the Heart Breaks. *The Guardian*. Retrieved from http://niemanstoryboard.org/stories/covering-the-last-days-of-aleppo-even-from-afar-the-heart-breaks/.
Stearns, P. (1994). *American Cool: Constructing a 20th Century Emotional Style*. New York: NYU Press.
Thorsen, E. (2008). Journalistic Objectivity Redefined? Wikinews and the Neutral Point of View. *New Media and Society*, *10*(6), 935–954.
Tumber, H. (2006). The Fear of Living Dangerously: Journalists Who Report on Conflict. *International Relations*, *20*(4), 439–451.
Tumber, H. (2011). Reporting Under Fire: The Physical Safety and Emotional Welfare of Journalists. In B. Zelizer & S. Allan (Eds.), *Journalism After September 11* (2nd ed., pp. 319–334). London: Routledge.
Väliaho, P. (2014). *Biopolitical Screens: Image, Power and the Neoliberal Brain*. Cambridge: The MIT Press.
Van Der Meer, TGLA. et al. (2016). Disrupting Gatekeeping Practices: Journalists' Source Selection in Times of Crisis. *Journalism*. Epub ahead of print 16 May 2016. https://doi.org/10.1177/1464884916648095.
Van Leuven, S., et al. (2013). Foreign Reporting and Sourcing Practices in the Network Sphere: A Quantitative Content Analysis of the Arab Spring in Belgian News Media. *New Media and Society*, *17*(4), 573–591.
Van Loon, J. (2002). *Risk and Technological Culture: Towards a Sociology of Virulence*. London: Routledge.
Van Zoonen, L. (1998). A Professional, Unreliable, Heroic Marionette (M/F): Structure, Agency and Subjectivity in Contemporary Journalisms. *European Journal of Cultural Studies*, *1*(1), 123–143.
Vincze, H. O. (2014). 'The Crisis' as a Journalistic Frame in Romanian News Media. *European Journal of Communication*, *29*(5), 567–582.
Vos, T. P. (2011). 'Homo Journalisticus': Journalism Education's Role in Articulating the Objectivity Norm. *Journalism*, *13*(4), 435–449.
Wahl-Jorgensen, K. (2013). The Strategic Ritual of Emotionality: A Case Study of Pulitzer Prize- Winning Articles. *Journalism*, *14*(1), 129–145.
Wahl-Jorgensen, K. (2016). Emotion and Journalism. In T. Witschge (Ed.). *The SAGE Handbook of Digital Journalism* (pp. 128–143). London: SAGE

Publications. Epub ahead of print. Retrieved from http://orca.cf.ac.uk/87552/.
War College. (2016). The Road to Ward 17. *Reuters*. Retrieved from https://soundcloud.com/war_college/the-road-to-ward-17.
Yates, D. (2016, November 15). The Road to Ward 17: My Battle with PTSD. *Reuters*. Retrieved from http://www.reuters.com/investigates/special-report/ptsd-witness-yates/.
Zelizer, B., & Allan, S. (Eds.). (2011). *Journalism After September 11* (2nd ed.). London: Routledge.

Open Access This chapter is licensed under the terms of the Creative Commons Attribution 4.0 International License (http://creativecommons.org/licenses/by/4.0/), which permits use, sharing, adaptation, distribution and reproduction in any medium or format, as long as you give appropriate credit to the original author(s) and the source, provide a link to the Creative Commons licence and indicate if changes were made.

The images or other third party material in this chapter are included in the chapter's Creative Commons licence, unless indicated otherwise in a credit line to the material. If material is not included in the chapter's Creative Commons licence and your intended use is not permitted by statutory regulation or exceeds the permitted use, you will need to obtain permission directly from the copyright holder.

CHAPTER 2

Defining a Crisis: Boarding

James reached the decisive point. Or was it the point of no return? Either he could turn about and withdraw, or he could continue queuing for boarding, which had started a few minutes before, and get on the aircraft. Either choice would send him in opposite directions—handing the whole of his mindful body over to an unpredictable risk and to the machine of *The Mo*, one of those ambitious wannabe-progressive printed (plus online) news magazines James worked for, or putting his early professional reputation in danger. Both options might have different consequences for *The Mo*, as well: gaining authority and credibility, or going on with the trend of losing followers without any moment of fluctuation. Both decisions could also interfere in the catastrophe playing out on San Lorenzo, since its causes, the stifling materiality of the tragedy, and its effects were inseparable from their media representations (see Van Loon 2002). Therefore, James also knew that his decision would relate to the individual tragedies of San Lorenzians.

Vertigo. A sudden microsecond of panic, followed by an unwitting tug; and a flash of inspiration, during which James saw all the levels and bends of the entanglement of his own edgy situation, the liminal position of the printed press of *The Mo*'s kind, the catastrophe itself, the historically logical and spatially global roots of the crisis, and, above all, the crisis with all its sharp materiality.

At very first glance, crisis seemed to be a Gordian knot or at least to have a rhizomatic non-structure. As far as James remembered, "crisis"

© The Author(s) 2019
J. Kotišová, *Crisis Reporters, Emotions, and Technology*,
https://doi.org/10.1007/978-3-030-21428-9_2

could mean anything. His colleagues and the media in general were using the word to refer to so many different things that they had inflated the use of the term. "Crisis" seemed to have lost any meaning. And scholars have been doing the same: at least from the nineteenth century onward, the enormous quantitative expansion in the variety of meanings of the concept of crisis caused it to lose its clarity, analytical precision, and appeal for social sciences (Koselleck 2006; Vincze 2014). "The term 'crisis' has been too widely diffused in the social sciences to be used innocently any longer" (Wagner 1994: 30). As a result,

> 'The crisis' has become a catchphrase that can refer to various shortages of resources and goods, material or spiritual, but also the perceived breakdown of governance, institutions or indeed the fabric of society. ... This use of the term contributed to creating a sense of generalized crisis. (Vincze 2014: 567, 579)

The term has encompassed all spheres and has become a commonly employed expression that remains diagnostic but removed from its eschatological explanation (Koselleck 2006).

Yet, the catchphrase was there, in all its amorphousness, *defined by* its polyvalence and incommensurability of its diverse facets. Often used and always ready to be used. Therefore, understanding the emotional experience of "crisis reporters" without making a journey through the strata of meanings of the word "crisis" in "crisis reporting" would be a lost cause.

Once again, the long wait at the airport and the thought of the crisis that awaited James made him see stars; for a moment, he lost his balance and touched a young and elegant yet tired-looking woman, queuing behind him, with his shoulder.

The passing contact crowned his faintness. His nervousness in the presence of women was increasing with his every next amorous fiasco. Although his girlfriends were typically from within the branch—where else could he meet someone?—at some point, saying "Listen, I have to leave, today, tomorrow, all of a sudden" (a sentence that, as James' colleague Bob once insinuated, could have contributed to his divorce, especially because he used to say it repeatedly) largely complicated having any stable relationship. James had to accept that "Journalism is a way of living, at the end. You learn how to live without plans" (Ines).

The impossibility went well together with independence, his basic necessity, so that the impracticable mixed with the unwanted. Eventually, James stopped distinguishing the two.

THE POLYPHONIC NATURE OF "CRISIS" WITHIN "CRISIS REPORTING"

James' colleagues' varied understandings of the term suggest that "crisis" is defined precisely by its multiple meaning. The word is like a "Rorschach blot into which I can project diverse things" (Matouš).

For example, Josef discursively interconnected crisis in family (e.g. when someone is ill, which significantly influences a reporter's ability to work even in a non-crisis situation), temporary social crisis (the crisis "out there," involving individual crisis biographies), global risks and crisis of the modern state (from which more and more temporary, local, and biographical crises follow), technological crisis (such as a wrong cable, "God forbid that it's your fault!"), crisis for a media organization (e.g. redoubling the demands on management and personal capacities during crises "out there"), and, above all, personal crisis (none of these circumstances "won't give you a lift," and a personal crisis may result from an emotionally demanding work context such as work with refugees, who themselves are undergoing personal crises). Astrid stressed a diffused technologically driven media crisis residing in poor-quality journalists and more reliance on social media; Louis and Matouš, focusing on national media systems, saw a crisis in the financial problems of media organizations and shrinking newsrooms; Matouš also added media oligarchization, while Jacob spoke about the division of Belgian society. All of these crises resonated and were mutually reinforcing—or otherwise related to—each other to the extent of blurring boundaries between the meanings:

> Crisis reporting is when one is sent somewhere, to Baghdad, something is going on—then one is definitely in hard conditions. Not only in difficult life conditions, in danger of one's life, which is the most essential thing, but also seeking information. And the crisis that we go through on work trips is, say, whether we will make it or not, whether we have connection or not—this kind of non-comfort, *that* is crisis reporting. (Astrid)

Although the boundaries between the diverse meanings of James' colleagues' use of the word "crisis" were often unclear, some distinctions could be made. Or rather, one could trace a few dialogues between the types. In other words, crisis is always contextual, contingent, transcending, and invalidating the inside versus outside, momentary versus permanent, constructed versus real, and global versus local dichotomies.

Inside-the-Media Is Outside-the-Media Crisis

As Josef, a permanent foreign correspondent said,

> a reporter faces two types of crisis, you know? (...) Either there is a crisis consisting in something that happens, an acute event that of course entails stress, and you must act fast. And the second crisis consists in nothing happening.

Indeed, when James talked with his former and present colleagues about the specifics of crisis reporting, they usually first asked him to clarify whether he meant a crisis inside or outside-the-media: "Well, the question is, whether you mean a crisis situation in the world or in reporting," said Marie, who spoke, similarly to Šimon, Astrid, or Ines, of technological breakdowns or logistic impossibilities during on-the-spot crisis reporting or inside the newsroom. The distinction between inside-the-media and outside-the-media perspectives reflects the difference between two positions/roles: whether the event in question is a routine or non-routine event from the point of view of the journalists themselves, and whether the event is defined as a crisis from the perspective of the affected actors (Olsson and Nord 2015).

Nevertheless, the distinction is not absolute, partly because journalists are actors, too (Peters 2011; Tandoc and Takahashi 2016). Sometimes, these two types resonate, or, conversely, interfere. A foreign crisis such as the earthquake on Haiti, Astrid said, was perceived primarily as an event that could facilitate newsmaking processes, and thus prevent a potential inside-the-media crisis. Similarly, Ema said that "crisis" meant, above all, better teamwork, much more fun (including tacit permission to smoke in the office!), and the desire to stay at work longer. On the other hand, Čestmír pointed to the danger of inside-the-media crisis and the threats to professionalism following from covering an outside-the-media crisis:

> From a purely journalistic point of view, crisis zone news is unprofessional, because it introduces only one side of the conflict. (...) Simply because there is a frontline between [the two sides], and it's very hard to cross.

In any case, crisis can be an event that "changes the news fundamentally" (Kryštof). This view is consistent with media researchers' observations that due to the essence of crisis-ness—negativity, high levels of uncertainty, surprise, lack of preparedness and routines—coverage of crisis events is of lower journalistic quality than other types of reporting

(Falkheimer and Olsson 2015; Nord and Strömbäck 2006; Olsson and Nord 2015; Van Leuven et al. 2013).

James looked above the boarding counter at the screen announcing his destination. The name of the capital of San Lorenzo was missing; instead, the screen was showing the heads of various politicians and officials, reacting to the event. A special broadcast. They knew nothing, maybe even less than James; yet the channel reasoned them into empty performances.

The hollow statements laid bare the resonances of inside-the-media and outside-the-media crisis. The crisis out there sometimes triggered what could be called an organizational crisis: much higher time pressure, chaos, involuntary improvisation, fundamental reassignment of tasks and responsibilities. Authors writing on organizational crisis and crisis management find it difficult to draw a clear line between outer crises, sources of uncertainty, disruption and change that form parts of larger events/states, and internally harmful organizational processes (e.g. Sellnow and Seeger 2013). For example, BP's 2010 Gulf of Mexico oil spill harmed its reputation and financial performance, and its relationships with customers, local communities, and governments (Bundy et al. 2017). Similarly, a major crisis that a media organization was supposed to report on, although not caused by the organization itself, brought about chaos, disruption, and change in newswork routines.

James recalled a situation when he, a rookie beginning at ČT, went to cover an anti-immigration demonstration in Prague with experienced reporter R and cameraman C:

> The meeting in the production department alone is very chaotic. I am waiting in the tunnel. Diverse reporters pass by, picking up cameramen and taking up their technical equipment. All are in a hurry—running here and there, taking something from behind countless doors and putting it back somewhere else. But the camerapeople are smiling and joking. R is coming, we are looking for a cameraman and a driver. R is twice set right about with whom we are going. No one really seems to know who, with whom and where she shall go, what to shoot and what equipment to bring. Tripod— yes, or no? "This is a crisis situation," R tells me and smiles somewhat crossly. (…) C is always returning to the people present at the demonstration. 'They make me wanna puke. I think I will throw up on them,' he says. (…) He doesn't throw up, but always throws in an evaluation of the attendees and of the speakers standing on the stage. 'Goddamn motherfuckers. The fucking bastard Zeman[1],' C grinds out. (Field notes)

---

[1] Czech president, known for his anti-immigration rhetoric.

Of course, in comparison, the journalists' published (written, televised) discourse was always much more acritical and homogeneous (cf. Pedelty 1995).

Needless to say that standing in a media pen in the middle of the front rows of demonstrators from Pegida—who came from nearby Dresden to support their fellow Islamophobes—and the like, among the banners and placards with ridiculous but terrifyingly bizarre combinations of symbols, James himself felt very uncomfortable. He took a few pictures (Images 2.1 and 2.2).

And this was a stupid demonstration, James thought. In more serious crises, the disorganization was even more obvious. For example,

> Whenever there was a development [after the terror attacks in Paris in November 2015]—like when Abdelhamid Abaaoud, one of the instigators of the attacks, was killed—people [in ČT] started to move fast and frenetically, and even ran across the newsroom. They were speaking in an agitated way and the tension was almost palpable. (Field notes)

Image 2.1 Demonstration on 17 November 2015, Prague, organized by Bloc Against Islam (Blok proti Islámu), to support Czech president's opinions on immigration and Islam. Picture taken by the author as a part of her fieldwork in *Czech Television*

Image 2.2 Demonstration on 17 November 2015, Prague, organized by Bloc Against Islam (Blok proti Islámu), to support Czech president's opinions on immigration and Islam. Picture taken by the author as a part of her fieldwork in *Czech Television*

Similarly but even more apparently, as Jacob and Lotte recalled, the attacks in Brussels in March 2016 disturbed the daily routine in Brussels newsrooms to the extent that the whole newsroom started organically to work on the same topic. The domestic and external affairs desks united; the people from the cultural and sport desks went to interview witnesses and families of the victims, so that political reporters could make the "hard news."

For some media researchers and journalists, it is precisely the disorganization, chaos, and anomia that create the intersection of inside-the-media and outside-the-media crisis, and what lies at the core of "crisis." Crises—situations in which a major change, decision-making time constraints, limited information, and uncertainty are coupled with threats to core values at the personal, group, or state levels—fundamentally challenge journalists' practices (Ben-Yehuda et al. 2013; Van Der Meer et al. 2016). Thus, as Olga said, crisis is a "moment threatening a standard state in which the journalist works. Any situation that poses significantly higher demands on the work that we do."

A similar—organizational and professional—challenge is experienced by those who cover crisis events on the spot:

> It's not only to get there, not only to arrange all the permissions, not only to approach all the people, make the report, write it, cut it, but I must also reserve some time to send it. Which is somewhat more stressful than in normal situations. (Tomáš)

Tomáš hinted at technological difficulties related to making or sending a report. Indeed, sometimes these reached the level of a technologically induced "crisis." Tobiáš recalled his experience of reporting the terror attack on Charlie Hebdo in Paris:

> Speaking of technology, it was because of my photographer. Because I came to the hotel, wrote an article, and then he borrowed my computer (…) to send the photos. But while sending them, he switched something over and I couldn't start up the wifi at all. And now … you know the deadline is approaching and you have to send it in 30 minutes, the wifi is not working, in an internet café you can't get to your professional email. … (…) It was a crisis situation, but more a crisis for the people here [at the headquarters] than for me, but for me as well, a bit.

The crisis out there made the technological difficulties more likely—as Josef said,

> In a crisis situation, you are more in a hurry, see, the technical equipment is more endangered, there are bigger problems with the signal, the internet connection (…), and the first thing the authorities do in riots is switch off mobile network operators, so you find yourself cut off from the newsroom, which makes your life quite complicated.

In this sense, the less technological equipment one works with and the lighter one travels, the less difficult her situation is. Not least because one cannot move around that easily with more objects than pen and paper (Judith). James instinctively touched his trouser pockets with his palms. Almost empty. Like many times before, he felt relieved and lightweight. A scribbler, as more loaded-down TV reporters used to call press people. He recalled Čestmír speaking about reporting on the Haiti earthquake: whenever his cameraman pointed a camera at the wounded and homeless, the latter felt much less comfortable,² which, as he suggested, hindered him from doing his job. The same thing was experienced by Lotte, Ernest, and Tomáš, mainly in refugee camps across Southeast Europe, the Middle East, and North Africa. Moreover, as TV reporters, Čestmír, Josef, Sam, Carl, Vítek, and their cameramen had to go to the most affected—and still dangerous—places. "You have to shoot it. Because otherwise what? Otherwise you'd have a view from your hotel and an interview with a taxi driver" (Čestmír).

In turn, the technological crisis was equally traceable at the media-organizational level. James remembered two moments at *ČT*:

> Main morning meeting. Evaluation. Obviously, there was a problem with broadcasting the breaking news on the Paris attacks. "We had a problem with the thematic bars, they didn't work for two hours!" Martin, the boss, discusses with the others how to deal with such a "crisis situation," and "how to prepare crisis management." Then, Martin concludes: "For the news, it's a tragedy." (Field notes)

> Control room. Marie announces: "The Tomáš looks bad."—"How, bad?" someone asks. "He is not ready yet." [Tomáš, a correspondent from the Balkan route, has not sent his report.]—"Shit! Are you kidding? It's a part of the overview!"—"I know it, but the Macedonians obviously don't care," Marie says. (Field notes)

Furthermore, the organizational and related technological mishaps and breakdowns were connected to the broader context within which they occurred—mainly the economic and political aspects. Thus, press people (Louis, Astrid, and Richard) spoke of the crisis of the paper press being challenged by online news outlets, which causes organizational crises—fatal lack of personnel and insufficient resources to cover international affairs, including wars and conflicts. "When the Russian aeroplane crashed over Egypt," Richard from *LN* told James on their way out to lunch,

> I was alone in the newsroom. So I could cover it only briefly. And he [Richard's boss] came and told me to make it more balanced. [The boss told

---

²The masses of reporters invading the grieving community can indeed cause further stress and have psychological impact on survivors of crises. For example, Siri Thoresen et al.'s study of survivors of the terror attack at Utøya Island (Thoresen et al. 2014) associated negative experience with media participation with increased post-traumatic stress.

me] that if it had been an American aeroplane, we would have filled four pages with it. But he didn't realize that it was caused by the personnel situation. (Field notes)

The same could happen in television, in case the tragedy happened in the middle of July when the TV station produces fewer programs and many people go on vacation:

> When Russians started to … be in Crimea, and then when the pro-Russian rebels shot down the MH17 above Ukraine, when almost no one and only one of the bosses was at work, I was here from 8am to 11pm, trying to make the staff work. *This* was a crisis. (Šimon)

The typical silly season, which recently has not been that silly, though. In the case of Ernest's and Cyril's workplace, a newsroom of one of the most read Slovak dailies, the lack of personnel was long-term and thus had more systematic and structural effects. The two journalists together constituted the *whole* of the foreign affairs news desk. Neither of them could afford to cover crises in the field, because only one person would be left in the newsroom.

In sum, Nicolas from *LS*, speaking to James shortly after the terrorist attacks in Brussels on 22 March 2016, described the interconnection of the organizational and personnel crisis, the crisis out there, the crisis of the press, and the economic crisis:

> At the newspaper *LS* at the beginning of the year 2000, we were 110. We are now 90. So we lack. … We lost 20 percent for economic reasons, but we also have the pressure of the economic crisis, and at the same moment, we have the fatigue of this war stress. So what did we get? We got burnout. And we got people that are just on medical treatment, who are ill. Why are they ill? They are ill at the same time because of the economic pressure, post-economic crisis, because of the management that is more brutal, but at the same time, the coverage of crisis. And you just have to try to distinguish now what is due to the economic crisis—this happens in every newsroom in the world—and what is due to the new threat related to the kind of trauma you have within your work. It's not that easy. (Nicolas)

Nicolas' summary not only puts in a nutshell the interconnection of the outside-the-media and inside-the-media crises but also shows well some specifics of crisis reporters' precarity, that is, their existential, financial,

2 DEFINING A CRISIS: BOARDING   39

and/or social insecurity, consisting in irregular and informal jobs, erratic work schedules, overwork, low levels of safety, and high risk—and implies how deeply the precarity is rooted in media and cultural production (e.g. De Peuter 2011; Hesmondhalgh and Baker 2011).

James glanced to the left. Through the glass door he could see the spot where he was waiting a while ago. Nicolas touched upon the issue that James had already given a thought: work-related traumas and personal crises.

Crisis Outside Is Inside a Journalist

It was not that easy, as Nicolas said, to understand where stress and traumas come from. Yet, it was equally difficult to distinguish between inner and outer crises.

Many journalists—mainly TV reporters—said that on-the-spot crisis reporting meant long-distance traveling, lengthy, "endless" business trips, working up to 18 or 20 hours a day (cf. Pedelty 1995). "One pushes oneself to the limit, several days in a row. (…) Reporting on an exhibition of rabbits does not bring one to such a state. Only reporting on an international crisis can do that," Matouš said. When Josef stated that "at the other TV channel, they promoted 'No sleep during working trips,'" James was taken aback. Tomáš told a story of feeling the limits of his own body after his cameraman collapsed in Hungary during the heat wave in 2015, and Tomáš had to run eight kilometers with a ten-kilo camera on his shoulder, to shoot a milestone of the "refugee crisis." Sparkling with stories from the spot, he also recalled how he tried to report on the financial exploitation of refugees on the Balkan route by Serbian villagers: "They nearly smashed my face in when I was trying to shoot it with the little camcorder, so. And many other colleagues had the same problem" (Tomáš).

But the journalists experienced more kinds of dangers that followed from the commitment to witness, directly or vicariously, the suffering of other people:

> And you really see so much suffering, and you know, you get to know a lot of people, and sometimes you stay in touch with people, for example when I meet Syrian refugees in one of the neighbouring countries, they keep informing me on their way to Europe and how it's working, especially on how it's not working. (Lotte)

James noticed a weak weeping sound coming from around the corner, reminding him that he was just about to board a flight to a focal point of a catastrophe, an event that epitomized the fragility of life on Earth. Sure, this was true for any catastrophe; but this time it felt different. Ice-nine was potentially the most destructive matter that had ever been invented. Never had there been so much uncertainty over the nature and scope of a crisis.

Casting his eyes on his own endangerment would have been unbearable, so James looked outward and returned to his thoughts. Like the distinction between the outside- and inside-the-media crisis (see the previous section), the distinction between the psychological and the physiological crises, risks, and dangers, in which his colleagues found themselves, seemed unclear and sometimes even non-existent (see e.g. Scheper-Hughes and Lock 1987).

Some things "can get you" and trigger or resonate with a "personal crisis" (Ester), like

> when you find out that … right into the people visiting a concert in a club, where they have gone to have fun, someone starts to actually … shoot. Out of the blue, and many people have no chance. It's just something that really gets you. (Matouš)

Matouš was speaking about the attacks in Bataclan, Paris, that occurred on Friday, 13 November 2015. Another journalist, X, admitted—insistently "off the record, but really off the record"—that terrorism, but also violent riots and conflicts, caused him panic attacks that he carefully dissociated as a "disease":

> I do have it from watching … whether or not the policemen have collided with them on Maidan, see? (…) But alcohol helps, I guess. Because it blunts your … Look, I don't drink here, ok? But when you have, say, two glasses of wine in the evening, you may be able to sleep and you don't think about … that tomorrow there will be something like that again, actually.

The journalist Y hinted at a similar thing on the way to another smoking break, accompanied by Z:

> "The main thing is that the crisis event grows into a health crisis. I have a backpack full of pills," says Y, while motioning to his backpack. Indeed, full of something. Both Y and Z look serious—it seems that he is joking only partially. "But don't write it anywhere," says Y, giving a saddened smile. (Field notes)

James thought, what else would have X admitted if he had smoked?

Y was one of those who stayed in James' life even after they were no longer colleagues. They became friends—or something like that. They once went for a beer after work and ended up talking about French poststructuralists, which apparently happened to create an implicit alliance even before they knew "it" about each other. In the months and years that followed, they used to meet every now and then, holding existentialist conversations (that proved to be even more binding).

Apart from "having to be ready for getting yourself as a reporter into trauma" (Nicolas), journalists frequently encounter or interview people who are in much bigger trouble or trauma, which often places the former into moral dilemmas and quandaries (see Boltanski 1999; see the section "Moral Dilemmas and Guilt") and makes the lot even tougher. At the same time, the very experience of meeting people from outside the European "privileged bubble" often makes them realize that "Our particular emotional reactions to those situations are not as significant as that of the people who are genuinely moving through those conditions" (Farrukh). Face to face with their sources' bad deals, the reporters' trauma seems either vanishing in obscurity or absurd. Taken together, the experienced trauma, guilt, consciousness of one's self-pity, and sense of ludicrousness can create a vicious circle.

Perhaps because of its relative "insignificance," said Matouš, "stress is something that one is used to, that pumps you up, it's not that it immediately ruins you. It ruins you a bit later."

After passing through the thorough control of James' ID card and boarding pass at the boarding counter, our hero set foot on the zebra path to the backdoor steps. Going to San Lorenzo, he said to himself aloud. It immediately occurred to him that he must have seemed ridiculous to the young woman who was still two steps behind him. Everyone here was going either to San Lorenzo, or to one of the neighboring islands that were expected to be contaminated by the ice-nine very soon—long before their arrival. For a second, the nervousness he experienced was bodily again. He shivered, felt the urge to erupt into laughter, and jump, pull a face, or cry

His mood again debased the distinction between psychological and (or even "versus") physiological categories. After all, most of his fellow journalists did not distinguish the two. Like Nicolas, working on the Panama Papers: "The problem is not to avoid the contract killer. The problem is to discuss it with your wife. And children."

As Nicolas' words suggest, such an experience—the dialogue between personal and outer (lethal) crisis—follows directly from the "dual state" as actors and observers which journalists are expected to simultaneously maintain (Peters 2011; Tandoc and Takahashi 2016). Or, to put it more precisely, the reporters' lived experience proves that a reporter is an actor—even more inevitably and obviously when she finds herself in danger. For example, as Annabelle Sreberny (2011) argues, September 11 canceled the hierarchy of significance of journalists' inner psychological worlds and the actual dynamics of global state systems; the outside crisis and collective trauma merged with the interior shocks. The very notion of the "dual state" is thus based on the fallacious assumption that journalists are, because of their professional authority (which is, in turn, based on the objectivistic illusion of truth), able to step out from the world—albeit only with one foot—and to look at events from above—even though only with one eye. Journalists' actorship resides in the potential political implications of their action (Ben-Yehuda et al. 2013; Van Der Meer et al. 2016), but also in their roles as witnesses and victims.

An extreme level of active involvement was apparent among journalists covering suicide bombings in Brussels, the city where they lived:

> I recall March 22, that day I was working in shock in the medical sense of the word, even. I didn't expect. ... Because as a journalist, of course, we are used to reporting the crises, that's even our [job description]. Wars, etcetera, etcetera. We're used to that. Then, suddenly, it happens in your own city. That's completely different. (Jacob)

The reporters' involvement went so far as to erase the distinctions between their professional and personal identities (Du Gay 1996; cf. Pedelty 1995). This was not without consequences for the particular kind of objectivity-as-a-practice (Carpentier and Trioen 2010; see the section "Professional Ideology and Its Critique") that they performed.

The issue of the interrelation of crisis "out there" and the personal crisis of a journalist formed the core of what the research questions address, and what will the chapter "The Emotional Experience of Crisis Reporters: The Journey" deal with in more detail: crisis reporters' emotional labor.

Before entering through the back door of the aircraft, James stopped for a moment and glanced at the four fighter jets passing diagonally across the sky. The young woman behind him frowned at him and pursed her lips, but then she lowered her eyes. Her face seemed familiar to James, but he could not place her. He passed by a flight attendant with dark hair tightly tied back, popped eyes, and grotesquely strained smile, and hid himself from the macabre masquerade on board.

The Crisis Out There Is a Locally Lived Moment Is a Global State
Anytime James was on a plane, he felt he had changed his territory, widened his realm. Here, he was on his own. He loved the intense feeling of being alive: putting himself on the line, betting on himself, isolating himself with his responsibility and power—leaving *The Mo* behind and going toward a shrouding mist which, in this particular outside-the-media crisis, was incomparably vaguer than ever before.

Typologies of Crisis Moments
At first glance, the outside-the-media crisis seemed to be an obvious thing. "Something went wrong in a big way," threw in Bob, the minimalist. According to more talkative Julian, Čestmír, or Ema, crisis is a rather unpredictable event that cuts across short- and long-term processes and causes a deviation in society from normality toward a very negative direction. Natural disasters, wars, conflicts, big leaks, terrorist attacks, "and the like" (Čestmír)—these were the most commonly mentioned crises. Some reporters were more concrete and gave the examples of terrorist attacks in Paris during the year 2015 and Brussels in March 2016, parts of the Russian-Ukrainian conflict, the failed states in Egypt, Syria, and across Central Africa, the earthquake in Haiti, and "too many refugees in such a short period of time" (Tomáš). What all these understandings of the concept of "crisis" have in common is that they stress the temporally and spatially limited character and negativity of the event or situation. Most of all, they resemble the somewhat narrow definition of crisis as a more or less unpredictable event with potentially negative effects on its environment/surroundings/milieu—a turning point, a threat (Coombs 2010; Walaski 2011). As mentioned earlier, such a sudden and unpredictable event may also pose a danger to society and create high levels of confusion, as well as time pressure (see the section "Inside-the-Media Is Outside-the-Media Crisis").

Imagining the ice-nine-caused catastrophe, James finally found his seat. It was the same as the last time.

Although crises are "*always* about the people" (Marie, Lotte) and, being aware that it is them who make sense of the particular event and who structure the unknown (Weick 1995), the journalists *always* try to give the most truthful representation of what happened even more than in "normal" times (Kryštof, Sven, Cyril), each crisis is different "depending on the time when it happens and the place where it happens" (Olga).

> each of them requires a slightly different approach, different preparations, different type of behaviour, different style of reporting. (Čestmír)

Thus, as Olga suggests, from the journalistic point of view, it makes more sense to distinguish crises based on their temporality and spatiality then based on their origin and nature (e.g. Cottle 2009; Sellnow and Seeger 2013). Most accurately, Nord and Strömbäck (2003: 71) suggest that there are four types of crises based on their predictability, the surprising character of the crises, and their newness or repetition: new and surprising events, new but expected events, surprising events that have happened before, and expected events that have happened before. The individual types are distinct in terms of the media representation of the given event. Indeed, the reporters say that they work differently with short- and long-term situations; with events that happen in the morning, at noon, in the evening; or during working hours and weekends; whether it happens in a neighboring country or in, say, Pakistan, Yemen, Nigeria:

> when in Sana'a a bomb explodes at a market place and kills fifteen people, it has no chance to get anywhere. It would have to be 450 people and a children's choir, ideally. ... These shifts, it's called 'Arabic numbering.' When Europeans die, then it takes less. ... Well, it's terrible. (Astrid)

Also Farrukh, Ida, Tobiáš, at least four women from *ČT*, Ben, Sven, Ernest, and others in one way or another reflected upon the disproportion in the viewing of culturally close and distant deaths. By evaluating such an approach as "terrible" and "cynical," they implicitly—often by the way or on the way out to lunch (Field notes)—criticized news values of bad news, magnitude, relevance, and the power elite (Harcup and O'Neill 2001). At the same time, by expressing their criticism by the way and outside the newsroom, most of the reporters proved their adaptation to the somewhat bloodthirsty mainstream media logic: it was just the normal way it goes.

Farrukh, pointing at "the grossest exploitation of dead black bodies" and talking about the camera as a weapon of "European Western power, let's be clear about that," pronounced more thought-through criticism. He partly evaded the iron cage of the Western mainstream media logic by going independent and working on stories that "standard magazines wouldn't buy." (An act which he could afford after reaching a certain level of fame and after collecting a number of awards for his work for Western mainstream media.) Similarly, for Ida, the very negotiation of geographical-emotional closeness/distance relative to enough corpses was sufficient as a reason to explain why she was uncertain about her future journalistic career:

> I don't want to get to the stage where I won't consider fifty dead in Afghanistan sad. To be so ground down that I won't care. ... I want to keep the feeling that all human lives have the same value.

Both of them deliberately refused to accept that crisis events and tragic stories are more newsworthy if they refer to elite people, elite nations, and to culturally close regions (see Harcup and O'Neill 2001), and adapted/ were ready to adapt their biographies accordingly.

For the rest, the "twenty bits" (meaning "casualties") in, say, Baghdad, according to Tobiáš, had to stay in the zone of detachment, unlike for example Charlie Hebdo, "because taking all these attacks like [one takes] Charlie Hebdo, one'd go nuts." "It's impossible to carry all the weight of the world on our shoulders," Kryštof summed up.

James wondered whether the specific combinations of newness and repetition had also some consequences for journalists' emotional engagement in the event. Did they react to (potential) death with laughter or with explicit resistance to insensitivity only because they were caught unawares? Was a surprising event necessarily also more emotionally shocking? Is it possible to get emotionally used to a long-term crisis? Can good preparation reduce the stress?

Belgium, Czechia, and the Closeness of a Crisis
The grasp of the contact between Europe and the Global South was not the only important aspect of the spatiality of crises. The European mediascape comprised miscellaneous regions. James knew at least something about the varied European media systems (while working mainly in two of them), each of them dealing with specific challenges.

There was Belgium: Belgique, België, and Belgien. Some of the Belgian journalists talked about an inherently critical context of their work, stemming from the reoccurring conflict between Wallonia and Flanders:

> Belgium is not a particularly ... peaceful land. We are not fighting. But ... crisis has always been there. The differences between the two communities fuel a rampant crisis. (Louis)

Moreover, the Belgian reporters had a somewhat specific experience with covering a major crisis event—a terrorist attack—that happened in their own country. "War, it's not just going on there. It's just coming back here," said Sam. The difference from "just another bombing" over there (Lotte) and when "the crisis came home" (Jacob) resided in its "surrealism": an internationally relevant negative event that the reporters were accustomed to reporting on from afar suddenly occurred in their own country. Finding themselves in the middle of the type of event that they had previously experienced as temporary visitors, they had difficulty realizing, or at least found it "very strange," that it was happening in Brussels:

> So I was invited by *CNN* twice, and that was a very strange experience. Because then it's kind of surreal. Because this is a place where I often go. ... It really felt strange to talk about your own country as a ... Because the questions were really like a bit combat zone questions. (Sven)

Sven's statement illustrates his feeling of the unusual nature of the double status as both an observer and a member—even spokesperson—of the community (Peters 2011; Tandoc and Takahashi 2016). His (and others') "surreal" feelings and thus emotional difficulty were determined by several dimensions of closeness at play (Tumber 2011), mainly by the materiality of the situation and its technological circumstances and by the fact that it affected loved ones and fellow citizens, about whom the reporters were worried.

First, the usual experience of crisis reporting was altered by the materiality—the geographical and technological circumstances—of the situation. The space where the reporters commonly performed their work merged with a meaningful, personally relevant place:

> The problem is that the airport was always for me a bit like a homecoming. That airport. Because it's mostly my starting point and the end of my journey. ... You see a lot of misery, but when you come to the airport, you feel safe, home, secure, you know? (Carl)

2 DEFINING A CRISIS: BOARDING   47

Moreover, the reporters' sense of existence was intensified and confused by technology. Carl further recalled that the first night after the all-day reporting from Zaventem Airport, he went to his favorite bar for pilots and flight attendants not far from the spot:

> And the TV was playing. … That was already strange. Because you were seeing yourself reporting on a place which was only half a mile away, [and] you were still there. … So it was like becoming all one.

Other journalists, besides reporting on the attacks, became objects of others' reporting, which disturbed the outer boundaries of the profession (see Carlson and Lewis 2015). Sven turned into a talking head (see earlier in the chapter). Ben was helping US journalists find their way around Molenbeek, a neighborhood where he and the perpetrators lived. This experience of convergence seemed to reach an uncanny extent which appeared to transcend reality.

Second, for the interviewees, the difference resided in their emotional closeness to people who were directly or indirectly affected, such as children, friends, parents, siblings, and their perceptions:

> it's very different, because I have a family and I have two children who go to school in Brussels, so my son was here, my little daughter just had a school trip, a tour of Brussels, and the whole school was actually in the metro. (Sven)

> And then there comes an e-mail from the school, it says 'everything is ok, but children can't go out during the [recess], so they have to stay in.' … So that's, of course, that's very emotional. (Jacob)

All of the journalists were also well aware of their active role in the construction of narratives about the attacks, the perpetrators, and the victims, and thus of their political authority within the community. Moreover, they were well aware of the construction mechanisms used by terrorist organizations via various media (e.g. Falkheimer and Olsson 2015) Finding themselves in the middle of the struggle among narratives meant that their incentive to produce the best possible news (McDonald and Lawrence 2004) further resonated with the emotions they felt as Belgian citizens and inhabitants of Brussels. For example, Sven and Sam were frustrated when their analytical accounts were misinterpreted or misunderstood:

> It's like a puzzle. Many pieces of the puzzle, as many as you can, different angles, different views. What is affecting me, or touching me, is when … they don't treat it with proper respect. … I was anxious. Society has divided. You have Islamophobia, so I think it's extreme. … A war zone, even for me, is less tiring than that. Because this is part of my own society. (Sam)

Both the social and the material dimensions of closeness and identification constituted membership in the imagined community of Brusselians/Belgians sharing the trauma and the not-so-imagined community of family members and neighbors (Anderson 1991; Hutchison and Bleiker 2008). The combination of the material context and social ties thus significantly intensified the surreal duality of the journalists' status as observers and as community members (Peters 2011; Tandoc and Takahashi 2016) while simultaneously triggering bodily feelings of fear, worry, and anger. To put it differently, the closeness challenged the border between the reporters' personal and professional identities. Since the identity of (media) professionals constitutes itself in relation to personal identity (Du Gay 1996), their socio-materially mediated integration raised questions about the journalists' fit within professional boundaries (Carlson and Lewis 2015).

Interestingly, some Belgian reporters were not astonished and talked instead about confirmation of their predictions, or even spoke about "release of tension" in their Brussels newsrooms.

> To my surprise, people were really … I wouldn't say satisfied, I'd say eased, because what we were feeling for years just happened. And we knew what exactly the form that it took was. … It just concretely happened, and you just said, 'Uff, okay. So we work.' (Nicolas)

After the long-term vague and constant threat and anxiety were condensed into a concrete attack, the journalists found relief in the clear task that had landed in the newsroom.

In sum, reporting on a crisis close to home ultimately resulted in the journalists' stronger identification and closeness (cf. Tumber 2011), as the latter constituted "surreal" feelings related to the ambiguous and self-contradictory relationship between professional and personal contexts and identities (Alsup 2005; Peters 2011; Tandoc and Takahashi 2016; Van Zoonen 1998). On the one hand, their tasks placed the reporters in an emotionally demanding position and required much effort. On the other hand, the tasks needed to be performed despite the emotional thrill of the moment. Thus, the work itself forced (or helped) the reporters to avoid fully realizing the tragedy and to suspend their feelings.

Nevertheless, even an emotionally shocking event of this kind did not come completely from out of the blue. A mere week before the attacks on 22 March 2016, Louis anticipated:

> We are confronted with the fact that it could also happen here in Brussels. Yes. Now, this is maybe the most difficult thing to accept. Because we've got to live with this threat. This is maybe a new paradigm. (Louis)

The recollection of Louis' prediction gave James the shivers. However, what gave him the shivers in the blink of an eye were the Czech specifics of covering crises.

Czechia used to be a very calm place. In a way, it was isolated in its homogeneity and lack of (media) interest in foreign affairs (Vítek, Josef). No crisis on the horizon; so some journalists had the feeling that they needed to create one.

Like on an especially silly seasoned day in June 2015, after doctors suppressed the MERS (Middle East respiratory syndrome) virus. Marek, head of one of the newsrooms, being nervous about the lack of breaking news, was marching around the newsroom, jokingly ordering his subordinates: "We need another disease today, come up with another one!" (Field notes). The feeling of the need for a crisis was reduced to absurdity by one of the commercial TV channels. In autumn 2015, its management expressly ordered the staff to report on refugees as a threat (*The Economist* 2016). The strategy of such a purposive, deliberate, and literary securitization of migration (e.g. Bigo 2002), or rather institutionalized xenophobia, broke all ethical standards. Not only the action of the management of the TV channel, but also other processes of building a security threat from nothing was harshly criticized by many colleagues of James (not only from Czechia), such as Astrid, Tobiáš, Richard, Čestmír, Josef, Ema, Ernest, Giuseppe, Bob, and Diego.

Such creation of artificial, sensational news emerged partly from another specific of the Czech media system. Many times James had been told and made aware that the Czech post-socialist media environment was "distorted and deviated" (Matouš), fatally marked by the "wild privatisation" after 1989, oligarchization, and the neoliberalist turn (manifesting itself, among other things, in the opinion that public service media are superfluous, and by the lack of media attention paid to foreign affairs) (see Balčytienė et al. 2015; Örnebring 2009). As such, the Czech media system was seen as inherently critical as well, by both paper press journalists and public service TV reporters, in particular, because the nature of the national media system was seriously affecting the quality of journalism:

> In this country—when I leave aside the economic aspect—this [media ownership and political influence] is a much bigger crisis. That many really important topics do not appear in the media. Which is simply really dangerous for the society. (…) And the truth is that a lot of journalists are bribed. (…) Now, switch it off—really. (Y)

James did not know what to switch off, but cared rather about his vanishing naiveté. Even now, when he recalled the moment, he saw his gullibility fading into the distance of front rows. To James, this conversation worked as an initiation ritual. As if the information was labeled "staff only," similar to the warning sign he had spotted some minutes before inside the tail next to the uncanny flight attendant.

To put it in a nutshell, both the media systems suffered from nationally specific defects. Each of them had its own way of being inherently critical.

Importantly, a terror attack in one's own country or inventing a threat is not the only way how a crisis can come closer. It can also get closer, for example, by language. Kate Adie, a reporter covering Northern Ireland, recalled that threats issued in her own language were far more frightening than threats delivered in a foreign language by people who look different (Tumber 2006). Likewise, Sven recalled that it was "too much" when, a few days after the Brussels attacks, he was asked to write an article about the first Belgian Daesh fighter who killed somebody execution-style, and he needed to watch the Daesh video:

> I mean, it's a horror, it's horrible. And then I watched it, and that felt like the information was too much. … Of course, it was the killing of the person, but also. … Originally, I am from Antwerp. It was also his accent. … The accent of my schoolmates.

By sharing the accent with the perpetrator, the crisis came unbearably close to Sven. By comparison, Lilah, reporting on refugees and speaking Arabic, grew closer to the victims of the "refugee crisis": she became the medium between refugees and audiences, and even European offices, in yet another sense.

A level of closeness stemmed also from the journalists' professional ecosystem (Abbott 2005). For example, after the murder of Slovak journalist Ján Kuciak and his fiancé Martina Kušnírová, James' colleagues from Slovakia perceived a certain determination and interconnection among the community of journalists—mainly the investigative reporters. The sentiments raised by recent attacks on journalists could even transcend national borders. Indeed, journalists often felt themselves as members of a transnational mediascape that transcends all borders, rather than as employees, falsely self-employed or contractors of a particular media company and working in a particular country. This included also fixers—often local journalists or activists—who sometimes found themselves much more endangered than the European reporters, and for whom the reporters felt responsible (Gloria, Ernest, Sam). The most evident case of the professional unity was the terror attacks on the staff of Charlie Hebdo:

> I mean, the Charlie attacks were also ... felt harder here in the newsroom, because it was colleagues. Then it comes closer. ... I think that Charlie had a deeper impact on the professional things we do here than the other Paris attack, which ... Charlie was just an attack on people like us. (Jacob)

Jacob expressed the sentiments of many of his colleagues from all around Europe. The unprecedented nature of the Charlie attacks was also apparent in the newsrooms where James worked. He took out his cell phone and scrolled through the gallery. He found a picture of a column behind which he used to sit when he worked at *LN*.

On the best visible side of the column, above a notice board of the foreign news desk, there was hanging the iconic green title page of Charlie Hebdo with Mohammed holding "Je Suis Charlie" sign. On the square, someone pasted an even bigger black poster with Mohammed's caricature.

He scrolled down a bit more and ran into another photo from one of the labyrinthine corridors of *ČT*. It depicted a door that he used to pass several times a day. On the door, there hung a photo of one of his distant colleagues, saying "Je suis Jiří." The second picture made him laugh—good old times!

Individual Tragedies Within the Broader Picture
Making fun of the Charlie Hebdo case did not necessarily mean that the reporters were wicked and unsympathetic (see how crisis reporters defend themselves from constantly facing others' suffering in the section "Coping

Strategies"). Quite the opposite: for many of James' colleagues, crisis is defined primarily by the death or suffering of people. For example, to Sven, a political crisis, a natural disaster, and a social crisis were only words referring to the prelude to "crisis as a situation where human beings end up in a very vulnerable and dangerous and harmful situation" (Sven). Such an understanding of crisis paved the way to rich storytelling: "I try to pick out a human story to tell the broader political view," Lotte said. Judith even believed that putting the human story into context forms the core of "valuable journalism" and an answer to her students' question: How not to feel as a vulture?

Correspondingly, the level of crisis-ness consists in the nature and context of the event. Crisis must have "a wider societal impact" (Tomáš). The crisis-ness of an airplane crash, for example, depends on whether (the media have known from the beginning that) it was a terror attack (and acted accordingly—gave it much more space) or not. A single terror attack, a local conflict, or an environmental catastrophe epitomizes a broader dramatic story of modernity (Heaphy 2007; Wagner 1994), and the task of a crisis reporter is to show the relation of the two. In turn, for Sam, as for Vítek, Jacob, Sven, Josef, and Lotte, connecting the immediate, local level with the long-lasting, global, "broader picture" (Lotte) was the source of their passion for crisis reporting. "It has to be rooted in complex societal evolution. And then it's interesting," Sam said.

James put his hand into his pocket, pulled out an almost finished pack of chewing gum, and stuck the last piece in his mouth, trying to protect his middle-ear micro-mechanics against the air pressure. The aircraft was supposed to take off in a few minutes.

The link between the contemporary crisis of modernity/risk society (Beck 1992; Giddens 1991; Wagner 1994) and locally and individually experienced crisis situations has been thoroughly theorized. As Anthony Giddens argues while speaking about global threats, most notably the latest fads of the industrialization of war, these

> social circumstances are not separate from personal life, nor are they just an external environment for them. ... Changes in intimate aspects of personal life, in other words, are directly tied to the establishment of social connections of very wide scope. ... The wholesale penetration of abstract systems into daily life creates risks which the individual is not well placed to confront. ... Greater interdependence, up to and including globally interdependent systems, means greater vulnerability when untoward events occur that affect those systems as a whole. (Giddens 1991: 12, 32, 136)

2 DEFINING A CRISIS: BOARDING 53

Similarly, Ulrich Beck and Elisabeth Beck-Gernsheim note that

> social crisis phenomena such as structural unemployment can be shifted as a burden of risk onto the shoulders of individuals. Social problems can be directly turned into psychological dispositions: into guilt feelings, anxieties, conflicts and neuroses. (Beck and Beck-Gernsheim 2001: 24)

All the global threats/risks thus become localized and materialized in the emotional lives of individuals, who then feel anxious. High-consequence risks especially shake the foundations of ontological security, the basic secure sense of reality and continuity (Giddens 1991), which influences the capacity of individuals to deal with existential questions. To be sure, as Giddens stresses, the point is not that everyday life is more risky than before; rather, the risk climate means that thinking in terms of risk is everyone's ever-present exercise. Thus, many neuroses and anxieties emerge as a response to risks and threats and their biographization—that is, their incorporation into individual biographies (Beck and Beck-Gernsheim 2001). In other words, although individuals may be required to resolve the potential neuroses and anxieties on their own, perhaps with biomedical help, these are individualized and psychiatrized *social* changes and *systemic* problems (Heaphy 2007; Lasch 1991; Scheper-Hughes and Lock 1987).

James' colleagues were aware of this dialectic in the case of their respondents, talking heads, interviewees—in short, the unfortunates, among whom the journalists were rather spectators or interlopers (Boltanski 1999). Like Lotte, speaking about Syrian children in Turkish refugee camps:

> But you just know that this generation is so damaged because of what's happening now. That it's not good for the future either. And that's just why it frustrates me so much. Because it's not just happening now, it will have consequences for at least one and probably two, three generations. (Lotte)

Nevertheless, the dialectic of global and locally lived crisis is relevant also for the "crisis reporters" themselves. For them, the generalized crisis of modernity (see later in the chapter) goes hand in hand with the everyday contact with its real, "already destructive consequences" (Beck 1992: 33; see the following section "Crisis is Media-Constructed Is Real") such as floods, limited wars, and terror attacks, which together lead their individualized psychological consequences on a leash.

James looked out the window. In the distance, he saw the last passengers of a just-landed flight striding into the airport building. A tall, slim man was leading two little children by the hands. Nostalgia for his father overwhelmed him—his childish sense of humor; silent conspiratorial bursts of laughter; his huge warm, dry, lined palms that he used to put on anthills when James was a little boy; ants would climb up his hands—the swarming astonished James; and his habit of shaking the walnut tree in the garden, so that James could pick up the nuts. It was more than a year since his father passed away.

Losing him led James into an even greater need for independence. And, here he was: ready to make good use of it. Although the pain was still stabbing.

In the newsrooms, the response to situations of mass death and suffering that implicitly reminded the staff of the potential destruction of the whole planet was often humorous (see the section "Cynics and Kynics: Pissing Against the Idealist Wind"). James soon learned the "typical morning joke" that journalists say to each other after entering the newsroom: "No airplane crash yet today?" (Olga).

An airplane crash was something that James really did not want to think of at the moment. His will to life was too strong. It made itself heard: his stomach rumbled.

The World and Journalism After September 11, 2008, 2011, 2014, 2015, and 1750
Rather, James recalled another situation from the *LN* newsroom that made him laugh:

> Searching for something at *The Independent*. After clicking on a headline, a stereotypically Arabic melody wafts through the open space. The entire editorial staff immediately stops working, falls silent, stands still and starts staring at me. I apologize, shrug my shoulders and have to start laughing. "Since Charlie Hebdo, everyone gets afraid when they hear something like this in the newsroom," an editor, scared stiff three meters away from me, explains. "Is it your ringtone?" I say, "No, it's started to play at *The Independent*." Then he starts joking with the colleagues: "Guys, let everything be, we're gonna have a moment of prayer!" (Field notes)

Many of the crisis reporters talked about the contemporary changing, complex, non-stable world. As a turning point, they usually cited

September 11—a day that shook to its foundations the familiar notions of how best to practice journalism and what it means to be a journalist (Zelizer and Allan 2011). A milestone after which international reporting became more important, because the West realized that even distant conflicts can have impact (Anthony). Some of them saw as another milestone the so-called Arab Spring in 2011 (mainly for journalists specialized in the Middle East), the beginning of the Russian-Ukrainian war in 2014, and the aforementioned attack on Charlie Hebdo in 2015. In their view, short-term crises were interconnected with failing states, the population explosion, or lack of resources. As focal points, they saw the MENA (Middle East and North Africa) region and the "unclear zone between Russia and the rest of the world" (Josef). Jacob and Josef thought that

> It's a kind of avalanche of crisis that we've seen and still see. It started in 2008 with the bank crisis, and it hasn't stopped since then. … professionally, it's very attractive, to try to analyze these big movements, the financial crisis, the migration crisis, the institutional crisis with different instruments, so that's intellectually very attractive—that's the reason why I am a journalist. On the other hand, of course there is the terror crisis. (Jacob)

> the relatively stable state is more and more relative and the crisis is kind of permanent. (Josef)

The fast pace of change is also reflected in media practices and required journalistic skills. While "15 years ago we needed a war correspondent, now we need an expert on terror, and the next generation will need geeks," said Nicolas.

James pulled his computer out of his backpack and smiled faintly at his relative technological incompetence. Interested in analytical work, he was not a geek and never wanted to be. So far, he had managed to disguise his reluctance and a kind of technological conservatism that he self-legitimized as romanticism. But if Nicolas was right, James knew he would need to find another job in a few years.

This understanding of permanent crisis is fully consistent with the way of using the concept of crisis from the second half of the eighteenth century onward: as a word describing a generalized modern experience, to the extent that it becomes a permanent concept of history. "The concept of crisis has become the fundamental mode of interpreting historical time. (…) 'Crisis' becomes a structural signature of modernity. … an immanent, permanent condition of the world" (Koselleck 2006: 371–372). And since then—thanks to Rousseau, Diderot, Paine, and Herder—the term has gained a religious connotation akin to the "Apocalypse" and "Last Judgement"; albeit used in a post-theological mode, history has incorporated eschatology. Periods of exception and crisis have become the norm (Agamben 2005 in Kaleta 2017); also reporters have normalized the abnormal and routinized the absurd and extraordinary (Pedelty 1995; Zelizer and Allan 2011).

"In the unlikely event of landing on water" James listened to the metallic voice casually wafting from the loudspeakers. The theatrical flight attendant was performing the robotic dance on emergency exits.

The generalized crisis of modernity has been widely discussed by the sociological successors of the dark-minded enlightened philosophers. Although, as stated earlier, the word "crisis" itself is not favored by the social theorists of late modernity for its excessive use and vulgarization, Peter Wagner proposes to keep it to describe periods of modernity "when individuals and groups change their social practices to such an extent that major social institutions and, with them, the prevailing configuration of institutions undergo a transformation" (Wagner 1994: 31)—in other words, for periods of de-conventionalization tendencies (cf. the positioning of crisis versus "normal times" by McDonald and Lawrence 2004, or Schudson 2011) accompanied by lack of integration, a sense of decline, rupture, or ending. Others, such as Ulrich Beck (1992) and Anthony Giddens (1990), characterize the late/reflexively modern world as a place full of globalized, universalized, and vague threats where people live in a state of permanent endangerment and loss of ontological security (Beck et al. 1994). The most current eschatological vision that they put forward thus consists in the "heightened sense of 'man- made' risks that cut across old boundaries of class, generation, geographical location and the like" (Heaphy 2007: 9) and in the view that "Modernity is self-critical and self-destructive" (Touraine 1995: 100).

Which is not inaccurate. Although James was too young to be able to compare the level of today's crisis-ness with premodern periods, he would agree with Giddens that there were some new trends. "The possibility of nuclear war, ecological calamity, uncontainable population explosion, the collapse of global economic exchange, and other potential global catastrophes provide an unnerving horizon of dangers for everyone" (Giddens 1990: 125). Similarly, Beck draws attention to the continuous threat of environmental and technological risks accompanying the attempts to increase and utilize Western techno-scientific rationality (that has been believed to help with overcoming the risks emerging from prior modernization; mainly poverty, social stratification, and unemployment). As a consequence of these attempts to deal with the risks of early modernization, catastrophe becomes an inseparable part of the "second" or late modernity (Beck 1992). The risks are multidimensional: the environmental and technological threats are inseparable from those of a social, economic, or political nature (Beck et al. 1994).

The case of San Lorenzo was emblematic. It was simply impossible to delimit the disaster caused by ice-nine as an event affecting—but also caused by—one particular "material." Above all, as ice-nine was a scientific invention, the catastrophe was nothing but an extremely concentrated outcome of modern thought (see Van Loon 2002) (Image 2.3).

The spreading of ice-nine, like other individual crisis events, then, can be seen as a *spatially and temporally limited realization of new risks*. This definition emphasizes, first, the *real* aspect of new risks, and sidelines the potential and unreal ones (Beck 1992), and second, the dialectics between the contemporary crisis of modernity, or risk society, or reflexive

Image 2.3 A frozen city. Drawing by Peter Van Goethem, 2017. Courtesy of the artist

modernity (Beck 1992; Giddens 1991; Wagner 1994) and locally lived crisis situations.

While putting his worn carry-on suitcase into overhead storage, James saw her face. The young woman who had always been two steps behind him was now sitting right in front of him. No doubt it was her. Sophie Schlesinger, *the* crisis reporter. He had seen her yesterday on TV while watching the first flashes on the San Lorenzo catastrophe.

In crisis reporting, women were either not visible enough or were too visible, depending on the level and face of patriarchy permeating the social context. "Crisis reporting is generally considered a male job," his Italian colleague Giuseppe explained. But Sophie seemed to be everywhere. At the same time, she stood out among the other "little girls in bullet proof vests"—young female celebrity war reporters criticized by Bob for contributing to the spectacularization of Danish crisis reporting—by her erudition. She was always equipped with thorough knowledge of the context. Taken together, it gave the impression that she was gifted by some preternatural capabilities.

In fact, it was she who inspired James not only to become a journalist, but, which is crucial, to try to do his best. But most importantly—and this was something that James did not realize—her somewhat moral and responsible approach to the profession was what kept alive James' hope for the existence of some basic values and principles. And now, she was sitting here, toughing it out.

Crisis Is Media-Constructed Is Real

The risks Beck talks about are rather global, vague, invisible, all-embracing. Yet—although Beck and his followers emphasize the "not-yet-event" (Beck 1992: 33) and the "potential" character of new risks—the plastic soup, the fall of MH17, the BP oil leak in the Gulf, sinking islands, or the Fukushima nuclear catastrophe are painfully localized and affect the everyday life of many people (e.g. Allan et al. 2000). Beck himself states that

> Risks of course do not exhaust themselves in the effects and damages that have already occurred. There must be a distinction between *already destructive consequences* and the *potential element* of risks. (…) In a fundamental sense they are both *real* and *unreal*. On the one hand, many hazards and damages are already real today: polluted and dying bodies of

2 DEFINING A CRISIS: BOARDING 59

water, the destruction of the forest, new types of disease, and so on. On the other hand, the actual social impetus of risks lies in the *projected dangers of the future*. (Beck 1992: 33–34; italics original)

James looked at his mobile for the last time before selecting flight mode. He opened Signal, recommended for internal communication. A message from Fred: "Good opportunity," Fred wrote. "Don't screw it up." The whole management of *The Mo*, as with other media organizations James knew, and maybe even for the media in general, had a somewhat love-hate relationship with crisis events. Mainly love:

> When there is an international crisis or something happens, like Haiti, one doesn't tell oneself, this is crisis, but rather simply, this is an event! (Astrid)

> There seems to be a tendency towards more conflict reporting. (…) And there is always the element of crisis. (Jacob)

This means that—somewhat contrarily to the aforementioned definition of crisis—it is not only the inherent characteristics of an event that constitute crisis-ness, negativity, and thus newsworthiness (Harcup nad O'Neill 2001). The crisis-media entanglement also works the other way around: media can define, sensationalize, deny, or hide crises (Cottle 2009; see the section "Emotions in Crisis Coverage"). "What is worth covering is decided at the meetings" (Josef). The newswork and the process of becoming of a crisis overlap. For some, crisis is even defined by the visual form it takes on the screen: "It's me, who decides, *this* is a crisis, and puts there the yellow banner," said Olga once, as if it was taken for granted.

In general, it can be said that modernity and its crises have always been inseparable from their media representation: the birth and development of modern institutions have been bound up with the increase in mediation of experience by printed text and, subsequently, by electronic signal, nullifying spatial-temporal distantiation, emptying time and space. "Intrusion of distant events into everyday consciousness" (Giddens 1991: 27), together with the nomadic nature of life spent in trains, cars, and airplanes, and then on the Internet (Beck and Beck-Gernsheim 2001), has been one of the major defining features of (late) modernity. Media, evoking the sense of reality inversion, have blurred the boundaries between "real" events and their representations. Expert knowledge and abstract systems have become accessible to lay actors, introducing to them the risks and the new forms of danger they have to accept.

In particular, invisible risks "initially only exist in terms of the (scientific or anti-scientific) *knowledge* about them. They can thus be changed, magnified, dramatized, or minimized within knowledge, and to that extent they are particularly *open to social definition and construction*. Hence the mass media and the scientific and legal professions in charge of defining risks become key social and political positions" (Beck 1992: 23; italics original). As the risks are self-fulfilling by definition and have been co-constructed, spread, and shared via sharing reflexive knowledge and communication technologies, the (news) media can be understood as a risk-constitutive force: "media are part of the technological constellation through which risks come into existence" (Van Loon 2002: 12; see also Cottle 2009). This is what Sam meant when he spoke about today's Europe and the Middle East:

> you have the wars in the Middle East, you have the terrorism which is happening here, and the extremism, and Turkey and the migration. And all these three are linked together. You cannot solve one without solving the others. But what is happening in the media, in the minds of the people, is that they isolate one of the three and give a very strong aggressive answer to it. … You cannot solve one without solving all the three of them. … I think the responsibility of media and politicians in these days is so enormous, to keep our society from slipping into times like before.

Although Beck explicitly emphasized the socially constructed (i.e. media-defined) character of new risks, the subtheme of media influence remained under-theorized in his work (Allan et al. 2000; Cottle 1998; Tulloch and Lupton 2001). Later, Beck himself acknowledged the insufficient attention he had paid to the media, given their importance in the risk society:

> the key significance of mass media in the risk society (…) is something I have addressed again and again, if only with bold theories (…). This is clearly not sufficient given the significance of the subject and is to be attributed to my limitations alone. For the risk society can be grasped theoretically, empirically and politically only if one starts from the premise that it is always also a knowledge, media and information society at the same time. (Beck 2000: xiii–xiv)

2 DEFINING A CRISIS: BOARDING 61

Nevertheless, it was not only his work but sociological and anthropological research in general that has paid surprisingly little attention to the role of the media within the process of defining and constructing new risks and the crises that arise from them (Allan et al. 2000; Tulloch and Lupton 2001; Van Loon 2002).

"Do you mean the second live update and the third one?" James heard Sophie Schlesinger talking to somebody, maybe a shift leader, on the phone, scheduling the dosage of the San Lorenzo catastrophe. Probably the last chance to plan live broadcast before taking off. Her voice was much softer, calmer, thoughtful, and more tired than he had imagined.

The reporters and journalists were well aware how much of an active role they played in construction of crises. Like Ema, who complained about the relationship between media routines and the way of handling the "refugee crisis" in Calais:

> Our correspondent is on vacation. ... We thought, no hurry, it had already been happening for a few days. Nevertheless, yesterday, *iDNES* published the news. And this is the moment when the crisis situation is created a bit artificially. ... This is the moment when the crisis situation emerges from the competition. Before, it wasn't a crisis, in my opinion. It was a phenomenon that was already continuously happening. But in this way, it was turned into a crisis; suddenly six people simultaneously got engaged in it, discussing who will fly there first. (Ema)

Once a crisis is constructed, the reporters and media organizations know they have gotten involved in its politics as well; therefore, the Flemish national public service broadcaster even employed an official policy of "constructiveness." To be "constructive" meant to avoid spreading fear and firing up emotions by "trying to explain ... why something didn't go right, apparently, ... without, of course, ignoring the facts, even if these facts are inconvenient" (Jacob).

Such a constructiveness, officially proclaimed or not, was considered a principle of public service media in general. A moment that partially exemplifies it happened at *ČT*:

> Afternoon meeting. Discussing today's action of a host in the studio. Her guest, a military psychologist, interconnecting the Paris attacks with migration in his speech, said that radicalization of Muslims was genetically encoded. The host was apparently shocked: she opposed him and said,

"Let's talk about something else." Nevertheless, she was criticized by some people at the meeting for opposing the guest "rudely." Čestmír argued that "He won't be invited anymore, it's open racism in broadcasting!" Martin, one of the heads of news, said: "She disassociated herself from it, (...) I think it's good that she opposed and distanced herself. (...) She is a professional, but she is also a human." (Field notes)

Opposing a racist "expert" was the host's way of being constructive. James both witnessed the live broadcast and took part in the following meeting and debate. He admired the host's strength and readiness.

Obviously, journalists' political involvement and political opinion on or expertise in a certain situation go hand in hand with their emotional engagement (see "The Journey"). More specifically, the personal indignation against racism or resentment toward people and groups whom the journalists have to meet, talk to, or to whom they are supposed to give voice in the news despite their evident extreme right or even racist ideas/rhetoric (such as Pegida and Bloc against Islam), together with a more or less vague idea of the active political role of the media and reporters themselves, results in the journalists' strong emotional response, as in Sam's case:

> Sometimes you can, behind the false kind of objectivity, hide the truth also, eh? If you say, for example, 'the so-called occupied territory in Palestine.' What the hell 'so-called' occupied territories!? These territories are occupied, one country occupies the territory of somebody else! What is wrong with clear linguistics? ... There has been a lot of pressure, for many years, to not call it 'occupied' territory, but to call it 'territory.' ... So linguistics or language is power. It's a part of the narrative, a part of the defiance, who is right and who is wrong.

Cf. Vítek's equally emotional statement on the same territory:

> This is totally simple. But *totally simple.* Both the nations have the right to be here. ... Who is right? Not any one. Both of them. Are they able to reach agreement? Well, *not right now.* So, is it a problem, when you deal with specific situations, to agree with one or another side? For God's sake, why? There's no reason.

At the same time, the journalists' inevitable involvement in the process of defining a crisis meant that, according to Cyril, in crisis it was more important to "distinguish who is more probably right and who is more probably wrong," while not being biased (e.g. Gloria). Which was a task for a superhuman.

The no man's land of the departure lounge that James could see through the little oval window was about to stay behind. While James' train of thought was constantly, as if inevitably, turning to his colleagues' emotional experience, James' airplane was about to head toward the catastrophe. James fastened his seat belt and tightened his grip on the computer on his knees.

An Overview

The "crisis" in "crisis reporting" does not have only the non-problematic, at-hand meaning of a situation "out there" that reporters and the media are supposed to "cover" and "transmit." On the contrary, for journalists, crisis is defined by its polyphony and multi-level scope.

To James' colleagues, "crisis" meant an inside-the-media, usually organizational, technological, professional, or personnel situation not far from a breakdown; at the same time, it meant an outside-the-media temporary or continuous major negative event with a wide impact on society and the suffering of individuals, including the psychological state of the journalists themselves and even calling into question the very essence of the current phase of modernity with its global risks and insecurities (that are further individualized). It also meant the real and the media-constructed: media did not need crisis less than crisis needed media. All these meanings of "crisis" were interconnected, and resonated or interfered with each other.

As a result, the crisis is a ubiquitous, all-encompassing phenomenon, an environment for life; the journalists live *inside* the crisis, rather than with it or next to it (cf. Deuze 2011). This also means that journalists simply cannot be mere observers and non-actors. The idea of detachment, impartiality, or professional distance that still forms the core of the objectivistic professional commitment is fallacious (from the epistemological point of view) and utopian (from the point of view of media organizations). Journalists are humans and actors, too (Tandoc and Takahashi 2016; Zelizer and Allan 2011). The journalists' very actorship, the political relevance of their accounts, their endangerment, their witnessing are of crucial importance for their emotional experience—sorrow, moral dilemmas, fear. *What* is the emotional experience will be explored in more detail in the next chapter.

The decisive moment, where James could still turn back and choose to withdraw, or to continue, had just passed. He could hear the engine firing up. The plane was about to take off. James was slightly pushed into the softness of his seat by inertia. In a few seconds, he was supposed to lose his footing.

References

Abbott, A. (2005). Linked Ecologies: States and Universities as Environments for Professions. *Sociological Theory, 23*(3), 245–274.
Agamben, G. (2005). *State of Exception*. Chicago: The University of Chicago Press.
Allan, S., et al. (Eds.). (2000). *Environmental Risks and the Media*. London: Routledge.
Alsup, J. (2005). *Teacher Identity Discourses: Negotiating Personal and Professional Spaces*. London: Routledge.
Anderson, B. R. (1991). *Imagined Communities: Reflection on the Origin and Spread of Nationalism*. London: Verso.
Balčytienė, A., et al. (2015). Oligarchization, de-Westernization and Vulnerability: Media Between Democracy and Authoritarianism in Central and Eastern Europe. A Roundtable Discussion. *Journal of Media, Cognition and Communication, 3*(1), 119–141.
Beck, U. (1992). *Risk Society: Towards a New Modernity*. London: SAGE.
Beck, U. (2000). Foreword. In S. Allan et al. (Eds.), *Environmental Risks and the Media* (pp. xii–xiv). London: Routledge.
Beck, U., & Beck-Gernsheim, E. (2001). *Individualization: Institutionalized Individualism and Its Social and Political Consequences*. London: SAGE.
Beck, U., et al. (1994). *Reflexive Modernization: Politics, Tradition and Aesthetics in the Modern Social Order*. Cambridge: Polity Press.
Ben-Yehuda, H., et al. (2013). When Media and World Politics Meet: Crisis Press Coverage in the Arab–Israel and East–West Conflicts. *Media, War and Conflict, 6*(1), 71–92.
Bigo, D. (2002). Security and Immigration: Toward a Critique of the Governmentality of Unease. *Alternatives, 27*, 63–92.
Boltanski, L. (1999). *Distant Suffering: Morality, Media and Politics*. Cambridge: Cambridge University Press.
Bundy, J., et al. (2017). Crises and Crisis Management: Integration, Interpretation, and Research Development. *Journal of Management, 43*(6), 1661–1692.
Carlson, M., & Lewis, S. C. (Eds.). (2015). *Boundaries of Journalism: Professionalism, Practices and Participation*. London: Routledge.
Carpentier, N., & Trioen, M. (2010). The Particularity of Objectivity: A Poststructuralist and Psychoanalytical Reading of the Gap Between Objectivity-as-a-value and Objectivity-as-a-practice in the 2003 Iraqi War Coverage. *Journalism, 11*(3), 311–328.

Coombs, T. W. (2010). *Ongoing Crisis Communication.* London: SAGE.
Cottle, S. (1998). Ulrich Beck, "A Risk Society" and the Media: A Catastrophic View? *European Journal of Communication, 13*(1), 5–32.
Cottle, S. (2009). *Global Crisis Reporting: Journalism in the Global Age.* Maidenhead: Open University Press.
De Peuter, G. (2011). Creative Economy and Labor Precarity: A Contested Convergence. *Journal of Communication Inquiry, 35*(4), 417–425.
Deuze, M. (2011). Media Life. *Media, Culture and Society, 33*(1), 137–148.
Du Gay, P. (1996). *Consumption and Identity at Work.* London: SAGE.
Falkheimer, J., & Olsson, E. K. (2015). Depoliticizing Terror: The News Framing of the Terrorist Attacks in Norway, 22 July 2011. *Media, War and Conflict, 8*(1), 70–85.
Giddens, A. (1990). *The Consequences of Modernity.* Cambridge: Polity Press.
Giddens, A. (1991). *Modernity and Self-Identity: Self and Society in the Late Modern Age.* Cambridge: Polity Press.
Harcup, T., & O'Neill, D. (2001). What Is News? Galtung and Ruge Revisited. *Journalism Studies, 2*(2), 261–280.
Heaphy, B. (2007). *Late Modernity and Social Change.* London: Routledge.
Hesmondhalgh, D., & Baker, S. (2011). *Creative Labour: Media Work in Three Cultural Industries.* London: Routledge.
Hutchison, E., & Bleiker, R. (2008). Emotional Reconciliation: Reconstituting Identity and Community After Trauma. *European Journal of Social Theory, 11*(3), 385–403.
Kaleta, O. (2017). Migrační režim EU v kontextu trvalého výjimečného stavu. *Mezinárodní vztahy, 52*(2), 57–74.
Koselleck, R. (2006). Crisis. *Journal of the History of Ideas, 67*(2), 357–400.
Lasch, C. (1991). *The Culture of Narcissism: American Life in an Age of Diminishing Expectations.* New York: W. W. Norton & Company.
McDonald, I. R., & Lawrence, R. G. (2004). Filling the 24×7 News Hole: Television News Coverage Following September 11. *American Behavioral Scientist, 48*(3), 327–340.
Nord, L. W., & Strömbäck, J. (2003). Making Sense of Different Types of Crises: A Study of the Swedish Media Coverage of the Terror Attacks Against the United States and the U.S. Attacks in Afghanistan. *Press/Politics, 8*(4), 54–75.
Nord, L. W., & Strömbäck, J. (2006). Reporting More, Informing Less: A Comparison of the Swedish Media Coverage of September 11 and the Wars in Afghanistan and Iraq. *Journalism, 7*(1), 85–110.
Olsson, E. K., & Nord, L. W. (2015). Paving the Way for Crisis Exploitation: The Role of Journalistic Styles and Standards. *Journalism, 16*(3), 341–358.
Örnebring, H. (2009). *Comparative European Journalism: The State of Current Research.* Working paper. Oxford: Reuters Institute for the Study of Journalism.
Pedelty, M. (1995). *War Stories: The Culture of Foreign Correspondents.* London: Routledge.

Peters, C. (2011). Emotion Aside or Emotional Side? Crafting an 'Experience of Involvement' in the News. *Journalism, 12*(3), 297–316.

Scheper-Hughes, N., & Lock, M. (1987). The Mindful Body: A Prolegomenon to Future Work in Medical Anthropology. *Medical Anthropology Quarterly, 1*(1), 6–41.

Schudson, M. (2011). What's Unusual About Covering Politics as Usual. In B. Zelizer & S. Allan (Eds.), *Journalism After September 11* (2nd ed., pp. 44–54). London: Routledge.

Sellnow, T. L., & Seeger, M. W. (2013). *Theorizing Crisis Communication*. New Jersey: John Wiley and Sons.

Sreberny, A. (2011). Trauma Talk: Reconfiguring the Inside and Outside. In B. Zelizer & S. Allan (Eds.), *Journalism After September 11* (2nd ed., pp. 292–307). London: Routledge.

Tandoc, E. C., & Takahashi, B. (2016). Journalists Are Humans, Too: A Phenomenology of Covering the Strongest Storm on Earth. *Journalism, 17*(1), 1–17.

The Economist. (2016, September 13). How a Media Mogul Helped Turn Czechs Against Refugees. *The Economist*. Retrieved from https://www.economist.com/news/europe/21707125-politics-central-and-eastern-europe-are-increasingly-driven-businesses-own-media.

Thoresen, S., et al. (2014). Media Participation and Mental Health in Terrorist Attack Survivors. *Journal of Traumatic Stress, 27*, 639–646.

Touraine, A. (1995). *Critique of Modernity*. Oxford: Blackwell Publishing.

Tulloch, J., & Lupton, D. (2001). Risk, the Mass Media and Personal Biography: Revisiting Beck's 'Knowledge, Media and Information Society'. *European Journal of Cultural Studies, 4*(1), 5–27.

Tumber, H. (2006). The Fear of Living Dangerously: Journalists Who Report on Conflict. *International Relations, 20*(4), 439–451.

Tumber, H. (2011). Reporting Under Fire: The Physical Safety and Emotional Welfare of Journalists. In B. Zelizer & S. Allan (Eds.), *Journalism After September 11* (2nd ed., pp. 319–334). London: Routledge.

Van Der Meer, TGLA. et al. (2016). Disrupting Gatekeeping Practices: Journalists' Source Selection in Times of Crisis. *Journalism*. Epub ahead of print 16 May 2016. https://doi.org/10.1177/1464884916648095.

Van Leuven, S., et al. (2013). Foreign Reporting and Sourcing Practices in the Network Sphere: A Quantitative Content Analysis of the Arab Spring in Belgian News Media. *New Media and Society, 17*(4), 573–591.

Van Loon, J. (2002). *Risk and Technological Culture: Towards a Sociology of Virulence*. London: Routledge.

Van Zoonen, L. (1998). A Professional, Unreliable, Heroic Marionette (M/F): Structure, Agency and Subjectivity in Contemporary Journalisms. *European Journal of Cultural Studies, 1*(1), 123–143.

Vincze, H. O. (2014). 'The Crisis' as a Journalistic Frame in Romanian News Media. *European Journal of Communication, 29*(5), 567–582.
Wagner, P. (1994). *A Sociology of Modernity: Liberty and Discipline*. London: Routledge.
Walaski, P. (2011). *Risk and Crisis Communications: Methods and Messages*. New Jersey: John Wiley and Sons.
Weick, K. E. (1995). *Sensemaking in Organizations*. London: SAGE.
Zelizer, B., & Allan, S. (Eds.). (2011). *Journalism After September 11* (2nd ed.). London: Routledge.

Open Access This chapter is licensed under the terms of the Creative Commons Attribution 4.0 International License (http://creativecommons.org/licenses/by/4.0/), which permits use, sharing, adaptation, distribution and reproduction in any medium or format, as long as you give appropriate credit to the original author(s) and the source, provide a link to the Creative Commons licence and indicate if changes were made.

The images or other third party material in this chapter are included in the chapter's Creative Commons licence, unless indicated otherwise in a credit line to the material. If material is not included in the chapter's Creative Commons licence and your intended use is not permitted by statutory regulation or exceeds the permitted use, you will need to obtain permission directly from the copyright holder.

CHAPTER 3

The Emotional Experience of Crisis Reporters: The Journey

Ten-minute vacuum of gaining altitude. In his thoughts, James returned to San Lorenzo for a while. The last news he had got was the growing number of the dead. In one of the pictures, he saw a dreamlike, once civilized but now decaying square. Since the catastrophe had burst out, many hours before the picture was taken, polished surfaces turned dingy, bright paints faded, and healthy plants went black and dusty. There was no life. Everything looked broken, like 30-year-old forgotten scenery from a low-budget Western film. Never had James seen such a fast downfall. The square was full of petrified-frozen corpses in a line.

Yet, he still knew little about the nature of the catastrophe. Will it resemble a war zone, a natural disaster, an attack? He recalled a very strange week, during which there was a terror attack in Saint Petersburg; Syrian troops launched a chemical attack killing dozens of civilians including children; the US president then "sent a message" to the Assad regime by bombarding a Syrian air base; on the same day, a terrorist hijacked a truck and drove it into a Stockholm department store; on Sunday, the Daesh bombed two Egyptian Coptic churches with, again, tens of victims.

And this happened only in "his world"—Europe, the US, the Middle East. There were also all the thousands who were dying due to draught and much more severe conflicts or bursts of violence in South Sudan, Somalia, Central African Republic, Yemen, Ethiopia, Kenya, Nigeria and DR Congo, Mexico, Myanmar, North Korea. Europeans, including European journalists, had pitifully little information about them. Local

© The Author(s) 2019
J. Kotišová, *Crisis Reporters, Emotions, and Technology*,
https://doi.org/10.1007/978-3-030-21428-9_3

journalists, who could have raised awareness, lived in a different, far more dangerous world (see e.g. Høiby and Ottosen 2015), and only recently started to be in touch with their privileged Western colleagues (Sven, Farrukh). All in all, the Global South remained an unknown zone.

The catastrophe at San Lorenzo could resemble any of the crises that James was aware of or any of those that he couldn't even imagine.

Thinking of all this, James almost fell asleep. The pressure in his ears woke him up. He, finally, immersed in the thoughts about his colleagues' emotions. What is crisis reporters' emotional experience?

Bored in a News Hole

A significant part of journalists' professional ideology is based on their on-site presence (Andén-Papadopoulos and Pantti 2013). A prospective excitement and the opportunity "to be there" also lie at the core of the attractiveness of the profession: as a reporter, Ema said about herself and her colleagues at a journalism school, "We'd all wanted to be war correspondents." Anthony explained: "I wanted to see how the planet rolls." Indeed, working as a war correspondent tends to be particularly appealing for journalistic rookies, since it means becoming a part of a myth (Pedelty 1995). Moreover, it's just fun: "it's fun to be in these emotionally powerful situations, there is an adrenalin rush" (Farrukh).

However, face to face with the daily routine work on non-crisis coverage that the journalistic profession largely consists of, the attractiveness may transform into frustration, boredom, and disappointment (as Ema continued: "No one was."). The disappointment is accompanied by disillusionment and disenchantment with the real journalistic practice. This was explicitly stated by Olga during her fight with Marek (both of them in leading positions in one of the *ČT* newsrooms), when she criticized his submissive way of gaining information:

> Marek, but you are a great journalist! [But your practice resembles the] work of an *upscale assistant.* And I am really fed up with that. I am terribly demotivated. (Field notes)

Indeed, frustration arising from the everyday nothingness, the boredom, and ennui were related to job dissatisfaction or enactment of organizational structure and were particularly on exhibit among Czech journalists. Did their post-socialist, less traditionally professionalized, still less independent, more politically manipulated and oligarchic milieu, that was undergoing a problematic "transition" from an authoritarian media system to a liberal system (Örnebring 2009), play a role? Probably yes—together with the concrete organizational settings. The ennui was particularly visible at *ČT*—a business that was, according to some *ČT* professionals, less flexible due to its leviathan-like clumsiness, residual practices, and heavy materiality. How symptomatic it was that until recently, the company allegedly had maintained its Department of Typewriters (cf. Czarniawska 2011). One of James' *ČT* friends even came up with a perfect motto for the company: "*Czech Television*—you die here" (Field notes). Another colleague, Viktor, agreed:

> I'd call KH[1] a building of totally burntout people, absolutely, totally. And no wonder. Eeeh. ... The people sink into a terrible routine. I have a terrible problem with that. (Viktor)

According to Viktor, a young reporter, the company would use the beginners' enthusiasm—"suck the people dry"—so that after eight years they would have to leave. They would not be able to bear the health costs of the job.

As a consequence of the disenchantment, some described the everyday atmosphere in the newsroom as "sleepy" (Viktor, Ema), a "standard lethargy" (Matouš), a "dearth" (Richard), or "pure boredom" (Josef).

Surprisingly, the boredom was not limited to domestic and parachute reporters; it also appeared among permanent correspondents and sometimes also among those war correspondents who had reached Ema's dream position and, at first sight, seemed to be ceaselessly interested in "their" territory. For the reason for the lethargy, was "routinization" of the coverage of suffering (Vítek), which arrived even when face to face with turbulent events and the suffering of other people. It was caused by the awareness that "it's not the first time" (Čestmír), "it's not the first trouble of this kind. It's not. Nor is it the last one" (Vítek).

---

[1] The *ČT* headquarters.

The default mental state of most and not only Czech crisis reporters was thus already marked to some extent by compassion fatigue (Moeller 1999): the simultaneous feeling of overstimulation and boredom caused by constant bursts of crisis newsfeed. At the same time, the lethargy could emerge just because the reporters had a gut feeling that there *will be* another crisis, that no crisis is the last one, that is, that they—compared to the non-privileged reporters, victims, and witnesses who are anything but global citizens—remain *relatively* safe. Even if they are in the field, even when they do feel endangered, as Europeans, they can withdraw at almost any time: "as journalist, a Western journalist, you are privileged, in most situations you have at least food, hotel, certain security, and you know you will be out of the situations. ... [You tell yourself,] 'but you, my friends, you're gonna sleep on the ground'" (Bob). At some point, they would come back home.

This feeling of privilege that—together with the routine involvement in crises—made the boredom possible, also created conditions for guilt feelings—see the section "Moral Dilemmas and Guilt."

The plane's loudspeakers were now transmitting another voice, notifying the passengers of possible refreshments. The voice sounded more human than the metal voice of the robotic flight attendant. It was tired, with imperfect pronunciation and changing rhythms. James could not decide whether the humaneness of the voice was calming or made him nervous.

Indeed, he was nervous. But it was rather the malfunctioning loudspeakers that made him worried. "De-de-de- dear passengers," the loudspeakers stammered, announcing refreshments distribution. Bored and hungry, James felt like ordering panini.

It was not only the boredom of the eternal return of crises. As Nord and Strömbäck (2006: 88) have noticed, nothing happening causes also problems, because the media has a new "hole" which has to be filled. As a consequence, during field work, any "something"—an event or a development that could be considered newsworthy, that is, that was conflicting, negative, surprising/unexpected, of a certain magnitude, and relevant, or in close (cultural) proximity (c.f. Galtung and Ruge 1965; Harcup and O'Neill 2001)—was welcomed as an enlivening break from routine and the most interesting part of the job. As a perfect opportunity to "feed the Hydra" (field notes). These breaks were obvious during the observations: whenever a crisis event happened or developed, people either froze and together silently watched an agenda setter such as *CNN* on the screens in the newsroom (e.g. after 9/11) or started moving and speaking faster (see the example of the killing of Abdelhamid Abaaoud, one of the instigators of the Paris attacks, in the section "Inside-the-Media Is Outside-the-Media Crisis"). The organizations always got a kick out of an event such as the Brussels terrorist attacks:

> It's a bit silly to say that, but the newsroom never works better than in such a kind of crisis. (Jacob)

For media organizations, the terrorist attack was an easy piece of news; it just happened and helped to fill in the news hole (McDonald and Lawrence 2004; Nord and Strömbäck 2006). Thus, in Brussels newsrooms after the Brussels attacks, everybody was agile and ready to give a helping hand, so the collective worked perfectly, fast, vigorously. Moreover, the attacks helped to resolve the everyday competition between the digital and paper editions, as they clearly distinguished the respective roles (following the minute-to-minute developments vs. bringing contextual analyses; cf. Reinardy 2011).

Likewise, these breaks were explicitly—and positively—reflected upon by James' colleagues:

> Something like that [such as the gun attack in the Paris music club Bataclan] must happen to shake one from that kind of. ... From the cynicism and lethargy. (Matouš)

Any technological unpreparedness of both newsrooms and individual journalists shrinks to vanishing points with time and experience:

> The first war, it's terrible. It's like the first love. When you divorce for the fourth time, you know how to go to the lawyer, etc. (Gloria)

Nevertheless, after several days, the non-action developments, for example the continuing state of emergency in Belgium, lost their ability to rouse the journalists from lethargy, as described in the field notes just a few days after the Paris attacks.

> Marie says that "we don't look into anything except Brussels, so we are going to work hard today." (...) Marie sits back against the armchair and sighs: "Oh, what a day again. Nothing happens...." (...) After a while, Marie says in a bored way: "I should've brought the knitting with me." (Field notes)

This ennui was similar to the case of the "migration crisis" with its particular temporality (duration). Since it had started to be tagged as a "crisis" among journalists themselves around March 2015 (as Ema said), it became a constant ongoing event, raising no exceptional emotions. "When hundreds of thousands refugees are coming to Europe three straight months, you just keep it on top until it touches you, even though we all are so fed up with it and tired of it that we don't feel it any more," said Šimon, and returned to his default boredom.

In sum, the journalists James knew often oscillated between boredom and arousal, fatigue, and thrill. "Adrenalin is just like a drug, and you need your shot," said Anthony and draw Russian Mountains with his hand in the air. While the excitement of unpredictable and surprising events (Nord and Strömbäck 2003) disturbs some of the daily emotional routines, Sam Dubberley et al. (2015) point out that the unexpectedness and surprise of the brutality of acts (often in user-generated content) are also those qualities that, according to journalists, trigger the worst emotional shocks.

A strong turbulence. Right in front of James, a flight attendant had to hold onto the cart with sandwiches. James admired the skill with which he, being used to turbulence, avoided falling down.

After ordering his panini, James returned to his thoughts. Never before did he realize that the default emotional style of many of his colleagues was boredom and compassion fatigue (Moeller 1999). Only sometimes, this kind of mood was weakly and temporarily disrupted by an event that triggered distinct emotions.

Emotionally Engaged

As suggested above, journalists cannot step out of the world. In many respects, they exist in the situations they "cover" as actors. Thus, the reporters James knew could be emotionally engaged in politics. Being aware of the political potential of media, they were becoming indignant over their colleagues' bad journalism or the doubtful ethics performed in other media organizations. Giuseppe, for example, could not stand "the dehumanization of refugees" into a faceless mass and "the brutal lies" about them. The reporters were sometimes passionate about the technological details of the crisis event—like Julian from *LS*, who lost himself in the technological aspects of the nuclear catastrophe at Chernobyl—about the complexity of the crisis, about the truth, and The Truth. Many of the reporters were anxious about sticking to professional standards; for example, Sven talked about the "irrational responsibility not to make errors" he felt while reporting on the 2016 Brussels attacks; Tim, writing a news series on a trauma issue, recalled he was "very fearful about the responsibility ... I would have panic attack the night before we would publish the story. ...What if that detail was wrong?" (Tim slept very poorly that year.) Some others were saddened by members of the audience who misinterpreted their accounts (see Sam's quote in the section "Belgium, Czechia, and the Closeness of a Crisis"). Sam was especially angry when in 2013, after he had been involved in an attack in Syria that killed a French fellow journalist, he received hateful reactions:

> It made me very angry. *Very angry.* Very stubborn, but mostly very angry. And very emotional. ... It gave me higher blood pressure. Because of the tension. But mostly because ... afterwards. (Sam)

Indeed, as Marte Høiby and Rune Ottosen (2015: 67) have illustrated, "harassment and threats directed towards journalists in social media, on e-mail, SMS and voicemail is reported to trigger reactions such as insomnia, depression, frustration and anger." The emotions are particularly strong when the criticism is related to the journalists' professional performance, and they also have a greater effect on their ability to work than physical dangers on the spot. Correspondingly, Klas Backholm (2017) lists public debate and criticism related to journalistic work among stressors affecting journalists' well-being.

In short, James' colleagues' emotional engagement was always related, in one way or another, to their strong feelings of professional responsibility, their awareness of the political potential of the media, and their existence within their audiences' community. Thus, many of these emotions were directed toward the journalists' own social space.

By comparison, what follows fully focuses on the journalists' emotional identification with the on-site situation and the on-site tragedies of people. It addresses those emotions that the reporters feel when they are in contact with the crisis as such, its victims and direct witnesses, and mainly those emotions that are most obviously related to the mistaken yet practically existing paradox of reporting and witnessing. The paradox is particularly irrelevant when journalists find themselves in danger or when they bear witness to the pain of others (see Boltanski 1999; Sontag 2003).

Strangely, it was getting dark. Through the window on his right, James saw a distant land. An island of interconnected light spots. It resembled a drawing of the nervous system: nerve fibers, nerve endings, and lots of points.

Identified

What and why exactly, then, did the reporters feel once a crisis disrupted the boredom? Sadness, indignation, pity, sorrow, anger, fear, anxiety, panic, stress, tension, empathy, tiredness, compassion, horror, depression, shock, and guilt—these were the most common emotions that one could see and hear when digging into the phrase that covering the Haiti earthquake, the Brussels or Paris attacks, the war on Ukraine, refugee camps, 9/11, the war in Liberia, hurricanes, the aftermath of the Greek debt crisis, famines in Central African countries, and so on was "emotionally demanding" and "affecting" (e.g. Lotte, Nicolas, Sam, Kryštof, Matouš …; cf. Dubberley et al. 2015; Hight and Smyth 2003; Pedelty 1995).

Most often, the emotions the reporters feel emerge from their identification, and thus empathy—an emotion Antje Glück (2016) considers central to journalistic routines—with the victims and witnesses. In turn, the identification stems from their physical or vicarious presence in the field, with physical presence leading, not surprisingly, to stronger identification.

For example, the reporters very easily identified and empathized with the people on the move, fleeing their countries. Giuseppe recalled an existential moment he experienced while reporting on refugees on their way to Western Europe through Serbia and Hungary:

> Once you are in the field, you get involved. … At some point, I experienced that I was not a reporter any more, I was one of them. [After travelling nine hours in the forest,] our aim was not to report on that trip any more, but just to make it. So it was a feeling of fully embodying yourself in the shoes of the refugees.

Giuseppe stressed that he knew he was never in their shoes, but it was *the feeling* that he had after spending time with them in the forest. Diego went through exactly the same experience, made some friends among refugees, and pointed to how it contrasted with what he had learned at the university. On the spot, not being a part of the story was impossible for him. As mentioned in the section "Belgium, Czechia, and the Closeness of a Crisis," Lilah had one foot in the community of refugees because she spoke Arabic. Similarly, Farrukh said it was important to experience a conflict from within a community, without claiming that the reporter—in his case, the photographer—suffers alongside the unfortunates.

Although every single one of James' colleagues was different and reacted differently to being in the field, there were diverse streams of emotions typical for one or another crisis situation.

Thus, the identification and empathy felt while covering the refugee crisis would typically turn into sorrow, pity, sadness, compassion, grief, anger, or even depression (e.g. Diego).

Correspondingly, the reporters would feel rage about manifestations of extremism and hatred (see the section "Inside- and Outside-the-Media Crises Resonances").

They would feel despair and revulsion in the aftermaths of natural disasters. Similarly, the aftermaths of armed conflicts, bursts of violence and wars, for example the conflict in Syria, often triggered hopelessness, depression, injustice, and overload:

> Sometimes [the Middle East] is a very depressing region to cover, especially the last few years. Sometimes I really feel that for a while I want to do something different. ... Because you really think, uff, this never stops, it never stops! And you really see so much suffering, and you get to know a lot of people. ... And they confront you with their frustration, their anger and hopelessness. ... So sometimes I have this period that I think it's really hard to keep on dealing with it. I just want to shut it out for a minute, just to be able to keep going on. (Lotte)

More precisely, Čestmír talked about the feeling of overload when he saw little hands sticking out of the rubble after the 2004 Haiti catastrophe; Anthony, covering the earthquake in Pakistan in 2005, forever remembered children with amputated extremities and the omnipresent smell of death. Ernest could not stand watching a Catholic church in Rwanda full of Tutsi and Hutu moderates'—men's, women's, and children's—bones and skulls, with blood stains on its walls. Ernest needed to take a break, leave, and breathe.

James took a deep breath as well. What about Rwandan journalists? He knew only about those who took part in fueling the 1994 genocide, claiming at "Radio Machete" and in other "hate media" that the "graves are not yet full" and urging Hutus to "go to work" (*The Guardian* 2003). Those journalists who lost their lives received far less publicity.

The reporters would feel transfixion, consternation, anger, and fear in terror attacks (Felix, Jacob, Sven, Matouš, Ernest).

They would be left without any energy, exhausted (Tim, Finn), and would feel a strong sense of responsibility (Judith) while covering individual trauma issues.

Importantly, being on the spot and empathizing with the victims often meant that James' colleagues experienced a sharp contrast between the two worlds—the privileged, "superficial" life in European fashion and food capitals and the crisis zones. In the first, people were troubled by being unable to book a holidays trip; in the second, people were starving and dying. In turn, this existentialist feeling of facing more real humanity during crises strengthened the contact, identification, and empathy with the people affected by a crisis: "I felt more connected to the people I met in the crisis zones—people in big difficulties. Looking at them, you see the real face of a human." (Bob) This feeling leads to developing very deep (albeit often short-term) relationships in the field (Bob, Anthony, Diego, Ines, Giuseppe, Gloria).

But it also means that when you come back, as Anthony expanded on the contrast, few people can understand you. "You get in the shower, you turn on the water, and you're crying, because you have hot water and they don't." (Gloria) In the end, you want to go back. To be sent back, "you are just pretending that you are ok" (Anthony). You cannot show any weakness (see the section "Cynics, Stoics, and Brokens").

Some of the reporters stressed that even mediated crises had the capacity to trigger strong emotions. They argued that given the immediacy, ubiquity, and fidelity of the recording, transmitting, and displaying technologies that the journalists use, the difference between "parachute reporters" (e.g. Cottle 2009) and "armchair journalists" sitting in the comfort of their media organization's headquarters, that is, between immediate and secondary or vicarious emotions, is not that significant any more (Dubberley et al. 2015):

> [The relevance of emotions applies] not only [to] people in the field, but also people working in the newsroom. ... You are looking at those screens every day, the whole day. And you know, the horrific scenes that are coming to our screens, it's unimaginable sometimes. ... you don't want to see a beheading. You really don't want to see it, because you will never forget it. ... When there are days and days and days and weeks and months, and it just keeps on coming, even here at your desk, these images after another bomb attack with bodies blown all over the place. It's really horrible to see it. (Lotte)

Indeed. Although the trip to San Lorenzo was James' first experience with on-the-spot crisis reporting, he had already covered crises from afar. The footage he sometimes needed to watch was nothing nice. Some of his colleagues were able to eat their lunch while watching gory details on their computer screens when they did not make it to eat in the canteen. They could chew their smoked salmon salad while watching people being burned to death in cages. For James this was unthinkable—the cocktail of emotions that this type of footage triggered was too dense.

All in all, the types of emotions the reporters felt varied greatly depending on the nature of the crisis, its duration, its newness, and on whether the reporters witnessed it directly or vicariously.

As the bubble of James' colleagues was rather reflexive and self-critical, some of them condemned the falseness of their fellow media professionals' empathy. As always, the pithiest was Farrukh, who based his disbelief in the media workers' empathy—and his concern about the serious effects such false empathy had for the quality of news—on his knowledge of their work and its political-economic context:

> I don't take claims of the emotional disturbance, PTSD, to be serious. Because I don't see people in the industry who are actually concerned, committed to the issue they claim to be covering. ... People are walking over each other and walking over dead bodies to get to the emotionally powerful photograph.

For Farrukh, most people in the industry were ignorant of the situations they were covering and only stooped to politically motivated, lucrative, and self-seeking journalism.

James recalled how enlightening speaking to Farrukh was: his position was unyielding, determined, and defiant. His criticism, often publicly expressed, was well-meant. Friendly fire.

James had to acknowledge that there was something suspicious about empathizing with the victims, yet simultaneously using empathy as a professional resource (Judith) and as a way to protect oneself from guilt feelings (Gloria; see the section "Moral Dilemmas and Guilt").

Parenting
The narrated identification with the tragedy of the people experiencing the crises was usually the strongest when it came to children. Particularly those reporters who themselves had (small) children often recalled how

desperate they felt while witnessing the suffering of these little people who were civilian and innocent by definition. The reporters unwillingly identified the children who were suffering, for example, in refugee camps, natural disasters, or civil wars, with their own children. The extraordinary impact of seeing suffering children affected reporters ranging from the openly highly sympathetic (e.g. Lotte, Nicolas, Anthony) to journalists focused on factuality and technological processing of crises (e.g. Tomáš, Jesse, Marie):

> I have seen so many stories like this, and so many children, and yeah. I have children of my own, and you just want to give them every. ... All the love of the world, and you want them especially to feel safe and to feel secure. And you know that those children do not feel safe and do not feel secure. ... Yeah, it makes me angry and frustrates me. (Lotte)

> I must say, having children by myself, things have become more difficult. If I now see children, I see that I look at that with another point of view than I did ten years ago. Before having children. And I know that working with children or seeing children or reporting on children makes me more vulnerable than 10 years ago. ... The point is that to see children ... because it of course always makes the projection onto your own situation. And what if it would have been my daughter. Well, if you see a dead soldier, you never think, what if it would have been me. Because I am not a soldier. (Jesse)

Children created a link between their personal lives and their professional tasks.

Thus, for Jesse, Čestmír, Richard, and others, having children was also a milestone in their professional career, which further blurred the border between personal and professional identity (Rosen 2011; see also Van Zoonen 1998). Vítek explained the milestone at the end of a long and heated talk:

> "The birth of my first child was an absolutely essential moment that formed me as a journalist. Because it, in the best moment, kicked my ass and shot me down from the ... bumptious journalistic cynicism of a young journalistic nitwit. ... It's not about the big picture (shakes his head). ... You must transmit—and it's the emotions—the emotion about what it means that there is no electricity in Aleppo. ... It's about this. About the individual, concrete people. And the fact that my first son was born made me come down to earth and I started to be interested in individual people, and I think

this makes me a better human. I'm not saying that I am a good person, but it makes me better than I was before (laughs), and when a human is a better human, it certainly makes him a better journalist." (Vítek)

As Howard Tumber (2011: 328) observed, the idea that emotional identification and responses to disasters—such as that of September 11—make better journalists marked changing attitudes toward the norm of reporting (see the section below, "Professional Ideology and Its Critique"); five years later, Glück (2016) proved that journalists attribute a great deal of importance to empathy.

Additionally, having children and a family could also help to maintain hope and fight cynicism: as a parent, "you rediscover the unconditional love. The love for what you are, and not for what you represent" (Anthony). Family (and friends) is the best safety net (Gloria).

Yet, having children is typically complicated for crisis reporters, especially for female reporters. In those countries that James knew something about (see "Creative Nonfiction and the Research Method"), women of a certain age either stopped doing the job because of having children (including some of his colleagues: Olga and Astrid) and never returned to the core of the news service team or stayed, like Lilah and Ines, and never had children. Alternatively, like Gloria, they had feminist partners doing nine-to-five jobs. But having children was hard not only because of logistics but also because, as Anthony suggested, having a "normal family life" is improbable. When you ride the Russian Mountains all the time, you can hardly be understood. Closeness becomes almost impossible.

This was something James was already deeply familiar with. As far as he knew, he did not have any children himself, yet he dared to think he grasped the meaning of the crisis reporters' parental experience. Partly because having children was not the only way by which the crisis came closer.

James took the panini from the flight attendant and started eating it eagerly.

Moral Dilemmas and Guilt

In less than five seconds, James was completely disgusted; the meal even made him indignant. He continued eating with resignation.

As suggested above, the reporters empathized with victims and witnesses of crises and vice versa: their identification and empathy were essential for having an authentic on-the-spot experience. In this context, Sven recalled his impression of Congolese government soldiers who had just come back from the front:

> their eyes were really eyes which you don't see in normal situations. I mean, they were like mirrors of what they just saw. They were like open, they were tired, and ... I think then it's also important to identify. If you don't make that kind of identification, you can't really ... if you don't empathize, you can't really be there.

The direct or indirect on-site presence is also at the core of journalists' professional ideology from which they draw their authority (Andén-Papadopoulos and Pantti 2013). To Sven, "being there" was impossible without empathizing and identification. But empathizing and identification in turn resulted in moral commitment that did not allow a reporter to witness suffering without taking action:

> I am a father. If I see a child that is in [trouble]—and I wouldn't do anything just to keep my story dogmatically clear—I think I would save the child and maybe think about, ok, should I write about it? Or is it too much? I don't want to be the hero of the story. I think I would start thinking in that way. But I think I don't want to be on the side and let the child jump and then write about it. But even more strange would be to not write about it and to say that you actually. ... Eeeh. ... Didn't help someone in danger. I think there is no shame in it. (Sven)

Although, again, it does not make a fundamental difference whether a reporter witnesses other people's suffering on the spot or from a distance, the commitment was the reason why, in the case of the child, Sven could not even imagine continuing to observe and deny his agency. The same commitment was at place in relation to refugees/survivors; the journalists thus ended up giving them a ride (within a country or behind the borders; Tomáš, Josef), lending them a mobile phone (Sven, Tomáš, Matouš), buying them food, water, tent, or sanitary items (Nicolas, Bob, Tomáš), taking care of a little boy who lost his father under the rubble (Nicolas), playing a mother's role for a refugee child for a moment (Lotte), and so on. Indeed, as Luc Boltanski (1999) argues, taking action (albeit in the form of speech) is the only morally acceptable response to witnessing unfortunates' suffering.

At the same time, as journalists, Sven and others are subject to the somewhat inactive journalists' professional ideology (see the section

"Objections to Objectivity: Emotionality and Professionalism"), organizational codes, and media logic.

The logic of their unavoidable and repeatedly experienced quandary thus looks as follows: Is a journalist allowed to help people in need? Can she commit herself through a speech? And in another way? Is *helping* the subjects of the story legitimate, in terms of journalists' professional ideology? Is *not helping* suffering people legitimate, with regard to journalists' humanity?

The reporters' narratives about all the above-mentioned situations revealed that the journalists were very well aware of two types of commitments—that of a Journalist and that of a Human Being, and even explicitly reflected upon the internal conflict of the two roles. Several journalists explicitly stressed the importance of the latter:

> The most important thing is to be a decent human being under any circumstances. (Lilah)

> I have full respect for the ethical rules of my profession, but I also have full respect for the duties of my condition as a human being. Maybe in five years I will do something other than be a journalist, but I know that in five years I will still be a human being. (Nicolas)

Eventually, some of the reporters therefore *did* take part in the situations, sometimes even physically; only few of them did not, because they were not sure what to do. Correspondingly, the reporters strongly condemned "vultures" who only use the victims of a crisis, grab a powerful picture, write a heartbreaking story, and vanish without a trace. This went hand in hand with criticizing the use of artificial, inauthentic emotions in news stories (Pantti 2010).

But by helping those who went through serious troubles—being friendly and supportive (Gloria), buying them this or that, or even supporting some of them on a monthly basis (Bob)—the reporters also reduced their sense of guilt of being privileged, being fine, being able to get out of a dangerous situation:

> How can you just say goodbye and then not feel guilty about being rich? I am guilty about being rich, we should be, in this part of the world. (Bob, sitting in a library in Copenhagen)

> You feel bad because of not crying. (Diego)

I felt guilty when we left in the evening. ... I was in trouble with them as long as I wanted to. But they had no chance to get out of it. (Giuseppe)

Bob, Gloria, Diego, and Giuseppe felt that by helping in one way or another, they were sharing the benefits they derived from the stories and images they obtained in the field. Obviating guilt feelings was also important for their mental well-being (see the section "Coping Strategies"), as guilt feelings and moral dilemmas are among important stressors (Backholm 2017).

Sometimes a dilemma and a guilt feeling stayed in a journalist's mind and heart for years, though. Indeed, as Hopper and Huxford (2015) point out, journalists can be deeply troubled by once-acute emotions that they merely deferred/postponed but did not completely suppress, even though the events that triggered the emotions happened years or decades previously. James recalled a memory Nicolas told him about, many years after he had experienced it. For James, this was one of the most emotionally powerful stories he had ever heard from his colleagues:

> I always saw it as a moral image, not a stressful image. It's a rape. (Pause) Ehmmm, a scene of gang rape in Africa. (Pause) I just arrived. ... The problem is not the rape itself. No. The problem is ... So this is very egoistic as a reaction—I arrive in a car, the village is burning, and I see that two gunmen are taking a woman from a hut, the hut is burning, and they start the rape. They have assault rifles, I am a journalist, I have no rifle, I am just arriving at the scene with my car (pause), the driver stops, because he feels there is something to be done, and I tap on his shoulder (makes knocking sound), I say, go. We leave. We cannot, we cannot do anything. We don't have a weapon, the wife. ... I don't know what will happen, or I can know, I can guess what will happen with the woman, we are in a war zone, the village is burning, they have weapons, and as a man you have to say, ok, I just *flee*. And after that, you just have to *live* with what you *did*. I was just thinking today it was a good solution. But that's something awful. Because I was not prepared to do that. I was not prepared. In all *morality*, you say, hey, I would get out of the car and ... Be shot. And be shot. That's it—be shot. So I just think about that, I think that I had no. ... When I came into that, I would say drama, I had no guideline coming from my boss, coming from another journalist, or from my environment. I just made mentally the calculation, saying, I *should*, but I *can't*. *Get away*. (Pause.) And after that, you just think ... (Pause.) So I know it's something I wrote, and it helped me to write it in order to confront what I did with public opinion. I wanted to know if one reader would say to me, hey, Mr. Bernard, you did a war crime. I don't know what. No?

Nicolas' apologetic way of telling about the situation—posing rhetorical questions, simulating a dialogue, arguing without any outer prompting—shows that the sense of guilt from reacting in an egoist way, as he said, stayed alive. Similarly, Julian from *LS* talked about a policeman who long ago committed suicide for reasons related to Julian's investigative reporting: "He committed suicide. Am I responsible? I don't think so."

Nicolas, Julian, and others made sense of the moral dilemmas and their solutions by retrospective justification of their action (Weick 1995). Such sensemaking was not built only on a mix of immediate calculation and instinct for self-preservation but clearly had an organizational dimension: namely commitment to and enactment of professional principles (ibid.). The journalists first of all had to stay alive and do their job. This kind of sensemaking helped them to reduce the (potential) strain following from both cognitive and emotive dissonance (Festinger 1957; Hochschild 1983): a discrepancy between thinking and/or feeling, and action. Nicolas, for example, drew the three closer together by rationalizing his spontaneous action and placing it into the media-organizational context (boss, other journalists, environment, articles, and readers). The media organizations thus worked as both poison and remedy: they were bringing forth moral dilemmas and guilt but also providing, sometimes insufficient, justifications of solutions. The reporters' personal and biographical sensemaking narratives often had this smoothing effect; never did a journalist come off badly, never did she play the part of an immoral, inhumane, or unprofessional character. On the contrary, she often fitted into the self-myth consisting of morality, adventure, and bravery (see Pedelty 1995).

However, the existence of moral dilemmas, guilt feelings, and the need to make sense of them through a personal narrative also illustrates well the above-mentioned individualization and biographization of risks and crises. Moral dilemmas and guilt feelings, emerging from a crisis and newswork (i.e. social phenomena), and perhaps also from a Western collective sense of "guilt of being rich" (Bob) at the expense of non-white peoples (Farrukh), can easily be shifted as a burden of risk onto the shoulders of individuals. Then, the guilt feelings turn into anxieties and neuroses (Beck and Beck-Gernsheim 2001; Scheper-Hughes and Lock 1987).

Behind the dilemmas and the help that the reporters provided to the unfortunates, there often was an attempt to reduce, albeit imperceptibly, the gap between the contrasting worlds, and a kind of vague, dispersed, everyday struggle for democratic principles of human co-existence, solidarity against populism, xenophobia, and inhumane living conditions. For example, Lotte's attempts to contribute to improving refugees' conditions by reporting on refugee camps worked as a strong professional motivation:

> And I really want to find energy to keep going, because you hope that you make a difference by sharing their story. (Lotte)

However, such open acceptance and performance of the journalists' active role in public discourse and perhaps also the social milieu was sometimes harshly criticized by colleagues, rivals, and superiors. Marta, an experienced foreign correspondent, was criticized for her "activism" by all these groups. For example, Vítek, a foreign correspondent from another media organization, said she had long ago ceased to be a journalist and became an activist; apparently, the two identities were irreconcilable in his view. Marta's superior also used the label "activism" for any reporters' practices that, in his view, resulted in distorted, "overly positive" news. Later, Marta left her very stable and comfortable position for a relatively uncertain and demanding job in an emerging progressive paper where she had more freedom. This kind of criticism lays bare the double humane and journalistic commitment that James' colleagues faced. Not only Marta's boss but also other editors-in-chief had problems with "activism," that is committed speech acts performed face to face with others' suffering.

The extent of openness about one's involvement often corresponded to the reporters' view of the place of reporters' emotions in their reports and news (see the section "'No Torn Children's Life Jackets': Good Taste, the Organization, and Morality"). Tomáš, for example, said he did not want to admit or include his act of buying food for refugee families in his report because he found it irrelevant and too openly partisan. On the contrary, Sven, who lent his mobile phone to a Syrian man who needed to call his family, then decided to admit it:

> I thought, oh, this is really strange for a journalist. Now you are participating in the story. And then I said, well, I'll just write it, and then the readers will know that I'm in the middle of it. (Sven)

Obviously, many of these decisions and attempted resolution of doubts about involvement/detachment, activity/passivity, and overtness/withholding were preceded by thorough reflections. These reflections on, and solutions of, the moral dilemmas and potential guilt feelings then directly reflected themselves in the journalists' work, mainly in the particular objectivity-as-a-practice (Carpentier and Trioen 2010) that the media professionals performed (see especially "Technologies of Sign Systems: Output Emotions").

James glanced at the top of Sophie's aesthetically appealing hair-do: what would she have done in Nicolas', Sven's, Tomáš's, Giuseppe's situation? Her gender must make a difference in these types of moments. James imagined her moral dilemma while witnessing a gang rape would have looked differently. She might also feel a different type of fear.

For a moment, he wanted to ask her. Then he swallowed the question. Not only was he nervous with women but he also realized how awkward and inappropriate asking a stranger about her feelings could be: "Hey, Sophie, aren't you afraid of your sources?"

Danger and Fear
> Here, it can be that you receive a blow from a cobblestone, but it means that you were standing in the way. There [in Ukraine or areas controlled by Daesh], you peek out and get a bullet blasted through your head. (Josef)

Danger and risk appear to be intrinsic conditions of conflict reporting. Media scholars increasingly speak about danger that journalists expose themselves to in the context of wider media professionals' precarity. For example, Silvio Waisbord (2019) sees the economic transformations, the precarization of journalists' labor, the rise of anti-democratic forces, and anti-press violence as the major vulnerabilities of contemporary journalism. More specifically, Mark Deuze and Tamara Witschge (2018) articulate how the networked character of newswork has become a common denominator of several aspects of the transformation of journalism, including the outsourcing of risks: the increasing reliance of new organizations from the Global North on local contacts or freelancers, with the tariffs for freelancers declining at the same time. Tim Rosenkranz (2019) then links this externalization of risks of crisis news production onto the freelancer to lean capitalism and the phenomenon of speculation.

James used to hear terrifying stories, some of which went public and turned their characters into heroes (and corroborated the myth of the war correspondent; Pedelty 1995). Abductions, assaults, bombings, intimidation, and being followed by a hired killer were only the most dramatic of the dangerous experiences that James' colleagues (at least Mario, Sam, Carl, Čestmír, Josef, Vítek, Nicolas, Anthony, Giuseppe, and Tomáš) survived—but not always their fellow reporters or photographers. The emotional counterpart of the dangers was fear:

> I feel the fear. Each time that I go [to the Middle East], actually. There are certain points, certain moments, when I feel it. Especially before arriving. The days before arrival, the hours before arrival. … And I don't like … because I go to Turkey, then to Iraq and then to the frontline, I feel … I especially feel the fear of the unknown. (Sam)

The danger, fear, and the self-preservation instincts and strategies—which, according to experienced conflict reporters such as Čestmír, Sam, Josef, and Vítek, could be gained through social learning processes and specialized education (such as hostile environment trainings for reporters)—have significant consequences for the news.

First, media organizations, prudently enough, have recognized some parts of Syria,[2] Iraq, North Korea, and so on, as "uncoverable" (Josef). However, this might not apply to freelancers, a group of journalists facing increased precarity (Creech 2018; Hesmondhalgh and Baker 2011), who at times go to uncoverable areas and into dangerous situations to succeed amidst competing media professionals and organizations, often without being able to afford, among other things, a fixer or insurance. Spanish journalists in particular told James that they either directly faced this heightened form of precarity and/or perceived it as a pressing problem. In Spain, a country with the second highest unemployment rate in the European Union (15.2 percent in summer 2018; Statista 2019), young reporters like Diego and Ines had little choice and often had to start as freelancers. Later, if they did well, they might obtain a regular salaried job (if they wanted to). However, they were often trapped in a vicious circle, because doing well while facing the dangers of a freelancer was more difficult than working their way up in a media company:

> because to cover news in a conflict is very expensive, insurance and everything. And when I was a freelancer, I couldn't … I have to say I didn't cover things in a proper way, sometimes. Because … for example, I didn't have the vest. Or I didn't have the helmet. … But I did it, which is not the best way to do it. (Ines)

[2] Syria is currently the most dangerous place for journalists and the level of violence directed to them is unparalleled, because, among other things, some parties of the conflict do not need journalists at all (Creech 2018).

Therefore, Gloria, who herself had a stable job for many years in one of the established Spanish media organizations, passionately argued that

> Media must pay and must insure these people even when they are freelancers. Freelancer does not mean a Kamikaze. And now they are like Kamikaze, because nobody takes care of them. … if they send them to the war or they accept the reporting from the war, they also must accept the obligation to protect them. (Gloria)

Protecting freelancers as well as employees could be a way to redistribute the risk and equalize the higher precarity of the former.

Yet, "the gravest threats are often felt by the reporters, photographers, bloggers, and fixers who call sites of conflict home" (Creech 2018: 576): for example, almost 90 percent of journalists who have been killed in Iraq were Iraqis, and almost all journalists covering Mexican drug cartels were Mexican. Western media researchers, busy conceptualizing the perceived crisis of contemporary (Western) journalism, tend to ignore the safety and other problems faced by local journalists (Hanitzsch 2019). Solving the problem of the most severe threats of violence faced by local journalists and fixers, who perform labor that is invisible to Western audiences, is far more complicated and at present involves mainly NGOs and foundation bodies (e.g. the Committee to Protect Journalists and Reporters Without Borders) that have advocated more comprehensive safety policies than media organizations (Creech 2018).

Second, as Ines and Čestmír suggested, it seems that sometimes the fear is inversely proportional to the quality of reporting:

> It's a permanent, permanent struggle of yes and no. Where you put the camera, and where you don't. If you go a metre further, or not. And this is the border that decides whether you come back, or you don't come back, and at the same time the border is often about whether the report will be even better, or not. (Čestmír)

Again, this has a lot to do with media competition and the transformation of newsrooms into "networks of loosely affiliated competitor-colleagues" (Deuze and Witschge 2018: 176), so that freelancers might be more willing (or pushed) to go the fatal meter further and fit into the newswork environment which "demands journalists today to be committed well beyond what any profession could ask for—without most of the securities, comforts, and benefits enjoyed by being a member of a profession" (ibid.). Needless to say, the endangerment tended to be physical and psychological at the same time.

Some reporters who frequently found themselves in dangerous situations dismissed their own position and focused rather on their subjects' and talking heads' danger and fear or even on the danger for equipment. On one hand, this stance logically followed from the comparison of the reporters' luxury (Lotte, Anthony) and privilege (Jesse, Bob, Farrukh, Giuseppe) and the misery of the unlucky subjects of the news: "I would make a distinction between what you have to feel as a journalist and what the victim you interview feels. It's far more important. ... How would you dare to think about your own trauma?" Nicolas once asked James.

On the other hand, journalists who refused to adapt their behavior to the dangerous circumstances and their fears were sometimes condemned by others as "adrenalin junkies": "the people who are so obsessed by the profession that they are able to risk their life for it" (Matouš). The reprehensible aspect of such conduct was that adrenalin junkies give precedence to their psychological needs over professional values: "if he searches for an adrenalin rush, he searches for excitement, not the truth" (Vítek). Correspondingly, Anthony listed such "feeding of one's ego and being in the centre of interest" among bad reasons to be a crisis reporter. By some, adrenalin junkies were perceived as similar to the vultures: feeding off of others' suffering, selling a powerful story, and moving on to the next in a heartbeat.

Yet "adrenalin" was a very ambiguous expression. First, those who were considered adrenalin junkies by their colleagues often spoke of other reporters using the same words. Second, even exceptionally thoughtful journalists such as Anthony or Farrukh admitted that adrenalin matters. Third, in the Czech context, the label of a risk and danger fetishist even resembled a challenge trophy (cf. Pedelty 1995) and was handed down from generation to generation. Jukes' findings about reporters involved in crisis reporting suggest that affective detachment has the same status in Anglo-American journalism: his interviewees wore and cultivated their detachment as a badge of honor having the magic property to validate journalism both to themselves and to the outside world (Jukes 2017). In a few cases, losing the image went hand in hand with parenthood (see the section "Parenting").

Waging Diffused Wars
Occasionally, the extent of identification and actorship reached a level at which the reporters were involuntarily waging diffused or hybrid wars (e.g. Hoskins and O'Loughlin 2010; Mejias and Vokuev 2017)—wars embedded in the media and produced by media—and they were aware of it, which intensified their sense of endangerment.

This started after September 11 and applied, for example, to the "war on terror": Josef, for instance, thought that "The ISIS is the first conflict in which the target is really journalists. Systematically." Lilah thought the same. Bob and Anthony believed that it was the case rather for American journalists, perhaps Brits, and that continental Europeans were still relatively safe. Be that as it may, since terrorism profits from media exposure, media professionals' quandary—the paradox of their involvement and detachment—is made more difficult by their active position and involuntarily political capital within the emergency state: either they lend terrorists legitimacy and credibility or they overly rely upon the interpretation framework offered by the public and military officials and experts (Falkheimer and Olsson 2015; cf. Hallin 1986). Being aware of this quandary, many of James' colleagues, and even whole departments, newsrooms, and media organizations, explicitly reflected upon and elaborated policies for reporting on Daesh and its European activities:

> Because we work here and have to weigh words. ... When you say 'terrorists executed a man'—execution is a legal act, right. ... so you basically put it at the level of ... the state, which has a monopoly on violence, on the use of violence. ... But it's not, it's a murder. It's a totally ordinary murder, what they were doing. So this is one of the things that is terribly sensitive. And, of course, we try, now mainly in relation to Islamic terrorism, we do our best to plan and not to play. ... *Not* to play the role and not to be simply a speaker of what they want. To spread the terror, spread the paralysis from whatever madness they've done again. So very ... We have set completely clear rules about what to show and what not to show. We don't show any moving images of the videos that they release. The person who is supposed to die, the victim, is always pixelated there, because it's ... It's precisely in accordance with the code, we don't show victims of crime acts—this is a crime act, it's a murder. ... We won't show him as the dehumanized object of the propaganda of ISIS. (Čestmír)

In his long explanation, Čestmír revealed a lot about how the involuntary role of the press within an information war becomes embedded in and reflected by organizational strategies: codes, rules on using footage and words, and so on. Indeed, words are a crucial weapon—Sven and Sam also stressed the power of "loaded words" that have the ability to "indoctrinate." The "war on terror" was thus an obvious example of journalists' active role in crises, which raised questions about the possibility of detachment, neutrality, and emotional disengagement.

However, the journalists became similarly (emotionally) embroiled in other conflicts—mainly the Russian occupation of Crimea and the "hybrid" war in eastern Ukraine (Mejias and Vokuev 2017; see also Rutten et al. 2013):

> Regarding Russia and Ukraine, it's … The number of [hateful] e-mails that you receive for each single report, it's simply unbelievable. (Ema)

James' Czech colleagues were also worried about the attempts of fake news outlets to discredit their work. James recalled a Pulitzer Prize-winning series of *New York Times* reports (*Russia's Dark Arts* 2016) on Russia's covert projection of power that he had read some time ago. In East Europe, the Russia's influence was an issue even before Donald Trump was elected, who knows with whose help, the US president.

To summarize, crises had the potential to disturb the newsroom/on-the-spot boredom and could result in closeness, identification, empathy—in particular when children and parenting were at play—and in strong emotional involvement (see Zelizer and Allan 2011). The possibility to stay emotionally detached further diminished with the moral quandaries and guilt feelings that the reporters often faced, danger they experienced, and diffused wars they involuntarily waged. At the same time, the corresponding emotional distress—the moral dilemmas, feelings of guilt, fear, and sense of responsibility—reflected itself in the media content.

The robotic flight attendant still looked pretty bored, though. Her neutral yet terrifying face and body—even more terrifying now, in its increasing tiredness—emerged from the nose, pushing a similarly angular waste cart. James collected all his waste and threw it into the precisely shaped cart.

Cynics, Stoics, and Brokens

"What is your research about?" asks Čestmír when I enter his office at ČT. "I'm interested in the specifics of crisis reporting," I reply. "You'll soon find out that we're a bunch of cynical psychos." (Field notes)

Thinking through the emotions on the output, James became aware that the reporters' emotions were carefully managed (see Hochschild 1983; Illouz 2007). As such, they fit into the realm of sociology and anthropology, rather than psychology. Being biologically preconditioned, but to a large extent culturally determined, defined and shaped practices of feeling and thinking, emotions are not substances to be discovered; rather, they are ways of practical engagement with social context, structured by our forms of understanding the context's cultural and historical specifics (Flam and Kleres 2015; Rosaldo 1984; Scheer 2012; Scheper-Hughes and Lock 1987). This does not mean that sociology and anthropology withdraw the body from the concept of emotions: quite the opposite. The body as a plastic, time-bound, socially situated, and adaptive phenomenon absorbs and is shaped by the wider political and social conditions of its existence (Scheer 2012; Scheper-Hughes and Lock 1987). This is how emotional cultures or styles (Illouz 2007), that is, ways of experiencing and performing emotions typical for certain groups of people and/or periods, emerge.[3]

Perhaps most importantly, what makes reporters' emotions a *sociological* problem is the very practice of their individualization and biographization (Beck and Beck-Gernsheim 2001) by the actors themselves: the practice of appropriating and taking responsibility for handling (or blaming oneself for not being to handle) certain emotions—often negative emotions, such as anxiety, guilt, and fear. While these emotions stem from the crisis reporters' professional context including crisis situations and newswork, they are shifted as a burden of risk onto the shoulders of individuals. Thus, the sociological problem, further addressed in the chapter "Touching Down," resides in the process of internalizing this professionally and contextually determined emotional culture and making it personal and private.

The existence of such emotional craftsmanship and the idea that emotions provide an important missing link between body, mind, individual, society, and politics also means that individual emotional response is structured by our forms of understanding. Emotions entail not only feel-

---

[3] Eva Illouz calls the capacity to display an emotional style "emotional competence." Each emotional style is defined by a specific emotional field: "a sphere of social life in which the state, academia, different segments of cultural industries, groups of professionals accredited by the state and university and the large market of medications and popular culture intersected to create a domain of action and discourse with its own rules, objects, and boundaries" (Illouz 2007: 62–63).

ings but also thoughts and cognitive orientations, our sense of cultural ideology, and public morality (Rosaldo 1984; Scheper-Hughes and Lock 1987). As Michelle Rosaldo (1984: 143) puts it, "Emotions are thoughts somehow 'felt' in flushes, pulses, 'movements' of our livers, minds, hearts, stomachs, skin. They are embodied thoughts, thoughts seeped with the apprehension that 'I am involved.'" Understanding emotions as practices including not only the self and other people but also language, material artifacts, and environment, practices involved in stories that we both enact and tell (Rosaldo 1984; Scheer 2012), allows us to bridge both the imaginary gaps between cognition and feeling and the discourse and action.

The food had been eaten, the waste had been thrown away. Nothing remained. The flight advanced to its second half. There was no obstacle between James' present bodily state and the catastrophe at San Lorenzo. He started to feel its imminence.

Following James colleagues' emotional paths, diverse strategies of dealing with emotions such as empathy, revulsion, consternation, sadness, fear, or guilt emerged, and the strategies' varied results.

Emotion Postponed and Accumulated

Typically, the journalists recalled that their emotional reaction to a crisis situation was inhibited and postponed until they came back/home from the site/the newsroom (from a refugee camp, from the Balkan route, from a screen with graphic consequences of terror). While being on location/at work, they felt less sorrow, pity, sympathy, and even less anxiety and fear than afterwards:

> On the concrete spot it's of course charged, a lot, it's emotionally demanding, because, of course, you're in the middle of mud with thousands of people and with children, see, and at the same time you realize that the people keep going and going and going. ... (...) Nevertheless, at that very place it did not affect me as much as when I was not there anymore. (Kryštof, speaking about a refugee camp in Hungary)

The journalists often postponed the emotions because they simply did not have enough time to be moved:

> 9/11 for example, I didn't realize what I was seeing. And what was happening. It was just on automatic pilot. You know? Very business-like.

3 THE EMOTIONAL EXPERIENCE OF CRISIS REPORTERS: THE JOURNEY 95

These are the facts. So many dead. And th-th-th. And th-th-th-. ... I shut out all emotion. ... And it was only afterwards that I realized [what happened]. (Lotte)

Similarly, Jukes talks about "putting himself on autopilot" as about a specific emotional style residing in distracting himself by working 18-hour days (Jukes 2017: 265; cf. Hochschild's term "going into robot" /Hochschild 1983/ mentioned in the section "Technologies of the Self"). Indeed, the task, the demanding mission, often overshadowed any possible authentic emotional experience of crisis:

It's very difficult to speak about emotion in a ... In a crisis moment. I would say. Because everyone is so focused on what is happening. (Louis)

You don't deal with it until you finish the report. (Ines)

As a result, the journalists often simply did not feel any emotion that they would need to put into cold storage, they acted not superficially but deeply, as Hochschild (1983) calls the practice of tricking even one's self into believing that there are no emotions to be felt.

This way of handling one's bodily emotions, their suppressing and postponing "for the sake of an ideologically driven, detached professional self" (Hopper and Huxford 2015: 38), became habitual:

Occasionally during the rush, when one realizes what has happened, the emotion comes back. But at the same time, it's a kind of ... state. In particular, in the foreign news, one works with these kinds of events on everyday basis. And there is a distance, maybe a defence mechanism. (Matouš, speaking about the Paris attacks)

Buchanan and Keats (2011) echo Matouš's view of the defensive effect of distancing oneself from a crisis by listing the self-control of the reporters' emotions among their coping strategies.

The level of predictability and newness (Nord and Strömbäck 2003) does not seem to make a difference when it comes to the habitualization of the emotional experience. The journalists James encountered were equally able to emotionally adapt to the tragic "state" of the "migration crisis" and to the subsequent developments of terrorist attacks (see the section "Bored in a News Hole"). At the same time, those who considered themselves less experienced could be strongly shaken by the sudden strike of the Paris attacks as well as by a working trip lasting a few days in Hungary or at the Greek-Macedonian border.

At that moment, James himself was strongly shaken: another intense turbulence occurred.

It took hardly four seconds, but the unpleasant surprise caused Sophie, who had just gotten to her feet, to stagger and catch hold of James' headrest.

"Another fall?" Sophie gave a laugh.

"Would be nice to have a point event before touchdown," James jested.

Sophie guessed right that he was a journalist too. "Two birds with one stone!" she replied.

Both laughed. The exchange, although rather predictable and not really hilarious, put them at ease. For James, this humor was a bit too much gallows, though.

He would never have confessed it, but the ease had a subtly hysterical aftertaste.

The flight was progressing, and James felt bodily unrest. He could not find a comfortable position. Every stimulus that would be hardly noticeable under ordinary circumstances felt suddenly unbearable. James took his shoe off and spilled a little stone out of it.

Although the reporters were able to postpone and shut out an immediate emotional response, crisis events were not without cumulative, stealthy consequences. As Nicolas precisely said,

> Every shock, every emotional shock you get, is not something you can get through with no problem. It is something that will. ... It's a little stone that you will have in your luggage. And all the stones are accumulating. So it is not true to say that everything that does not kill you makes you stronger. That's not true. Everything that you have, in terms of emotional stress, is something that makes you weaker and weaker. So you have to deal with that. At some point, you have to make clear, ok, you are just a human, you take things, and you have to get some distance from it. Ignoring it is not enough. You have to deal with it. (Nicolas)

Anthony agreed: it would have been much better for him to (try to) express what he felt each time he came back from a conflict zone. If he had done it, perhaps he wouldn't have nightmares now, he wouldn't smell the death that he still smells, he wouldn't hear the noises, he wouldn't continue to see the faces of the victims.

3 THE EMOTIONAL EXPERIENCE OF CRISIS REPORTERS: THE JOURNEY   97

The way of dealing with emotional shocks—or not—followed three ideal-typical paths, corresponding to three ideal-typical emotional styles (Illouz 2007).[4]

Brokens
James did not meet any journalists who were noticeably broken at that moment.
At least not at first sight. At second glance, as he traveled down the rabbit hole, he started to meet empty bottles, squeezed out blister packs and traces of other panaceas. Seldom, panic-stricken eyes flickered from the darkness, but immediately vanished, startled by other observing eyes.
A few times had James had the chance to meet someone Broken in person. Several reporters told him that they had had problems with alcohol or that they had been seeing a psychiatrist (which, after all, could show also strength). Often, he used to hear pitiful or condescending stories about the pasts of some of his colleagues and mainly his colleagues' colleagues, sometimes told by those in leading (Marek, Čestmír, Olga, Marie) or informally supervisory (Bob, Nicolas, Jesse, Vítek) positions:

And we have people that are just on medical treatment, that are ill. (Nicolas)

A half of journalists are alcoholics. ... I don't have a survey on how many journalists work only based on anti-depressants. Hard to say. (Marek)

As Hopper and Huxford (2015, p. 37) observed, "there was a lot of truth 'in the old stereotype of the reporter who heads straight to the bar at the end of the day.'" According to some, alcohol had a prominent position among the cure-all treatments, for it had therapeutic properties (see the section "Coping Strategies"). Some of his friends were so thorough in undergoing therapy that during their talks, James sometimes had a hard time keeping up with them.
James stopped the flight attendant, who was just passing by, and ordered a beer.

---

[4] This is to say that there were almost no "pure" Cynics, Stoics, or Brokens. Rather, according to the journalists' narratives, these were positions and roles that they entered and exited in different life periods and professional moments. At the same time, not every journalist had tried all the emotional styles.

Cynics and Kynics: Pissing Against the Idealist Wind

Luckily, probably most of James' colleagues were rather Cynics, the typical postmodern characters (Bewes 1997). More precisely, according to their own narratives about their emotional paths, suspending the emotional reaction and distancing oneself from the emotionally disturbing experience of witnessing close or distant suffering, as seen from a long-range perspective, led to cynicism:

> My father told me, 'haven't you become hard-bitten?' (...) You really get hard-bitten. (...) ... if I broke down every time, I couldn't do it. (Ester)

> I think that one displaces the emotions somewhere, and it must seem to you that we are a bunch of ironic fellows. But I think that without such an attribute one couldn't work here. (...) ... it is terribly cynical, but that's the way it is. I think that people gain experience and get tough. (Marie)

Cynicism, however, was a cause for concern:

> It is dangerous, see, because when you are living in it, you realize that the only rescue is cynicism. But cynicism means suppressing your own emotions, I'd say. And it's putting your ass on the line a bit, then. (Kryštof)

Anthony said that as a crisis reporter, one loses naivety with time. Principles, like justice, vanish face to face with the reality. When this happens, one must fight not to become cynical, because, "When it does not affect you, then you are a limited human being, you're not a good psychologist and probably not a very good journalist." (Bob) For Bob, like for Lilah, the moment of becoming cynical would be a sign of their need for a break. In short, becoming cynical, while being often the only way how to manage crises, threatens both good journalism (cf. Glück 2016) and the individuals' mental health.

Norbert Elias would agree: "only the insane can remain totally unmoved by what goes on around them" (Elias 1956: 226). Foreign correspondents interviewed by Mark Pedelty expressed similar worries about the long-term effects of sublimating emotions: "It has killed me, something in my mind," his interviewee Alonzo said, "We don't have any more feelings" (Pedelty 1995: 199–201).

Some of James' colleagues' criticism of cynicism as such, and of their cynical fellow journalists, was for the same reasons that they condemned the "vultures" (see "Moral Dilemmas and Guilt") and the "adrenalin junkies": the cynics "who are not affected by anything" (Bob), who feel responsibility neither to their sources nor to their readers, and who exploit dead and injured black bodies (Farrukh), are considered the bad guys of crisis reporting or crisis photography. However, while the vultures practice bad journalism for success, the adrenalin junkies do it for their ego, and the cynics are almost inevitable products of their working conditions.

Pedelty (ibid.) concludes that "Emotion, if not humanity itself, is the first element to be filtered out in the disciplinary process." Obviously, the crisis situation and the machine of newsmaking not only *condition* the emotional experience; crisis reporting also *requires* a certain emotional posture, finding the right balance of disengagement, nonchalance, and interest that Chris Peters calls "American Cool" (Peters 2011). Somewhat more dramatically, Mark Pedelty writes that

> this type of reporter, the war correspondent, is like the accountant who rides a Harley. He projects a renegade identity to himself and the world in a desperate attempt to live up to the American myth of the independent man. (Pedelty 1995: 24)

The use of "he" is not random in Pedelty's account. Male reporters in particular tend to be subject to the machismo in the myth. Carl said that "The macho culture formed me a bit" and explained how it helps in his profession:

> I have seen people being shot in front of my eyes. ... A lot of young reporters are trained in an academic way, so they have a lot of knowledge and know a lot of technical stuff, but it's the human aspect which makes it more difficult. ... [They have] more problems than people who are used to it.

James thought of how to escape from the cynical trap. In the very near future, he will most probably need to suppress his emotions to be able to work. Yet if he overdoes it and appears cynical, he will be condemned for bad journalism.

It is essential to distinguish two forms of cynicism here. The first one follows some of the principles of classical, ancient, intellectual cynicism, or kynicism (Bewes 1997; Navia 1996). Kynicism, an infallible strategy of shutting the emotions out, had a prominent position among all defense mechanisms (see the section "Coping Strategies"). It took the form of critical irony, mockery, satire, sarcastic remarks (cf. Fleming and Spicer 2003). Kynics were joking about mass casualties, suffering, or dangerous developments of international politics.

> I use it during terrorist attacks. You might have heard it: the word 'bits' for the number of dead. ... One would go nuts, so I somewhat cynically say, look, fifty bits there. (Tobiáš)

James took part in one of the most brutal cases of this "pissing against the idealist wind" (Sloterdijk 1987: 103) at *ČT*:

> Smoking. The head of broadcasting announces he cannot reach Vítek [one of the foreign correspondents, his colleague]. Vítek wrote to him from his Czech number some time ago, but not lately. The others—Matouš and Ema—are joking: "he's drinking in Prague and we think he's in Turkey!" ... Matouš asks again: "What about Vítek? Maybe he died! If he died, we'll make a special for him," Matouš laughs. I say that if he's in Prague, then he hasn't died. Ema says that a man, who, while on holiday, goes to do some shooting at a military camp, cannot die. ... We are laughing. The whole thing is conceived as a joke. Matouš asks whether any *ČT* reporter has died. On our way back, Matouš says that Vítek really disappeared. (Field notes)

In the end, Vítek, luckily, did not disappear. But behind every joke there is a grain of truth. For some days, James could not get rid of the idea that if Vítek had died, his colleagues would have been eager to prepare a special broadcast. They would have been able to work even on this issue and under these circumstances (see Sloterdijk 1987).

Essential for this classical cynicism, or kynicism, is truth-telling and care of oneself (Foucault 2005), and especially intellectual rebellion against many existing beliefs and practices, manifesting itself via satire, irony, mockery, and so on.

The second form of cynicism is inverted and contradictory: modern cynicism (Sloterdijk 1987). Modern cynicism is an ideology and a social phenomenon in which human aspiration is lacking (Navia 1996; Sloterdijk 1987). The modern cynic is apathetic, refuses to engage with the world (however antagonistic her position toward it can be), is resigned to her experience of alienation, and rather flees into solitude (Bewes 1997). Therefore, it fails to meet the moral commitment to take action when witnessing others' suffering (Boltanski 1999).

The posture of neglecting the emotionally demanding character of tragic events corresponds to Peter Sloterdijk's definition of the second form of cynicism as an ideology in which "the ability of its bearers to work—in spite of anything that might happen, and especially, after anything that might happen" (Sloterdijk 1987: 5) is central. At the same time, however, the cynical emotional posture is precisely one in which kynicism—irony, mockery, sarcastic remarks—has its place. As such, the cynical ideology does not only contradict kynicism. It also acknowledges and absorbs the kynical critique but insists on maintaining the existing state of affairs. The cynical ideology, which Sloterdijk calls "enlightened false consciousness" (Sloterdijk 1987: 5), is thus resistant to any critique, for it recognizes the particular ideological interests and the distance between the ideological mask and the reality, but it still finds it reasonable to retain the mask. In other words, it is a stance taken by people who realize the naïveté of those immersed in their activities. Cynics see the nothingness toward which everything tends (which constitutes their intellectual superiority), but keep doing it (what else to do?).

James was supposed to become, with most probability, one of those who were stolid and oblivious to the world. "No way," he said aloud. Reluctant to engage himself with the problems with (his) false consciousness, he rather turned his mind to the following situation that happened at *LN*:

> A meeting. The colleagues say that Tobiáš is in Odessa, southern Ukraine, on holiday with his family. Richard comments: "If anything happens, we have a war correspondent! But don't wish it on them." We all laugh. (Field notes)

Richard had a kynical moment. His satirical remark was pointing to the uncertainty and chaos of the Russian-Ukrainian conflict and primarily to how opportunistic the media in general can be. His bitterly joking tone signified a form of subtle critique of—euphemized aggression toward—both aspects of reality. At the same time, however, it was clear—Richard knew and all the others knew as well—that if another focal point of the conflict had burst out in Odessa, the media organization would have enjoyed the unprecedented immediacy of Tobiáš's reporting, the moment of earning a reputation for being the first, and, primarily, increased readership, despite the fact that Tobiáš himself would have suddenly found himself in danger (not to mention spoiled holidays). Thus, Richard also recognized *LN*'s interests. Similarly to the situation with missing Vítek, Richard and all his colleagues would have been ready to get involved in building the organization's reputation and increasing its readership.

James realized the everyday-ness of this enactment of the gap between front and back stages (Goffman 1956). In the back region, the journalists were rather kynics or the ancient philosophical Cynics:

> regardless of their apparent 'cynical' stance towards practically everything, [they] remained honest and truthful: they practiced, as perhaps no other human beings have, the art of truth-telling. (Navia 1996: 6)

Even James' colleagues' subtle, jokingly uttered critique of the news-making machine was a manifestation of the decision to use language in a truthful way.

In the front region, however, James' colleagues were often modern cynics: they maintained the consciously inauthentic mask, sticking to and reproducing the cynicism as an ideology (Sloterdijk 1987). They had got used to this specific emotional style and had learned to deploy the "defence mechanisms" (Matouš). These formed part of the journalistic emotional management techniques that the journalists were supposed to perform in order to be successful in doing their job (Illouz 2007). They merged with their emotional field.

In other words, being a comfortable (Sloterdijk 1987), cool (Peters 2011), and romanticized (Pedelty 1995) professional identity, such ideological cynicism was a result of the journalists' reflexive construction of self-identity (Giddens 1991) comprising their self-mythicization. In turn, the myth of a somewhat cynical, cool renegade was vital for the journalistic professional ideology:

> It is, in short, a 'myth'—but in a particular sense of that word. Far from being a mere lie or illusion, it is a deeply held system of consciousness that profoundly affects both the structure of the news organization and the day-to-day practice of journalism. (Hallin 1986: 23)

At the same time, however, Farrukh pointed out that it is precisely this myth what forms the core of the unethical, exploitative journalism that Western journalists often perform in Global South.

James realized that the relationship between the forms of cynicism, with their diverging ways of handling the truth, and the journalistic

3 THE EMOTIONAL EXPERIENCE OF CRISIS REPORTERS: THE JOURNEY   103

professional ideology was very complex. The traditional journalistic professional ideology seemed to him at least self-contradictory (see the section "Professional Ideology and Cynicisms").

Obviously, being a good journalist—a truthful and ethical one—requires a carefully balanced combination of staying detached and being immersed; letting the emotions in and sticking to the facts. A similar skill to keep the "right distance" is an expected feature of caregivers, doctors, and employees of funeral parlors (Bernard 2008; Castra 2004; Molinier 2009). Many of the reporters—Sven, Jacob, Nicolas, Sam, Čestmír, Kryštof, and so on—compared their position to that of medical workers, in the sense that they cannot let themselves be moved too much (see Peters 2011):

> I mean I have to just be a professional. Like a doctor, who has to be professional on the spot, otherwise he is not useful. You have to do what you have to do. (Sam)

The cynical emotional style, preserving the right distance, is thus a result of emotional labor (Hochschild 1983), or psychological "care of oneself," that was also crucially important for the classical Cynics (Foucault 2005).

Stoics

But taking care of one's body and soul was also essential for the Stoics: those of James' colleagues who had mastered emotional management to the extent that their emotional style was at first sight equable and peaceful and allegedly did not interfere with their personal life. Stoics were to be found mainly among the most experienced reporters; historically, they were the Cynics' philosophical successors (Sellars 2006). For the Stoics, emotions are judgments, things that are up to them, things that we can and should control. A typical Stoic, perfectly rational and indifferent to the influence of circumstances, was Jesse:

> I don't get stressed out often. And I find it easy in difficult situations to keep my cool. And these are skills that I have learned and that I have sharpened over the years, which are very handy now in my work. … I just know that in stressful situations I always stay very cool and I am quite rational and I rationalize. … I think I am quite rational, although other people say that I am quite rational as well, so that you rationalize the options, you know what you see. (Jesse)

Among James' colleagues, there were several Stoics who were either stoic by default or had learned to carefully measure their emotional engagement in crisis situations, or even got to stoicism via a breakdown. For example, Lotte, Marie, Carl, Čestmír, Josef, Tomáš, Sam, Sven, Tobiáš, Emil, Šimon, Nicolas, Judith, Anthony, Bob, Giuseppe, Tim, and Astrid, although certainly not emotionless, were able to take a good care of themselves and rationally assess their psychological risks. Such as Čestmír, speaking about his abduction:

> These are not emotions that would—at least for me—come back in a noticeable way or that would repeat themselves, or be deposited somewhere. I mean, of course I do have it somewhere in my head. You can never delete these pictures. And … It's not that I have PTSD. Because I also think that it's true that we don't spend as much time there as, for example, soldiers do. (Čestmír)

That Čestmír rationally assessed a traumatic experience and put it away is related to the stoic principle of "following the facts" (Becker 1998). The fact was that he was lucky and survived. Likewise, Bob, Farrukh, Nicolas, Gloria, and Anthony grounded their equilibrium in knowing that they chose to be in the crisis and/or that people that they met there were in much bigger trouble.

Rationality was essential, as both Jesse's and Čestmír's quotations suggest. Indeed, similarly to the ancient Stoics, the stoic reporters' actions and consciousness were driven not only by the effort to avoid physical death/pain but also by the need to keep their rationality and dignity:

> I wanted to go to Libya now, because Libya has a new frontline, but … it's Ramadan, first, and you cannot find anyone, they are fighting, blowing themselves up, or they are sleeping. So … You can't do anything with that (laughs). After that, you have these sports events here, and to my feeling there is no interest when everybody is watching football or cycling or the Olympics. So I mean, what's the use of going to Libya in 50 degrees when it's too hot anyways? So I'll try to go there in the second part of August. It's still hot, but at least I would have the attention. So that's … No, I mean I have to think economically. Also. My company. I have to do it at the right time. (Sam)

In a Stoic's words, "If I am to survive as a rational being and not merely as an animal then I must pursue those things that will help to preserve my rationality as well as those things that will preserve my body" (Sellars 2006: 108). Taking care of one's soul and body thus did not mean surviving at any cost but included living by a consistent set of principles. Only the possession of virtue, according to the Stoics, can bring us happiness (Sellars 2006). Correspondingly, only performing ethical journalism could satisfy the stoic reporters.

The panini did not bring James any happiness; in fact, he felt rather ill. He took the last sip from the can of beer.

Coping Strategies

Obviously, the development of various emotional styles and mind-sets, and also the potential problems mentioned above—anxiety, panic attacks, post-traumatic stress disorder, insomnia, alcoholism, and other types of mental ill-health (Dubberley et al. 2015; Feinstein et al. 2015; Hight and Smyth 2003; Høiby and Ottosen 2015; Reinardy 2011; Richards and Rees 2011; Sambrook 2016)—is a work-related phenomenon, articulated by the crisis context and by the news-production machine (see the chapter "Articulating Journalists' Emotional Experiences of Crisis: Touching Down").

James' colleagues had developed various strategies for coping with the strain: cutting oneself off from the newsfeed during days off (Marie), falling asleep in dangerous moments (Sam), long-distance running (Finn), and the above-discussed cynicism and kynicism/black humor (Matouš, Lilah). The most frequently mentioned way of dealing with traumatic experiences and other sources of work-related pressure was simply talking it through. There were two ways of talking through trauma.

Needless to say that James preferred talking with his male colleagues: he felt calmer and safe in the company of those fatherly or brotherly old hands. His male colleagues were used to debriefing with friends/colleagues over a glass of whiskey or beer (Jesse, Bob, Anthony, Nicolas, Josef, Sam, Vítek). A method tested and approved, for example, by Josef:

> Luckily, I went through a course on how to fight post-traumatic syndrome, and how to avoid it. Do you know what the most important thing is? To—immediately, ex-post, once again—go through [the traumatizing experience] in your head and tell it to someone, most preferably with alcohol. (Josef)

> Talking about it with colleagues with whiskey is a kind of therapy. (Bob)

You have to discuss with [your photographer], you have to take a beer, have a cigarette, and ... 'How do you do, are you happy with what you did today, what do you want to say?' (Nicolas, explaining how he takes care of his colleagues' mental health and averts their trauma)

For its qualities, some considered undergoing alcohol cures/rituals a specific feature of foreign affairs reporters' or international correspondents' emotional culture (see also Pedelty 1995); see also the section "Brokens":

I think there are lots of similarities [among foreign affairs reporters] and I also noticed that other people in the field sometimes smoke a lot or drink a lot. (Jesse)

This is also one of the reasons why alcohol is a bit like a crutch for the foreign correspondents. One must be careful, but it really, really helps. Of course, no one will tell you, because no one *can* tell you, to get drunk, it's impossible, but it was conveyed to me between the lines as an expert counsel. (Josef)

As already mentioned in the section "Brokens," some reporters were not careful and couldn't restrain themselves from drinking too much, which than had serious consequences for their personal lives.

A piece of good advice could help a lot, though. James found it nice that two of his experienced colleagues, Nicolas and Jesse, fulfilled for their younger colleagues, within their newsrooms and particularly within their parachute teams, the role of informal psychological mentors:

You have to discuss after that, in the meantime, at the end of the day. ... It's a very important thing, to discuss that, because the economic pressure on a journalist is so strong that no boss pays attention to the trauma of the journalists. (Nicolas)

The other type of talking seemed to be reserved to women. Gloria, Lilah, and Ines claimed that when they are haunted by graphic traumatic memories, they talk them through mostly with other women, typically female colleagues. Not even knowing that men have their own self-help groups, they thought that the habit of talking about trauma is a women's specialty and even advantage:

My female colleagues, when we go through a crisis, after that we talk a lot about emotions. And my male colleagues, never. I sometimes ask them. (Laughs.) Didn't this have an impact on you? But they don't speak about that. And it seems that they don't feel anything, but I am not sure about that. (Ines)

For a woman it's very easy [to cope with traumatizing experiences]. (Laughs.) It's much easier than for a man. … They must be the machos and stay professional. For women, it doesn't matter. … I am not ashamed of crying, embracing somebody. (Gloria)

Gloria also protected herself against trauma by openly empathizing with the victims already in the field (and by calling them after returning to Barcelona); the feeling that she had helped someone made her feel good (see the section "Moral Dilemmas and Guilt").

James gave a sigh. It was increasingly difficult to be a man, and it must have been constantly difficult to be a woman. Luckily, both the genders had their work.

Both Nicolas and Jesse, and also Čestmír, saw their professional tasks—writing and speaking—as a cathartic strategy in itself, allowing them let loose their emotions while working:

I have to write what I saw during the day. … So it is, in some way, a kind of therapy … then I say to my students, do not be afraid of weeping on the keyboard. (Nicolas)

As I work for radio, when a thing happens, usually within hours I must frame it and I must start talking about it. And I have noticed that for me that is the way to cope with trauma. And with graphic things. … The sound engineers, 'cause they, they're in the same trauma, they see the same things, but they can't talk about it. (Jesse)

In its essence, the final product works as a catharsis. (Čestmír)

In this sense, the crisis reporting worked like pharmakon (Stiegler 2015), "poisoning" the reporters and providing a remedy at the same time. To compare, Hopper and Huxford (2015) speak about a "cognitive loop": doing the job of a newspaper journalist helps suppress unpleasant and paralyzing emotions stemming from doing the job, while suppressing emotions helps to do the job (which, as such, triggers strong emotions). Quite a few (at least ten) of James' colleagues had published at least one nonfiction book that was meant to give a more complex picture, fuller stories of people—victims, witnesses—they met in crises and better account for their own position in the field. Diego and Vítek were just promoting their freshly released oeuvres; Sven's book was adapted as a stage play and was just being rehearsed. Bob was then gathering material for his new book, Ernest was planning his travels for a book-long report (a genre that was, after a decades-long break, on the upswing). Farrukh continued to write a brilliant blog about the distorted depiction of crisis zones in mainstream media, the ideology, and the myths behind it. To compare, Judith was just writing a manual of storytelling, advising (future) journalists how to travel down the rabbit hole. For Nicolas, the relief coming from professional, factual writing was not enough, so he started to write fiction and regularly published fictional books based on his real journalistic experience. This allowed him to express much more and subtler meanings than newspaper articles.

Taken together, the coping strategies were rather informal, individual, not institutionalized (see also Buchanan and Keats 2011 and Høiby and Ottosen 2015):

> The worst thing is that one must deal with it on his own. (Josef)

> One just lives the emotion through alone. ... It's a very intimate thing. (Marie)

Indeed, during his short career, James had not yet encountered any media organization that would tackle the issue systematically. Organizational documents related to breaking news and crisis reporting that James saw or heard about did not go beyond to-do lists and practical guidelines, only listing steps aiming at the highest possible organizational efficiency (see the section "'You Can't Leave Your Journalists Alone with Their Feelings': Organizational Identities").

Some media organizations (e.g. *VRT* or *DR*) did institutionalize a kind of support, which, however, came always ex-post facto. After coming from a conflict zone or a natural disaster, any journalist could call an external trauma specialist—without telling the boss—and arrange one or more debriefing sessions. The confidentiality was important, since potential psychological problems were considered intimate and gender-sensitive:

> [Y]ou know, especially maybe for men, or for some men, it's difficult after such a severe assignment to go and say, hey, I would like to talk to someone, because I am sleeping badly. (Lotte)

According to some, such a follow-up measure was all right ("We are really investing in that, because you see unimaginable things sometimes, when you are in the field"—Lotte), although the support could be better (Jesse). By contrast, Bob was not so impressed by that: psychologists cannot do so much. "Psychologists do not have an attitude to that; I do have an attitude." This is also why the best thing one can do is talking about her trauma with fellow reporters.

At least it's something, James thought. He was wondering whether *The Mo* or Fred himself would offer him a session with a therapist after his return from San Lorenzo. James thought Fred should. If James returns.

For crisis reporting is not (only and always) an individual pursuit of masochistic pleasure. It is a politically important business. Independent and quality media are vital for democratic processes: contemporary democratic societies, constantly reflexively constructed and reconstructed (Giddens 1991), are not conceivable without established information flows, including first-hand and mediated experience with risk and crisis zones. As Wahl-Jorgensen et al. write, "Journalism plays a key role in democracies around the world, acting as a watchdog on the state and informing citizens about the decisions that affect their everyday life" (Wahl-Jorgensen et al. 2016: 810–811). Simon Cottle observes that visualized narratives, emotive testimonies, and experiential accounts can play a significant contribution in the public enactment of communicative democracy (Cottle 2009; see also Boltanski 1999). In particular,

> the media's performative use of resonate symbols, dramatic visualization, narrative and embedding of emotions into ritual forms sometimes confront the strategic power of institutions and vested interests and can even lend moral gravitas to the projects of challenger groups within society. (Cottle 2009: 353)

On top of that, in crisis moments, journalists and quality media can fulfill other than purely informational roles in the affected community (e.g. Schudson 2011; Tong 2015). For example, given their embeddedness in decision-making processes (Hoskins and O'Loughlin 2010), media have a peacekeeping potential (Neumann and Fahmy 2016). Not to mention that the common mediated perception of global risks and crises underpin and mobilize an emergent global public sphere and global citizenship (Beck 2005).

The emotional risks of journalism in general and crisis reporting in particular not only follow from the practices that fulfill the democratizing role of media but also include the large number of new threats that limit journalists' ability to fulfill the watchdog role (Wahl-Jorgensen et al. 2016). At the same time, the multiple crisis environment, the institution of the media and its general logic, and the newsmaking processes and technologies (see the chapter "Articulating Journalists' Emotional Experiences of Crisis: Touching Down") have share in shaping the emotional styles, risks, and problems. Therefore, the risks and negative outcomes of crisis reporting should not be individualized but subjected to public, institutional, organizational, and professional prevention and resolution.

James himself came to the conclusion that we all should be more open about the journalists' *authentic* emotional experience. Secretly treating individual trauma and sweeping it under the carpet meant preserving the contrast between the privileged European bubble and the starving and dying Others: on one side, there is a cool, acceptably concerned yet still quite relaxed talking head from Europe, and on the other side there are thousands of dead, injured, and displaced civilians in Aleppo or the Rakhine state. The reporter narrates their story; for a while, the viewers/readers are horrified by the affairs in this or that geographically distant country. But they are not aware that the reporter cannot get rid of the smell of blood and decay (Lilah, Mario, Anthony, Ines, Jesse) and that in the next days, weeks, and months she will sleep poorly. Showing what the tragedies of the Others meant for a privileged visitor could help to build a bridge between the two worlds (see Usher 2019).

All things considered, the existing ex-post responses were not adequate to treat frequent and intense exposure to traumatizing circumstances, constant awareness of existential problems, and work-related pressure. Moreover, there was vicarious trauma (Dubberley et al. 2015), evident amongst staff working in newsrooms on the digital frontline. Exposure to graphic images and psychosocial risks were no longer limited to being on the spot, so that the common notion of subsequent debriefings as "therapy" was only partly grounded in reality.

Introducing *prevention* measures within media organizations—preparing the reporters materially and psychologically—could be more appropriate:

> the best thing would be to prepare the people before you send them. … you cannot send people to the war naked. (Gloria)

> I think you should not do these things unless you are well prepared to what you might experience. You have time to get in and out of the situation, you have enough time to interview the people, to interview them in a dignifying way, and you have time to write it. (Judith)

Lilah said that even having enough time to think what she might expect helps her.

Providing psychological training and education related to possible threats, together with normalizing one's response to psychological trauma (Buchanan and Keats 2011) could reduce the discrepancy between the emerging evidence on journalists' emotional risks, the developing policies, and poor organizational practice. Implementing emotion instruction to journalism courses and textbooks could be a starting place (Hopper and Huxford 2017).

There are also sufficient legal arguments—implementations of EU directives, country-specific acts and labor codes, and Customary International Humanitarian Law (CIHL)—for why media organizations should prevent related (mental) health problems caused by work-related risks. According to the CIHL, reporters covering crisis events such as wars and conflict zones have a similar status as medical workers, members of peacekeeping missions, and humanitarian relief personnel. As such, they should be a specifically protected group. "Civilian journalists engaged in professional missions in areas of armed conflict must be respected and protected as long as they are not taking a direct part in hostilities" (Rule 34; Henckaerts and Doswald-Beck 2005: 115). The UN General Assembly and the UN Commission on Human Rights have also deplored various threats to journalists' health and safety such as harassment, intimidation, attacks, acts of reprisal, abductions, police violence, unjustified imprisonment, threats of legal prosecutions and subjection to defamation campaigns, threats to treat the media as enemies serving foreign powers, and denial of full and unhindered access (Henckaerts and Doswald-Beck 2005: 117–118). Some measures directed to fulfilling the CIHL have already been advanced by the Dart Centre and UNESCO's handbook for journalists reporting on terrorism (Dubberley et al. 2015; Marthoz 2017).

An Overview

Drawing energy from the trace of anger raised by the literal injustice of the almost non-existent preparations of journalists suffering from workplace dangers, James now clearly saw all the ambiguities of the journalistic emotional journey through the Russian Mountains. Newsroom routine sometimes bored the journalists to tears. Crises had the potential to interrupt the newsroom/on-the-spot boredom and could result in closeness, identification, empathy—in particular when children and parenting were at play—and strong emotional involvement. The possibility to stay emotionally detached further diminished due to the moral quandaries that the reporters often faced, the danger they experienced, and the diffused wars they involuntarily waged. At the same time, the corresponding emotional distress—the moral dilemmas, feelings of guilt, fear, and sense of responsibility—reflected themselves in the media content. However, as the next chapter will illustrate, the reporters' emotions were supposed to reflect themselves in the media content neither too strongly nor too weakly.

Reporters reacted to the emotionally demanding nature of crisis reporting by developing diverse emotional styles: mainly cynical, stoic, and, rarely, broken. The convenient, cool, and romanticized professional identity of Cynics, encompassing modern ideological cynicism and classical kynicism, was a result of the journalists' reflexive construction of self-identity and their self-mythicization. In turn, the myth or image of a somewhat cynical, cool renegade was vital for the journalistic professional ideology (however, the complex relationship between cynical and journalistic ideology is to be further investigated). By comparison, Stoics were respecters of all kinds of rationality and of living according to a consistent set of principles.

Staying sane required the reporters to develop individual and informal coping strategies ranging from drinking-talking sessions to writing fiction and running marathons. Even though there were legal measures meant to deal with the health, safety, and stress of workers, James had not encountered any specific solutions for possible emotional distress or mental ill-health at the state, professional, or organizational level. The social and systemic problems were individualized and biographized (Beck and Beck-Gernsheim 2001) and the journalists carried their solutions on their shoulders (see Scheper-Hughes and Lock 1987). Media organizations did not respond appropriately to the frequent and intense exposure to traumatic circumstances, the constant awareness of existential problems, and the work-related pressure. Their negligence made the reporters' work increasingly precarious, all the more so when they worked as freelancers.

While turning left, the airplane banked. The overhead bin above James opened, and a steel case partly slid out of it, almost falling down before the robotic steward rushed to it and snapped the bin shut. It made James aware of all the technology he was dependent on.

He had no idea what was inside the case and wanted to find out.

REFERENCES

Andén-Papadopoulos, K., & Pantti, M. (2013). Re-imagining Crisis Reporting: Professional Ideology of Journalists and Citizen Eyewitness Images. *Journalism, 14*(7), 960–977.
Backholm, K. (2017). Distress Among Journalists Working the Incidents. In L. C. Wilson (Ed.), *The Wiley Handbook of the Psychology of Mass Shootings (Wiley Clinical Psychology Handbooks)* (pp. 247–263). Chichester: John Wiley & Sons.
Beck, U. (2005). *Power in the Global Age*. Cambridge: Polity.
Beck, U., & Beck-Gernsheim, E. (2001). *Individualization: Institutionalized Individualism and Its Social and Political Consequences*. London: SAGE.
Becker, L. A. (1998). *A New Stoicism*. Princeton: Princeton University Press.
Bernard, J. (2008). Bonne distance et empathie dans le travail émotionnel des pompes funèbres: L'analyse des interactions en milieu professionnel. *Journal des Anthropologues, 114–115*, 109–128.
Bewes, T. (1997). *Cynicism and Postmodernity*. London: Verso.
Boltanski, L. (1999). *Distant Suffering: Morality, Media and Politics*. Cambridge: Cambridge University Press.
Buchanan, M., & Keats, P. (2011). Coping with Traumatic Stress in Journalism: A Critical Ethnographic Study. *International Journal of Psychology, 46*(2), 127–135.
Carpentier, N., & Trioen, M. (2010). The Particularity of Objectivity: A Poststructuralist and Psychoanalytical Reading of the Gap Between Objectivity-as-a-value and Objectivity-as-a- practice in the 2003 Iraqi War Coverage. *Journalism, 11*(3), 311–328.
Castra, M. (2004). Faire face à la mort: Réguler la "bonne distance" soignants-malades en unité de soins palliatifs. *Travail et Emploi, 97*, 53–64.

Cottle, S. (2009). *Global Crisis Reporting: Journalism in the Global Age*. Maidenhead: Open University Press.

Creech, B. (2018). Bearing the Cost to Witness: The Political Economy of Risk in Contemporary Conflict and War Reporting. *Media, Culture & Society, 40*(4), 567–583.

Czarniawska, B. (2011). *Cyberfactories: How News Agencies Produce News*. Northampton: Edward Elgar.

Deuze, M., & Witschge, T. (2018). Beyond Journalism: Theorizing the Transformation of Journalism. *Journalism, 19*(2), 165–181.

Dubberley, S. et al. (2015). *Making Secondary Trauma a Primary Issue: A Study of Eyewitness Media and Vicarious Trauma on the Digital Frontline*. Eyewitness Media Hub. Retrieved from http://eyewitnessmediahub.com/research/vicarious-trauma.

Elias, N. (1956). Problems of Involvement and Detachment. *The British Journal of Sociology, 7*(3), 226–252.

Falkheimer, J., & Olsson, E. K. (2015). Depoliticizing Terror: The News Framing of the Terrorist Attacks in Norway, 22 July 2011. *Media, War and Conflict, 8*(1), 70–85.

Feinstein, A., et al. (2015). Witnessing Images of Extreme Violence: A Psychological Study of Journalists in the Newsroom. *Journal of the Royal Society of Medicine, 6*(2), 1–7.

Festinger, L. (1957). *A Theory of Cognitive Dissonance*. Stanford: Stanford University Press.

Flam, H., & Kleres, J. (Eds.). (2015). *Methods of Exploring Emotions*. London: Routledge.

Fleming, P., & Spicer, A. (2003). Working at a Cynical Distance: Implications for Power, Subjectivity and Resistance. *Organization, 10*(1), 157–179.

Foucault, M. (2005). *The Hermeneutics of the Subject: Lectures at the College de France, 1981–82*. New York: Palgrave Macmillan.

Galtung, J., & Ruge, M. B. (1965). The Structure of Foreign News. *Journal of Peace Research, 2*(1), 64–91.

Giddens, A. (1991). *Modernity and Self-Identity: Self and Society in the Late Modern Age*. Cambridge: Polity Press.

Glück, A. (2016). What Makes a Good Journalist? *Journalism Studies, 17*(7), 893–903.

Goffman, E. (1956). *The Presentation of Self in Everyday Life*. Edinburgh: University of Edinburgh.

Hallin, D. C. (1986). *The "Uncensored War": The Media and Vietnam*. Berkeley: University of California Press.

Hanitzsch, T. (2019). Journalism Studies Still Needs to Fix Western Bias. *Journalism, 20*(1), 214–217.

Harcup, T., & O'Neill, D. (2001). What Is News? Galtung and Ruge Revisited. *Journalism Studies, 2*(2), 261–280.

Henckaerts, J. M., & Doswald-Beck, L. (2005). *Customary International Humanitarian Law*. Cambridge: International Committee of the Red Cross. Retrieved from https://www.icrc.org/eng/assets/files/other/customary-international-humanitarian-law-i-icrc-eng.pdf.

Hesmondhalgh, D., & Baker, S. (2011). *Creative Labour: Media Work in Three Cultural Industries*. London: Routledge.

Hight, J., & Smyth, F. (2003). *Tragedies and Journalists: A Guide for More Effective Coverage*. Dart Center for Journalism and Trauma. Retrieved from http://dartcenter.org/sites/default/files/en_tnj_0.pdf.

Hochschild, A. R. (1983). *The Managed Heart*. Berkeley: University of California Press.

Høiby, M. H., & Ottosen, R. (2015). *Journalism Under Pressure: A Mapping of Editorial Policies for Journalists Covering Conflict*. Oslo: Høgskolen i Oslo og Akershus.

Hopper, K. M., & Huxford, J. (2015). Gathering Emotion: Examining Newspaper Journalists' Engagement in Emotional Labor. *Journal of Media Practice, 16*(1), 25–41.

Hopper, K. M., & Huxford, J. (2017). Emotion Instruction in Journalism Courses: An Analysis of Introductory News Writing Textbooks. *Communication Education, 66*(1), 90–108.

Hoskins, A., & O'Loughlin, B. (2010). *War and Media: The Emergence of Diffused War*. Cambridge: Polity Press.

Illouz, E. (2007). *Cold Intimacies: The Making of Emotional Capitalism*. Cambridge: Polity Press.

Jukes, S. (2017). *Affective journalism – Uncovering the Affective Dimension of Practice in the Coverage of Traumatic News*. PhD Thesis, Goldsmiths University, United Kingdom.

Marthoz, J. P. (2017). *Terrorism and the Media: A Handbook for Journalists*. Paris: UNESCO.

McDonald, I. R., & Lawrence, R. G. (2004). Filling the 24×7 News Hole: Television News Coverage Following September 11. *American Behavioral Scientist, 48*(3), 327–340.

Mejias, U. A., & Vokuev, M. E. (2017). Disinformation and the Media: The Case of Russia and Ukraine. *Media, Culture and Society, 39*(7), 1027–1042.

Moeller, S. D. (1999). *Compassion Fatigue: How the Media Sell Disease, Famine, War and Death*. London: Routledge.

Molinier, P. (2009). Temps professionnel et temps personnel des travailleuses du care: Perméabilité ou clivage? Les aléas de la "bonne distance". *Temporalités, 9*, 1 14.

Navia, L. E. (1996). *Classical Cynicism: A Critical Study*. London: Greenwood Press.

Neumann, R., & Fahmy, S. (2016). Measuring Journalistic Peace/War Performance: An Exploratory Study of Crisis Reporters' Attitudes and Perceptions. *International Communication Gazette, 78*(3), 223–246.

Nord, L. W., & Strömbäck, J. (2003). Making Sense of Different Types of Crises: A Study of the Swedish Media Coverage of the Terror Attacks Against the United States and the U.S. Attacks in Afghanistan. *Press/Politics*, *8*(4), 54–75.

Nord, L. W., & Strömbäck, J. (2006). Reporting More, Informing Less: A Comparison of the Swedish Media Coverage of September 11 and the Wars in Afghanistan and Iraq. *Journalism*, *7*(1), 85–110.

Örnebring, H. (2009). *Comparative European Journalism: The State of Current Research*. Working paper. Oxford: Reuters Institute for the Study of Journalism.

Pantti, M. (2010). The Value of Emotion: An Examination of Television Journalists' Notions on Emotionality. *European Journal of Communication*, *25*(2), 168–181.

Pedelty, M. (1995). *War Stories: The Culture of Foreign Correspondents*. London: Routledge.

Peters, C. (2011). Emotion Aside or Emotional Side? Crafting an 'Experience of Involvement' in the News. *Journalism*, *12*(3), 297–316.

Reinardy, S. (2011). Newspaper Journalism in Crisis: Burnout on the Rise, Eroding Young Journalists' Career Commitment. *Journalism*, *12*(1), 33–50.

Richards, B., & Rees, G. (2011). The Management of Emotion in British Journalism. *Media, Culture and Society*, *33*(6), 851–867.

Rosaldo, M. Z. (1984). Towards an Anthropology of Self and Feeling. In R. A. Schweder & R. A. LeVine (Eds.), *Culture Theory: Essays on Mind, Self and Emotions* (pp. 137–157). Cambridge: Cambridge University Press.

Rosen, J. (2011). September 11 in the Mind of American Journalism. In B. Zelizer & S. Allan (Eds.), *Journalism After September 11* (2nd ed., pp. 35–43). London: Routledge.

Rosenkranz, T. (2019). From Contract to Speculation: New Relations of Work and Production in Freelance Travel Journalism. *Work, Employment and Society*. Epub ahead of print 20 January 2019. https://doi.org/10.1177/0950017018793344.

Russia's Dark Arts: An investigative series on Russia's covert projection of power. (2016). *New York Times*. Retrieved from https://www.nytimes.com/series/russias-dark-arts.

Rutten, E., et al. (Eds.). (2013). *Memory, Conflict and New Media: Web Wars in Post-socialist States*. London: Routledge.

Sambrook, R. (2016, April 11). Newsrooms Should Prepare to Cover Terrorist Attacks. *International News Safety Institute*. Retrieved from http://www.newssafety.org/news/insi-news/insi-news/detail/newsrooms-should-prepare-to-cover-terrorist-attacks-1722/.

Scheer, M. (2012). Are Emotions a Kind of Practice (And Is That What Makes Them Have a History)? A Bourdieuian Approach to Understanding Emotion. *History and Theory*, *51*, 193–220.

Scheper-Hughes, N., & Lock, M. (1987). The Mindful Body: A Prolegomenon to Future Work in Medical Anthropology. *Medical Anthropology Quarterly*, *1*(1), 6–41.

Schudson, M. (2011). What's Unusual About Covering Politics as Usual. In B. Zelizer & S. Allan (Eds.), *Journalism after September 11* (2nd ed., pp. 44–54). London: Routledge.

Sellars, J. (2006). *Stoicism*. London: Routledge.

Sloterdijk, P. (1987). *Critique of Cynical Reason*. Minneapolis: University of Minnesota Press.

Sontag, S. (2003). *Regarding the Pain of Others*. New York: Picador.

Statista. (2019). Unemployment Rate in Member States of the European Union in June 2018 (seasonally adjusted). *The Statistics Portal*. Retrieved from https://www.statista.com/statistics/268830/unemployment-rate-in-eu-countries/.

Stiegler, B. (2015). Numérique, éducation et cosmopolitisme. *Cités*, *63*, 13–36.

The Guardian. (2003, December 5). Journalists Jailed for Inciting Rwandan Genocide. *The Guardian*. Retrieved from https://www.theguardian.com/media/2003/dec/04/pressandpublishing.radio.

Tong, J. (2015). Being Objective with a Personal Perspective: How Environmental Journalists at Two Chinese Newspapers Articulate and Practice Objectivity. *Science Communication*, *37*(6), 747–768.

Tumber, H. (2011). Reporting Under Fire: The Physical Safety and Emotional Welfare of Journalists. In B. Zelizer & S. Allan (Eds.), *Journalism After September 11* (2nd ed., pp. 319–334). London: Routledge.

Usher, N. (2019). Journalism's Biggest Challenge? Journalists. *Journalism*, *20*(1), 140–143.

Van Zoonen, L. (1998). A Professional, Unreliable, Heroic Marionette (M/F): Structure, Agency and Subjectivity in Contemporary Journalisms. *European Journal of Cultural Studies*, *1*(1), 123–143.

Wahl-Jorgensen, K., et al. (2016). The Future of Journalism. *Digital Journalism*, *4*(7), 809–815.

Waisbord, S. (2019). The Vulnerabilities of Journalism. *Journalism*, *20*(1), 210–213.

Weick, K. E. (1995). *Sensemaking in Organizations*. London: SAGE.

Zelizer, B., & Allan, S. (Eds.). (2011). *Journalism After September 11* (2nd ed.). London: Routledge.

Open Access This chapter is licensed under the terms of the Creative Commons Attribution 4.0 International License (http://creativecommons.org/licenses/by/4.0/), which permits use, sharing, adaptation, distribution and reproduction in any medium or format, as long as you give appropriate credit to the original author(s) and the source, provide a link to the Creative Commons licence and indicate if changes were made.

The images or other third party material in this chapter are included in the chapter's Creative Commons licence, unless indicated otherwise in a credit line to the material. If material is not included in the chapter's Creative Commons licence and your intended use is not permitted by statutory regulation or exceeds the permitted use, you will need to obtain permission directly from the copyright holder.

CHAPTER 4

Articulating Journalists' Emotional Experiences of Crisis: Touching Down

Revived by the curiosity, James pulled out his computer again and turned on a movie player. He had long planned to watch Viggo Mortensen's reading of Albert Camus' speech "The Human Crisis," written in 1946 (Camus 2016). The flight seemed to be a perfect opportunity, the only opportunity. He put on his headphones and plunged into the material-technological solution.

To do justice to James' feelings, thoughts, and primarily to the conditions that (were supposed to) shape(d) them, the analysis requires to make a few final steps. The previous chapter illustrated that and in which sense emotions are to a large extent *culturally* determined, defined, and shaped practices of feeling and thinking (Rosaldo 1984; Scheer 2012; Scheper-Hughes and Lock 1987). But a concept that seems to be most intrinsic to the modern Western culture, whatever stance one adopts (e.g. Beck 1992; Foucault 1978; Heidegger 1977; Van Loon 2002; Williams 1974), is technology. One more crucial question thus arises: In which ways does technology, constitutively entangled with human beings (Orlikowski 2007), articulate journalists' emotional experience of crisis?

In recent media studies, technology has been thought as an assemblage of people, technological devices, buildings, texts, meanings, organizations, roles, contexts, and so on (Hansen 2006; Lievrouw 2014; Van Loon 2002), a living milieu (Deuze 2011; Parikka 2010), or as a part of the crisis-technology rhizome (Deleuze and Guattari 1988). But the most suitable conception here seems to be the one suggested by Michel

© The Author(s) 2019
J. Kotišová, *Crisis Reporters, Emotions, and Technology*,
https://doi.org/10.1007/978-3-030-21428-9_4

Foucault: technology as a fourfold complex of technologies of production, technologies of sign systems, technologies of power, and technologies of the self (Foucault 1988). In an interview he gave late in life, Foucault insisted that we should not understand technology too narrowly as tools and machines. His words were interpreted by some as shifting the meaning of technology away from materiality toward methods and procedures for governing human beings (Behrent 2013) and by others as encompassing material technologies within practices and means of government (Altamirano 2014; Greene 2012; Hay 2012; Packer and Crofts Wiley 2012; see also Rayner 2001). This study follows the latter interpretation and understands technology as a concept dismantling the traditional bifurcation of nature and society and positioning material artifacts alongside, rather than against, social institutions (Altamirano 2014; Orlikowski 2007).

To be more concrete, James' colleagues' emotional experience at work largely resulted from their emotional labor (Hochschild 1983), so that it was their work in its full extent that shaped their emotional experience:

> The work is a filter through which you look at [the crisis]. In the moment, you are not there to get stirred up by what is happening, and the work helps you in it. (Čestmír)

> It gives you the reason to go to a place which is unreasonable. (Farrukh)

Their emotional experience was articulated by their position within the hierarchy and corresponding professional tasks; the means of making news, in terms of both processes and material resources; the work with words and images; the feed of disturbing content and the responsibility to tame it and pass it on; and, above all, the work on their selves, stimulating certain emotional reactions and suppressing others, trying to do their job well and to stay healthy at the same time. All these aspects together—all the technologies, or matrices of practical reason telling people how successful professionals should conduct themselves and operate their bodies, souls, and thoughts (Du Gay 1996; Foucault 1988)—constructed the forms of subjectivity that were most appropriate to the social practice in question, in this case the journalistic profession (Du Gay 1996; Foucault 1988, 2005).

Again, James found it clear as a bell that the emotional experiences, styles, and potential problems related to covering crises were *social* and

Image 4.1 Albert Camus' historic lecture, "The Human Crisis," performed by actor Viggo Mortensen, New York City, 2016. Source: *YouTube*, "Albert Camus's 'The Human Crisis' read by Viggo Mortensen, 70 years later"; channel: Columbia Maison Française. Screenshot taken by the author

systemic. They were engendered by the demands of the media-technological environment on one hand, and the crisis contexts on the other.

Camus—or rather Mortensen—was just saying that "nihilism has been replaced by absolute rationalism, and in both cases the results are the same." Did the guys equal the "human crisis" with "absolute rationalism"? James pondered (Image 4.1).

He paused the video for a while. His tranquil rumination about the absolute rationalism started to be disturbed by haunting thoughts of his future report on the catastrophe at San Lorenzo. He still had not planned how he would make the news.

Newsmaking Machine

Technologies of Production: Practices, Devices, and the Surreal

Foucault defined technologies of production as one of the matrices of practical reason "which permit us to produce, transform or manipulate things" (Foucault 1988: 18). Regarding the complexity of material/artificial and natural/human inherent in Foucault's notion of technology (Altamirano 2014; Orlikowski 2007), technologies of production are both institutionally embedded practices of crisis news production and material artifacts employed in the process. Both facets of the technology of crisis news production were observable in the newsrooms and narrated by the on-the-spot reporters, be they parachutists or correspondents.

In the newsrooms, one could *observe* the technologies as practices and material technologies in their interplay: the milieu of the *ČT* control room, full of "[not-always-]silent co-workers" (Czarniawska 2011: 40), screens, speakers, cables, keyboards, computers, sockets, control panels, partitions, light bulbs, microphones, spotlights, telephones, tilt chairs, computer mice, but mainly screens, screens, and more screens, was a unique stage of human-machine synchronization when an unexpected piece of news came in (and people started to use microphones and telephones more or to watch *CNN* or *BBC* on the ubiquitous screens) (Image 4.2).

Image 4.2 A control room in *Czech Television*, Autumn 2015. Picture taken by the author

Likewise, the *narratives* often touched upon concrete moments of negotiations, conflicts, and friendships between humans and their cameras, internet connections, batteries, and smartphones. How did the technologies of production articulate the journalists' emotional experience of crisis?

Same Principles, Different Practices
The practices of making crisis news were driven by the same principles as making news in peaceful contexts. Why wouldn't they? James thought, and he recalled the often resolute or uncomprehending look of his colleagues after he asked them about any specific practices he should do while reporting on a crisis:

> I think they are fundamentally the same. One simply tries to give the most truthful account of what happened. (Matouš)

The reporters referred to the principles of sourcing, verifying, and gatekeeping. Indeed, as Toni G.L.A. Van Der Meer et al. (2016: 13) observe, "[g]atekeeping theory and practices still hold during a crisis; ... Just as in non-crisis times, the findings indicate that journalists remain critical gatekeepers during crises."

"[H]owever, a more nuanced understanding is needed," Van Der Meer et al. (ibid.) continue. Indeed, after the initial denial, it always became clear that making crisis news can be very different from covering non-crisis events. Not surprisingly, there are many differences even between individual crisis events, depending on the extent of their predictability and newness (Nord and Strömbäck 2003; see the section "Typologies of Crisis Moments"). Previous research has illustrated that "[crisis press coverage] does not tone all crises in the same shades" (Ben-Yehuda et al. 2013: 87), which implies that each type of crisis requires certain specific technologies of news production and journalistic practices (e.g. McDonald and Lawrence 2004).

At the same time, however, all the crisis types are substantially challenging. James recalled his thoughts about the dialogue between—and sometimes resonation of—outside-the-media crises and inside-the-media crises (Olsson and Nord 2015; see the section "Inside-the-Media Is Outside-the-Media Crisis").

First, crisis events often fully fill the news hole (Nord and Strömbäck 2006) or even become a central theme for a relatively long time, so they either require immediate organic improvization and fast reorganization of pages/broadcasting (e.g. Emil), or, on the contrary, stir up long, thorough, and time-consuming discussions about accuracy, precision, and ethics (e.g. Čestmír). These contradictory time requirements generate organizational crises ending up in increased pressure felt by individuals.

Second, the reality of gatekeeping practice, in general, follows professional principles more loosely than in non-crisis contexts:

> During a crisis, journalists have the tendency to rely mainly on familiar sources such as news agencies and disregard certain other less familiar news sources such as the organization and the public. This journalistic inclination toward certain routine sources might result in a bias in terms of the framing of the event and an imbalanced coverage. (Van Der Meer et al. 2016: 13; see also Falkheimer and Olsson 2015; McDonald and Lawrence 2004)

As a result, sources tend to be mainly English-speaking, such as American news agencies and big international media organizations (Nord and Strömbäck 2003; field work). Again, the sourcing practices in crises depend on the existence of routines and the possibility to make adequate preparations. For example, in terror attacks the journalists tend to use more anonymous sources (Nord and Strömbäck 2003). But using (potentially) anonymous information and alleged eyewitness accounts flooding Twitter, YouTube, and Facebook—in times of crisis, social media hype tends to precede the "traditional" media hype (Pang 2013)—requires careful fact-checking (e.g. Ema, Marie). The pressure becomes even higher.

Third, crises also compel the reporters to perform intensified, often frenetic activity. The process of handling one of the events with the potential to become breaking news looked as follows:

> First, someone comes up with the information that something has happened, from Twitter via reliable sources—such as *CNN, Reuters, BBC*. He/she informs others sitting in the newsroom about it or calls the editor (in chief). They discuss how to make it, what shots to use first: archive footage? Illustrative footage? Then, an editor makes a call to the on-site reporter and arranges a live entry: when, where and sometimes what to say in case there is little information (depends also on the constraints on site—like the reporter having a broken leg etc.). Alternatively, if there is no foreign correspondent nearby the epicentre of the crisis, the boss "offers" a business trip to a parachutist (i.e. practically assigns her, or rather him). Then, the editor decides how to combine the live entry with other resources. All of this has to be done in a matter of minutes. (Field notes)

From the perspective of rhythm, such a sudden flurry of action points to time compression in the moment which makes present and turns real the latent crisis continuum, inherently linked to reflexive modernity and risk society (e.g. Adam 2003; see also above). Correspondingly, the speed requirements in newswork and journalism grow (Czarniawska 2011), particularly in breaking moments.

Fourth, consequently, the reporters are supposed to look at the issue/event from many different angles and to provide as many details as possible (e.g. Sam). The crisis thus has the potential to push the reporters to their limits, to radically change their working hours, and to shift or erase the border between personal and professional time (e.g. Ines, Louis, Josef; cf. Pedelty 1995).

James was by no means an expert on San Lorenzo. As a parachute reporter, he kept moving from topic to topic, with little chance to become an expert in any of them, and, like most other people, he had known very little about the island before he was "offered" to go there. He nervously moved a bit in his seat.

Fifth, in the case of reporting on the spot in hostile environments, reporters were sometimes thrown into physical danger (see the section "Danger and Fear"). This concurs with Høiby and Ottosen's (2015) finding that journalists' professional performance in hostile environments is accompanied by danger, risk, and threat and is corroborated by data and stories provided by the Committee to Protect Journalists and Reporters Without Borders. Nevertheless, Mark Pedelty (1995) persuasively shows that the haze of danger is also a part of the foreign affairs reporters' renegade image, and Brian Creech (2018) shows that the romantic ideal of a reporter marching to war to bring back stories is deeply rooted in European history and tied to colonial expansion. This seeming contradiction of precarity, constituted by the growing threat of bodily harm, and promise of fame and success, not only stems from the increasingly individualized risk (Beck 1992) that is accepted for the sake of one's own reputation and that of one's media organization but also reflects the distinction between international correspondents/parachutists and local journalists. The risks facing journalists are vast, and unequally distributed among staff international journalists, freelancers from Europe and the US, and local journalists, stringers, and fixers. While locals living and reporting in hostile environments, together with their families, are much more likely to be exposed to danger and usually face the most severe threats of violence (Creech 2018; Høiby and Ottosen 2015), the privileged international correspondents—

that is, James' colleagues and Pedelty's interviewees—rarely put their feet on "battlefields." Instead, they stay in relatively safe capital cities, the headquarters of international organizations, residences of local officials, press conferences, hotels, and restaurants (Pedelty 1995). Yet, at least Josef, Sam, Anthony, Jesse, Čestmír, Vítek, Nicolas, and Tomáš had gone through life-threatening situations.

The technologies of making crisis news also impose increased and specific risks on women: most of the threats to women consist in sexual harassment, verbal threats, abduction, rape, and forced "marriage." "Kidnapping, rape and violence is of regular concern for women journalists at work" (Høiby and Ottosen 2015: 66). Women face these dangers especially when covering local conflicts.

James was wondering why he had not heard anything about this from his female colleagues. If they complained, the reason was rather their invisibility (Ines).

As has been suggested in the section "Danger and Fear," due to the danger, conflict zone news sometimes relied on only one side of the conflict:

> Rarely can you show both sides in one report. Almost never. Because there is simply a front line between them, which is very hard to cross. (Čestmír)

According to Čestmír, and also some media scholars, this often results in "less professional" news (e.g. Olsson and Nord 2015). Alternatively, a reporter can devote a large amount of time and energy to travel to the other side of the conflict, as Sven did in Kosovo:

> There were really ... snipers etcetera, so it was really dangerous. So back in Brussels, I felt I had the Kosovo side, the Kosovo-Albanian side of the story. And I was a bit in a non-balanced situation. ... So after a couple of weeks, I travelled to Serbia to get the story from the Serbian-Macedonian side. And then, at the end, I felt, ok, I am in balance now.

As Nicolas, Sven, Jesse, Čestmír, and some others said, it is important in dangerous conditions for the reporters and all members of the team to have formal autonomy—the right to assess the risks on the spot and to decide what level of danger they are willing to accept. But in reality, the reporters themselves are on the top of the hierarchy, followed by editors-in-chief, photographers, sound engineers, and fixers, for whom the reporters feel responsible. This further intensifies the stress (Jesse, Gloria).

Finally, sixth, in crises, James' colleagues were also faced with and constrained by various legal restrictions (e.g. Sam or Tomáš). The saying that "the first casualty of war is truth" was true, due to legal and official restrictions under crisis circumstances, whether well-founded or introduced under pretense of security measures, and because reporters may be greatly distanced from events, first-hand witnesses, and participants (Pedelty 1995). Alternatively, they may be offered restricted access. This was the case of some Belgian and Czech reporters who, after returning from Syria, were harshly criticized by other journalists for going there "at Assad's invitation" and echoing the official, governmental point of view and conveying Assad's politics/justifications. A few of James' colleagues believed that the legitimacy of covering conflict zones in this way—say, interviewing Assad—"depends on the questions." (Sven, Ernest)

The specificity of the practical technologies for making crisis news was often reflected in the visible innovations on the pages or in broadcasting, as proposed at a meeting during the police interventions in Brussels after the Paris terrorist attacks in November 2015:

> Martin suggests, due to the extraordinariness of the affairs, to "disrupt" the format of UK (an evening programme): "…to enrich it with one more presenter, so that the people see that something strange, unusual is going on." (Field notes, *ČT*)

Through "disruption," "enrichment," and other subtle technologies of production (representation), the risk of global terrorism became visualized, signified—and valorized (Van Loon 2002).

James took a banknote out of his pocket and passed it to the flight attendant. Its value, James thought, exceeded the value of his nauseating snack by far, but at least *The Mo* paid for it—regardless of its chronic decline in readership.

Despite the obvious economically rational dimension of the adjustments Martin pushed for, James never noticed any difference between public service and commercial media in technologies of crisis news production. As Nord and Strömbäck write,

> it is hard to generalize from structural factors … neither media type (TV vs. newspaper) nor media category (tabloid vs. broad-sheet papers) or ownership (private vs. public service) can explain these patterns [of making crisis news]. (Nord and Strömbäck 2003: 67)

In contrast, according to James' colleagues, there certainly was a difference between Czech and Belgian media. Czech journalists tended to "look to the West" (Čestmír) instead of following Czech journalistic traditions, because in Czechia "it is not going in the right direction." The difference was particularly striking when James compared Lotte's (Belgian public service TV reporter) and Marek's (Czech public service TV reporter) narratives of September 11. Lotte said she had immediately started to work "on automatic pilot," while Marek recalled that "the whole newsroom had been totally appalled, watching *CNN* for 25 minutes before someone finally got the idea to go and prepare a special broadcast." Since then, the *ČT* journalists have learned to react much more nimbly (see the field notes above on the changing newswork rhythm under crisis conditions). According to Čestmír and Vítek, from the escalation of the Russian-Ukrainian conflict on, *ČT* has even approximated its Western and Western-like models.

Wishful thinking, ever-skeptical James thought, and he remembered that Sophie Schlesinger was just sitting right in front of him. He pricked up his ears and heard she was just scribbling something down. No doubt she was getting ready for the job she had at San Lorenzo. And so James too finally got down to sketching his future report. Possible types of sources to get, social media to use, structure to keep, potential conflicts to highlight. He only hoped to be able to work fast enough and to have a steady connection with *The Mo*.

To sum up, all six answers to the question "what is specific about technologies of *crisis* news production" intersect in one word: pressure—heightened pressure on accuracy, principles, speed, precision; investment of one's personal time; placing oneself at risk. These were all various sources of precarity.

It needs to be stressed again that the journalists' and reporters' precarity is unequally distributed among staff reporters, freelancers, and local journalists who call the crisis zone their home and whose labor remains largely invisible to European audience. As Brian Creech (2018) argues, the economic conditions and cultural logic surrounding crisis (mainly conflict) journalism—the exploitative relations between media workers and organizations together with the myth of an independent, brave truth-seeker—normalize journalists' increasing precarity and make it acceptable. Any intervention thus requires engaging critically with both the economic logic and the normative ideals surrounding crisis reporting.

Mediators Matter

The practices of crisis news production were entangled with things. The ways in which individual devices used for crisis reporting can influence—not only determine, but also "authorize, allow, afford, encourage, permit, suggest, influence, block, render possible, forbid, and so on" (Latour 2005: 72)—journalists' emotional experience, were particularly clear in parachute reporters' and correspondents' narratives. Artifacts like cameras, pencils and notebooks, recorders, smartphones, and transmission vehicles all intervened, in a deeply ambiguous way, in how their users lived out the process of covering a crisis. As such, the artifacts were mediators rather than intermediaries. Whereas an intermediary "transports meaning or force without transformation ... [m]ediators transform, translate, distort, and modify the meaning or the elements they are supposed to carry" (Latour 2005: 39). The material technologies of crisis news production did not merely passively capture and convey words and images, but actively influenced the journalists' experience.

Most typically, James' colleagues claimed that looking at graphic scenes such as mass graves through the viewfinders of cameras and camcorders made a significant difference:

> there were more than three hundred bodies. Dead people. And the smell was really strong. (...) I remember putting the camera in front of me because I couldn't watch the faces of the people directly. People who were shot in their head, or whatever. And when I remember that, I don't remember it as a real situation. It's like a movie. Because ... I couldn't watch it directly. (Ines)

> the picture is something that does not really exist. (...) So it's a way of having distance from what's happening in front of you. (Nicolas)

The material technology of production works as a means of distancing the media workers from their subjects and reality (cf. Richards and Rees 2011; Sontag 1977); as a buffer. The more technology the reporter uses, the more shielded she is; as Farrukh noted, "Camera and a press card are acts of power." Thus, in the case of television production, the complex technological equipment is "mentally more comfortable" (Vítek) because its presence implies that the reporter must follow simple steps.

However, the view that technological devices can help a reporter to stay detached from the crisis and reduce the mental strain was opposed by others, who stressed the fact that technology also necessarily brings the reporter closer. Anthony, living in Peshawar and using "only" a voice recorder, did not begrudge his photo-colleagues the need to march in the middle of angry crowd. Matouš, who worked as a reporter and editor at ČT, compared his technologically demanding work with his previous experience at a news agency where he was "merely" writing:

> [When I was working] for the [news agency], it enabled me—since I was writing—to often be rather like a fly on the wall, a non-participant observer of the situation. So the camera. ... Firstly, what one has not shot, one does not have at all. So the very fact of what television is, and the camera, forces one to be close to the situations, to enter them. And this changes everything.

The material technology of production allows much more than ten years ago and needs to be utilized; as Vítek evaluated based on his 17-year television career, "I can really see that the demands on the people grow terribly, because the technology simply *can* make it." New and social media are stressful for other reasons:

> You have satellite phones that we did not have some time ago, you have the possibility with the small devices to do the editing and send it quite immediately, so you are able to operate ad hoc, faster, and on the spot, and continue with your work without having to go out. (...) It gives you ... emotionally, I think it's like everything with social media now, now it's also ... It's more intense. Because it's immediate. (...) So I think it absorbs you more. I think it's affecting you more. Especially since the last. ... The Arab revolutions, and now Syria, after that, because we are ... Since then, we've changed our way of working. It became different. Before, you made a news story. Which is intense. But since then, we make news stories, we have to produce for online, for Facebook, for all these things, which is a duty that follows from your work, and we have to do it immediately. (Sam)

In Sam's opinion, the ever-progressing material technology, its opportunities and power, and related changing newsroom routines, working conditions, and the power of (new) media logic have together had a rather negative effect on the ability of reporters to maintain mental and emotional detachment.

In sum, the technological affordances, "opportunities for or invitation to actions that things present to actors" (Lievrouw 2014: 48) bring about very diverse effects on reporters' emotional experience. They can allow a reporter to take footage and to mediate her authentic experience of the on-site presence (Andén-Papadopoulos and Pantti 2013); keep her distant; make her cover as much as possible; allow/push her to approach the crisis scene from unprecedentedly close range, and thus place her into its focal point. In doing this, the material technologies of production and the practical/processual technologies of production are always embedded in each other, as succinctly expressed by Čestmír:

> For me the technology is not a physical filter. It is a psychological filter—in the sense that my mission there is different. (Čestmír)

The technology helped Čestmír to overcome stress by delimiting his organizational identity (Weick 1995). In this context, Wanda J. Orlikowski (2007: 1437) writes of the constitutive entanglement of the social and the material: "materiality is integral to organizing, positing that the social and the material are *constitutively entangled* in everyday life … the social and the material are considered to be inextricably related." Čestmír thus happened to be constitutively entangled with his media organization and the material technology of crisis news production.

The Sense of Surreal

James saw and heard several moments when the media material-technological complex of processual *and* material technologies of production totally seized a journalist's or James' own sensory field and made a crack in their sense of ontological security (Giddens 1991). These moments that James' colleagues described as "very strange" or "surreal" were always connected to the "abnormal" experience with a distant crisis and especially with close crises. As such, they were most explicit in the narratives of Belgian journalists who had reported on the terror attacks in Brussels (see the section "Belgium, Czechia, and the Closeness of a Crisis"):

> You're in a strange situation that you have, you see war correspondents—literally, I've seen war correspondents in my city. (Laughs.) Which is very strange! And Christiane Amanpour flying over to Brussels to interview the prime minister, and … We used to see it as just distant. … It's not only in Belgium. It's not a globalization of risks, it's a sort of everywhereness [of risks]. (Jacob)

Jacob perceived the uncanny omnipresence of the terror threat, reflected upon the changing distribution of risks, and hinted at the significance of their discursive construction by the global media (see Beck 1992; Van Loon 2002).

But the funny feeling was not limited to those who reported a crisis close to home. Rather, the feeling was connected to the contrast mentioned in the section "Identified": a more general and widespread sense of inconsistency, rupture, and difference between the ordinary everyday life of a contemporary middle-class, typically white, university-educated European, and the everyday living conditions in a conflict/disaster/war zone:

> in Kosovo or later, in Congo, for example, it's also very surreal. Of course it is. If you are standing on this side of the hill, and you know that you can't climb the hill, because otherwise they will shoot at you, it's. ... We are people from the peace continent. We never really experienced war ourselves. (Sven)

> I must be very disconnected from this world. Yeah. Because you are so long in that world, in another kind of world. I mean, you have so many roles. I cannot explain it. (Sam)

Likewise, Anthony, when he touched down in a crisis region, felt "as if [he] landed at another planet."

The odd feeling was thus related to the very essence of the risk society/technological culture (Beck 1992; Van Loon 2002): not only the dispersion, both physical and mediated, of uncertainties and suffering, emerging as an unintended consequence of ever-advancing technological knowledge, but also the connectedness (yet stark contrast) of different parts of the world. The technological knowledge needs to be stressed, since the core of the funny feelings, the merging of worlds, was largely shaped by new media affordances (Lievrouw 2014). Charlie Beckett and Mark Deuze (2016) have identified a kind of surreal, magical, even wonderful experience among audiences following from the ubiquitous and networked character of news. If this is the case for audiences, the journalists simply hold a much more intense position in the middle of the transitions:

> When I am there, I am here, because of [social networking sites], and when I am here, I am there. So I am always ... there, basically. ... Last year, two of my translators, one from Gaza and one from Egypt, had to flee because of the risk of torture. So now they are in Belgium. So now they are here. So that world has come here. (Sam)

Only a few reporters reflected on the relative newness of the experience as explicitly as Sam did in the last two quotations. Many, however, incorporated the gap between the two worlds and the sense of discrepancy into their kynical coping strategies, such as Richard during a meeting at *LN* and Čestmír in the *ČT* control room:

> Tobiáš proposes to write an article about so-called "children of the Islamic state": "Sixty children of the jihadists from Europe have already been born, and the Daesh doesn't know what to do with these children." Richard: "Ah, whether to put them in kindergarten, or a day nursery, right?" We all burst out in laughter. (Field notes)

> A conversation between Marie and Čestmír about some footage released by Daesh. "What crazy shots, there. So dreadful, how they burn the people to death in the cages," Marie says. "Fucking beasts. Now, they have pissed off the Chinese by executing their man," replies Čestmír. "Murdered, not executed," Marie corrects him. Čestmír gives a smile: "Thank you. Thank you for putting me in my place, instead of me myself," Čestmír replies, and continues: "Norway will get pissed too, and the Daesh will never get Nobel Peace Prize." (Field notes)

A few times, James felt the magic himself. It was when he saw a camel at the *ČT* headquarters, lazily walking into the main building (managers' entrance). Or when he came, through a heavy yet hardly noticeable garage-like door in the center of Liège, into a beautiful, expensive, decadent art deco residence of a former journalist and started to listen to stories in which the journalist was both the main character and the narrator. Or when he was sitting with Sven in Le Cirio, an art nouveau brasserie next to the Bourse in Brussels.

Sven was just speaking about 1989:

> I mean, you were part of another world. And I think that was also. ... That was also quite a difficult period to write about. And now we are talking about it, but for example. ... That man! (Points out the window.) He was too fast, actually, but it's a former colleague. An Eastern Europe expert. (Laughs.)

The man flashed past the door of Le Cirio.

> Actually, that's interesting. It's a pity that he doesn't come in, but ... Because he studied literature, and he was interested in Kafka. So he went to Prague and there, I think, he had a lot of contacts with the group around Václav

Havel. And so ... And the Charta people. And then ... he has been followed by the Czech security services in Brussels. (Sven)

James was once again reminded of the absurdness of the inertial past of the former Eastern Bloc, of the volatility of the distribution of risks, and of their iceberg-like invisibility (Beck 1992).

He heard the robotic flight attendant's voice emanating from speakers, and took off his headphones. "...and the number is constantly growing," she just said, most probably informing the passengers of the latest developments at San Lorenzo. The audience reacted by deafening silence. The voice was waiting for questions. No questions were coming. Was it anxiety or apathy (Van Loon 2002)? Probably both, James thought. It took less than half of a second, and the same flight attendant suddenly emerged from behind, imperceptibly singing a joyful tune with a hint of melancholy and striding toward the nose. Someone cut through the silence with a question. James rather aimed his attention back to the technologies.

Technologies of Sign Systems: Output Emotions

Foucault defined technologies of sign systems as a matrix of practical reason "which permit us to use signs, meanings, symbols, or signification" (Foucault 1988: 18). How do the ways of using words, images, sounds, mixed signs, and symbols relate to journalists' emotional experience of crisis?

James reached for the issue of *Le Soir* he kept carrying in his bag. It was the issue from 23 March 2016, and he thought it was adequately emotional. Which meant, a lot.

James perused the black title page, the strong headline "Tenir bon," the hopeful image. A person wrapped up in Belgian flag with a non-white child, both drawing, with chalks in their hands and watched by a grieving semi-circle, one of the supportive signs and writings of condolence that, after the attacks, colored all Belgian cities.

Then, he cast his eyes at the pleading editorial written by Christophe Berti (Berti 2016). It began with "D'abord, l'émotion," and contained many emotion words; the article was even structured by different emotional phases: emotional shock, fear, questions, and sentiment.[1] Reading the article, James felt the vivid memories.

---

[1] While "emotion" referred to shock and solidarity, by sentiment, the author meant strictness and primarily hatred—which needs to be fought.

Likewise, what follows focuses on exploring the technologies of sign systems within crisis reporting and their entanglement with emotions through focusing on the reporters' notions of the role and place of emotions in crisis news. The perceived ideal and real place of emotions in crisis news—in Nico Carpentier's and Marit Trioen's words, the position of emotion within "objectivity-as-a-norm" and "objectivity-as-a-practice" (Carpentier and Trioen 2010), can reveal motives, desired results, and conscious parts of journalists' emotional labor (Hochschild 1983), because the ideals/norms and practices co-determine (and are co-determined by) emotional engagement, identification, actorship, and the criticized "activism." More precisely, emotional engagement and identification can easily result in the open or covert taking of an active role within the story (see the section "Moral Dilemmas and Guilt") not only by helping people on the spot but also by subtly, unobtrusively making emotional news that can work as an appeal (Boltanski 1999). Furthermore, the reporters' ideals and ideas about emotions "on the output," that is, the practical reason permitting them (or not) to make emotions (in)visible in the news, are plugged into the other technologies. The images, sounds, words, hyperlinks, and so on that the journalists use largely depend on media affordances and journalistic routines (technologies of production); they result from the codified and non-codified regulations of journalists' practices, such as ethical codes, organizational guidelines, and shared professional ideology (technologies of power); they follow from the journalists' ability to discipline their emotions (technologies of the self).

In this context, Karin Wahl-Jorgensen's analysis of Pulitzer Prize-winning stories stirs up further sub-questions. Wahl-Jorgensen speaks about a "strategic ritual of emotionality" and suggests that "there is an institutionalized and systematic practice of journalists narrating and infusing their reporting with emotion" (Wahl-Jorgensen 2013: 130). The ritual operates alongside the analogous strategic ritual of objectivity. As a result, emotionality is profoundly constitutive of journalistic narratives (Peters 2011; Wahl-Jorgensen 2013). In particular, crisis news are designed in a subjectively impacted and emotionally driven way (Altheide 2006; Falkheimer and Olsson 2015; Lull 2007; Van Der Meer et al. 2016). Nevertheless, rather than expressing their own emotions, Wahl-Jorgensen suggests that journalists "outsource," police, and discipline others' emotional expression. The question remains, however, whether the emotions are really "outsourced." Is it only the emotion of a talking head, a victim, or the victim's relatives that colorizes the news? Is it rather reporters' own emotions? Or is it some kind of diffused feeling that is sublimated only thanks to the narrator (e.g. Culler 1997)?

"The Right Dose" of Emotion
The reporters' ideas of the role of emotions in the process and outcomes of newsmaking—that to a large extent expressed the kind of "objectivity-as-a-norm" (Carpentier and Trioen 2010) they respected—were considerably varied. On a scale with two ends, the "reports-should-be-objective" end, and the "emotions-is-one-of-the-facts" end, James was able to identify three ideal-typical positions of his colleagues: Positivists, Measurers, and Franks.[2]

The first group, Positivists, was composed of very few people. For Positivists—usually, but not exclusively, young Czech and Belgian reporters with journalistic education (i.e. possibly with fresh awareness of theoretically and traditionally conceived journalistic professionalism)—news should be completely free from subjective emotions, neutral, and objective. A journalist should keep emotional distance in order to either transmit pure information or retain a critical stance toward all sides of the conflict:

> it is of course emotionally difficult in a way, and ... Eee ... But ... (Silence) I think I succeeded, in this particular situation like in Tunisia, in keeping the distance from it. I feel that way. I was just describing reality. (Silence) And ... It really is difficult. Simply because you are thinking. (...) I *must* be objective and pass the reality forward. (Kryštof)
>
> *We are trying to* be very neutral, like water. (Carl)
>
> for the news, I really say what I see, without any emotional timbre. (...) It *shouldn't* be in the news. (Tomáš)

The Positivists thus revived and strengthened (Wiik 2015) the traditional positivist-realist version of objectivity-as-a-norm, valuing detachment, complete neutrality, and impartiality (Carpentier and Trioen 2010; Schudson 2001).

---

[2] The three groups were contingent in the terms of people—mainly because some journalists did not care about the inner consistency of their normative notions and opinions—but delimited regarding the typical view of the role and place of emotions in crisis news.

This position was considered obsolete by the Measurers, a much bigger group. For Measurers—typically more experienced, and thus more practically professionalized—emotions do have room in the news and reports, because their "right dose" (Sven) or "a layer" (Nicolas, Jesse) adds to the author's credibility and to the "humaneness" of reporting (Lotte):

> The emotions *must* be there. One can't avoid them, because it's an intellectual job, you work with words, with thoughts. … but you should be able to control it. (Astrid)

> I think *the work is better* if you let in some kind of emotion. Not all of it. You cannot be swept away completely by your emotion, because then you won't be accurate any more either. (Lotte)

> With the *right dose* of emotion, you add to your credibility. I mean, if it's too much, if you put yourself in the foreground and you talk only about your own emotions while the emotions and the problems of the people you're writing about are much bigger, it's a bit pathetic to me. If you're just trying to be a machine, follow the reader, it's also very strange. (Sven)

Sven directly links the control of one's emotion with avoiding egocentric news, news focused on the journalists themselves, news that do not express the different significance of European journalist's emotion and the Other's emotion accurately, that is, with avoiding the unethical journalistic performance that was so harshly criticized by some other reporters (see the next section).

This second position best concurs with Wahl-Jorgensen's notion of policing and disciplining emotions (Wahl-Jorgensen 2013); in contradiction to her findings, however, the emotions allegedly belong to the very reporters who invoke, suppress, and manage their emotions in line with the requirements of their profession (Hochschild 1983; Illouz 2007).

The third ideal-typical view—that of Franks—was also rather widespread and appeared in many discussions. Franks insisted that emotions "should be there" because they are "one of the facts" (Lotte). Many of James' colleagues perceived their own emotional experience, the emotions of their talking heads and the emotionality of the stories being covered a significant part of reality; their personal value added; the very reason for reporting on the spot; or even, as Josef said, the "raison d'être of the existence of television":

I think it's *wrong* not to include the emotions. It's stupid. Because that's what you can do if you make a report from Prague, based on agency materials. Sure. But the virtue … why the report from the place is better than from Prague, it's not only that you have a stand-up there by which you are proving the medium is there, but just because you experience it. And because you are not a perfect robot but a mere human, you are able to include the drive. (Vítek)

[A child trying to find her father's body in the rubble] is a thing that is so very loaded with emotions that not to describe the emotional dimension would mean simply to flatten it. To flatten it brutally, and basically to distort reality to the extent that it won't resemble what was really going on there. (Čestmír)

The scale in general tallies with Patrick Plaisance's and Elisabeth Skewes' finding that journalists are deeply ambivalent toward the so-called interpretive—that is, non-informative—function of the press. However, Plaisance's and Skewes' analysis shows that journalists perceive a negative correlation between the analytical, interpretive, and explanatory role of the media on one hand and their notion of responsibility on the other (Plaisance and Skewes 2003). By comparison, while few James' colleagues saw emotionality in crisis news as a sign of failure or bad taste, most of them did not consider impressions, emotions, and openly value-driven interpretation as a threat to factuality and professional responsibility.

It is necessary to stress again, however, that all the discursively constructed professional positions are a testament to "objectivity-as-a-norm" (Carpentier and Trioen 2010)—manifesting itself in "I must," "we are trying to," "it shouldn't be," "the right dose," "the work is better," "it's wrong," and the like—professional principles and values, rather than actual practice. One can only assume how these norms are enacted.

Nevertheless, the diversity of positions reflects a certain variety within journalists' professional ideology, a collection of shared but continuously challenged strategies and values guiding the construction of their expertise and authority (Andén-Papadopoulos and Pantti 2013: 962). While the traditional version of this ideology appreciates objectivity understood as detachment, impartiality, fairness, and professional distance, alternative and more recent approaches have been advocating for the acknowledgment of reporters' emotions as a legitimate part of their work (e.g. Pauly 2014; see the section "Professional Ideology and Its Critique").

"No Torn Children's Life Jackets": Taste, Organization, and Moral Commitment

All of the reporters were well aware of the danger of overdoing the articulation of emotionality—be it their own or the victims'/witnesses' emotions—and building a "melodramatic" story. Making a report about a shipwrecked boat full of migrants, about a bleak camp along the Balkan route, or about the victims of the Bataclan shooting means a constant search for the border between an "awkward," "emotionally blackmailing," "caricature-like," "cheesy," "syrupy" testimony, and a transmission of a serious, information-based, and accurate account of what happened (including the emotional level). For the primary goal of anything that appeared in the reports—including emotions—is to inform and not to take a standpoint:

> You have to control your emotions and use them only if they explain what happens. (Anthony)

> You must find the level where the emotion, whether positive or negative, strengthens the information that you hand over. But you don't do it systematically, because of the emotion, because of picking at it. (…) We are of course always trying to show [the news] through a story, through a person, instead of making it a cold list of facts, but not to rummage in torn children's life jackets. (Ester)

So, although some reporters even explicitly stated that "objectivity doesn't exist" (Sven, who, as a student, wrote a thesis on New Journalism) or that "neutrality is a joke" (Nicolas, who gave university lectures on narrative journalism), they knew they could—and should—be "factual." Factuality meant a different thing than neutrality and objectivity. "Never mess up with the facts," Sam once warned James. And by "never mess up with the facts," he meant not to distort and omit any proved information. He did not mean "be cold."

James *was* determined to stick to the facts. Any other strategy would be strongly condemned in *The Mo*. *The Mo* enjoyed the image of a quality paper, and James wanted to contribute to that impression—shaping also his own professional image—as much as possible.

Indeed, some of the journalists saw it as a distinguishing feature of "their" media organization be it one of the public service televisions or one of the serious newspapers—that its authors and reporters work carefully with sound background, word choice (e.g. they prefer using no comments to impassioned, "mournful" adjectives) or overly explicit footage that unnecessarily exploits viewers' and readers' emotions. They felt the responsibility to stick to the character of their medium: "we really don't want to be cheap television," Lotte summed up. Freelancers seemingly had more freedom, yet they needed to keep their fingers on the pulse and adhere to the style of the media they wanted to publish with anyways.

James, planning out the report more and more hurriedly, gave some thought to possible pictures. Of course he could take a photograph full of frozen corpses in unnatural positions; one of those he saw earlier on Twitter. Such a picture would certainly attract attention. But considering the image of *The Mo* and his own taste, he knew he would rather go for something discreetly powerful. Like a frozen, empty city (Image 4.3).

This strategy had a moral dimension. Some individuals and media organizations that James had encountered tried to avoid a plain spectacle of

Image 4.3 A frozen city. Drawing by Peter Van Goethem, 2017. Courtesy of the artist

suffering that would further increase compassion fatigue in audiences (Moeller 1999). On the other hand, in order to respond to the humane commitment, the journalists had to commit themselves through speech acts, by adopting a stance, by reporting both what they had seen and how it personally affected and involved them. As Luc Boltanski suggests, a morally acceptable formula for the communication of suffering involves the use of evaluative and emotive terms:

> in order to respect a rule of common humanity, the spectator of suffering cannot adopt the stance of a subject describing an object and speaking of what he has seen as a simple reporter. He cannot describe the execution of condemned persons, or the bodies of dead children during a famine, with the same kind of precision and detachment one would use to speak of a system of economic regulation, a policy of regionalisation, or a plan for a road network. (Boltanski 1999: 43)

Describing their internal states thus had three important functions: first, it could help the journalists to reduce tension stemming from the cognitive and emotive dissonance (Festinger 1957; Hochschild 1983) and therefore was psychologically helpful. Indeed, Giuseppe—although an employee—said that he did not need any coping mechanism *because* he had complete freedom from his bosses, and he could write what he found important in a way he found suitable. His freedom shaped his overall experience. Second, explaining their emotional states could help the journalists balance aperspectival objectivism (the position of Positivists) and moral involvement (the position of Activists; see Boltanski 1999: 41). Including some level of emotions was thus both psychologically helpful and necessary from the moral point of view. Third, and importantly, as Beckett and Deuze (2016) point out, including reporters' emotionality can be a step toward more effective journalism, as authentic emotion linked to news reporting helps journalists connect with communities and thus to foster objectivity and trustworthiness. Wahl-Jorgensen agrees: "rather than necessarily undermining the rationality of the public sphere, emotional expression may be a vital positive force in enabling new forms of engagement and identification among audience members" (Wahl-Jorgensen 2016, p. 2).

However, it needs to be stressed again that James, like many of his fellow reporters, hated placing the reporter in the center of the narrative. For example, Farrukh criticized the photographer Linsey Addario who was outraged by—and publicly spoke a lot about—being forced, while pregnant, to repeatedly go through an x-ray machine when she was covering Gaza:

> And she had nothing to say about the fact that every day, every month *thousands* of Palestinian women have suffered the humility. ... Many have had to give birth at checkpoint. Many have died giving birth at checkpoint.

According to Farrukh, her suffering was relatively insignificant relative to suffering of Palestinian women, pregnant or not, yet she behaved in an egocentric way. Similarly, Bob and Anthony thought that journalists should not be TV stars: "Journalists are not the victims, we should not be the protagonists, the heroes." (Bob)

Regrettably, the trend, according to the critics, seemed to be putting oneself in first place and (ab)using the tragedies of one's sources by giving them the status of mere scenery within which the reporters' story unfolds. Nikki Usher (2019: 141) has even assessed the increasingly tiresome and growing "obsession journalists have with journalism as its own story" as one of the reasons why journalists are the worst enemies of journalism today.

Thus, James did not fool himself into believing that all of his colleagues used emotional words in crisis news to fulfill their moral commitment or as a defense mechanism. Emotion in crisis reporting could be a result of pure economic calculation, notions of professionalism, or aesthetic sense. Most probably, it was a result of everything together.

Yet, who is the bearer of emotions *in the news*, still seemed unclear. It could be partly the journalists themselves, partly their subjects and interviewees, partly the speakers, and partly the narrator. As Sam said, "My sadness from seeing things guides me to witnesses who translate this. Because it's their sadness." Sam's words suggest that the talking heads, victims, victims' relatives—all the subjects and interviewees—are the reporters' mouthpieces, "spoken by" the reporters' genuine emotions and selected more or less intentionally according to the conformity of their emotions with those of the reporter exercising her gatekeeping role. In this sense, emotions in the news were outsourced indeed (Wahl-Jorgensen 2013) but predetermined by the journalist's specific demand. Steen Steensen (2017) solves the question of whose emotions appear in the news by distinguishing *source subjectivity*, that is, witnesses', victims', and other talking heads' subjectivity which personalizes and exemplifies the story, and *byline subjectivity*, referring to a situation in which it is the author herself who imbues the story with her subjectivity.

Alternatively, the emotion can be diffused throughout the different identities connected to the story, rather than expressed by a concrete person; it can exist solely through the text. In such an instance, emotion ceases to be emotion and becomes *affect*. As Brian Massumi (1995) writes, affect is a virtual and synaesthetic (i.e. not ownable by a concrete person) perspective anchored in and embodied by actually existing things (e.g. a text). Emotion, on the contrary, refers to "a subjective content, the sociolinguistic fixing of the quality of an experience which is from that point onward defined as personal" (Massumi 1995: 88). Thus, any feeling that circulated in the news and was not assigned to the physical author or one of the characters in the story was positioned in between affect and emotion: socio-linguistically fixed but not ownable. Captured in a piece of language but still dispersed.

Be that as it may, the perceived ideal of "output" emotions and affects directly shaped the way the reporters worked with their emotions; in turn, the emotional labor—driven by professional ideals and other criteria of success—influenced the actual, real form of emotions in the news.

For a moment, James put on his headphones again. Viggo Mortensen, Camus' mouthpiece, was just speaking about the most obvious symptoms of the "human crisis." "The first symptom is the rise of terror. A consequence of the perversion of values through which human beings and historical forces are judged not in terms of their dignity, but in terms of their success. The modern crisis is inevitable. Because no one in the West can be sure about their immediate future. And all live with the more or less defined view that they will be crushed a bit, one way or another, by history." James felt tiny and meaningless, and the very next thoughts were about to make it even worse.

Technologies of Power: Discipline and Publish

For there was the question concerning technologies of power. Foucault defined technologies of power as a matrix of practical reason "which determine[s] the conduct of individuals and submit[s] them to certain ends or domination, an objectivizing of the subject" (Foucault 1988: 18). Technologies of power is a more general category within Foucault's theory, given the scope of effort he dedicated to the conceptualization of power as a ubiquitous, active, and productive practice, permeating all subjects, coming from below and within, rather than encompassing subjects (Deleuze 1996; Foucault 1978).

Like other technologies, the technologies of power permeated many aspects of journalists' emotional experience of crisis and were connected to the other technologies. The reporters' ways of experiencing and handling emotions resulted from two broad areas of technologies of power. First, from journalistic professional ideology: the acquired theoretical notions of professionalism on one hand, and journalistic codes and other regulations of correct journalistic action on the other. Second, from the journalists' individual positions within the organizational hierarchies (as suggested by the very distinction between Positivists—typically rookies—and the Measurers and the Franks), that is, from the conduct of individuals within the media organizations, including various guidelines or to-do lists.

Professional Ideology and Its Critique
As has been outlined at the beginning of the book (in the section "Objections to Objectivity: Emotionality and Professionalism"), the traditional version of journalists' professional ideology, that is, a system of beliefs characteristic of the particular group, a collection of shared but continuously challenged strategies and values guiding the construction of their expertise and authority (Andén-Papadopoulos and Pantti 2013: 962; Deuze 2005: 445), includes a commitment to objectivity (understood as detachment, impartiality, fairness, or professional distance). Together with other norms and values, such as autonomy and public service, objectivity represents the core normative and ethical aspect of professionalism (Andén-Papadopoulos and Pantti 2013); some scholars even argue that the objectivity norm is central to the constitution of the journalistic field and works as a privileged signifier of "good journalism" (Carpentier and Trioen 2010; Vos 2011). Professionalism and objectivity understood in these terms, however, mean staying cool and unemotional (Schudson 2001).

In the shaping of professional ideology, the Foucauldian entanglement of power and knowledge (Foucault 1978) is clearly visible, as the professional ideology is reproduced by academic knowledge on journalism and media. Many studies are explicitly normative, promoting the traditional positivist version of objectivity. For example, Nord and Strömbäck evaluate Swedish coverage of the war in Afghanistan and September 11 as problematic due to certain media strategies specific for crisis reporting:

> the line between fact and fiction sometimes has become increasingly hard to discern, due to the frequent use of speculations, the blending of straight reporting and commentary, and the use of storytelling techniques following

from the media logic such as personification, simplification, and enhancement. If one relates this to what Kovach and Rosenstiel have defined as the elements of journalism, then there are surely reasons for concern. (Nord and Strömbäck 2003: 73)

Similarly, Carles Pont Sorribes and Sergi Cortiñas Rovira (2011: 1061–1062) fight against "defective journalistic practices" by summarizing ten recommendations aimed at "improving news coverage of risk and crisis situations by the communications media." Among other things, the authors stated that journalists "need to avoid coverage based on statements by institutional actors and persons directly affected by a crisis" or that they need "to be more rigorous and should avoid sensationalism and overly dramatizing information," without taking into consideration crisis situation as a work environment.

All in all, while Nord and Strömbäck (2003), Sorribes and Rovira (2011), and many others obviously provided their version of how a certain part of reality should look, they forbade the journalists from doing so. James rather thought that journalists have the right to do the same thing that the scientists did, namely taking a position, promoting certain values, and speaking and writing in an emotional/partial way. Moreover, if the obsolete understanding of objectivity was a part of journalistic professional *ideology*, shouldn't the academics rather criticize than reinforce it?

Luckily, there *was* a critique of the ideology, coming from both scholars and professional journalists. The one-dimensional notion of objectivity has been criticized for ignoring the journalists' point of view and for working as an object of desire that is impossible to reach, rather than as a practice (Carpentier and Trioen 2010; Post 2015). Objective reporting remains an unattainable point on the horizon: "the ideological construct of objectivity can never be fully captured by [the everyday journalistic] practices. These practices will always evade and escape the ideological lure of the concept of objectivity" (Carpentier and Trioen 2010: 317). (Feminist) media scholars have argued that, contrary to the professional mythology surrounding traditional journalism, subjectivity and its various manifestations do not contradict objectivity. Both values are constitutive and necessary elements of journalists' professional identities (Van Zoonen 1998).

Corresponding to this "affective turn" in journalism and media studies (Richards and Rees 2011), media professionals' attitudes toward the norms of reporting have begun to change (Tumber 2011). Emotions have become more acceptable within the recent mainstream of 'hard' journalism. Proponents of non-mainstream successors to the New Journalism of the 1960s—"narrative," "literary," or "attached" approaches (see e.g. Harbers and Broersma 2014; Pauly 2014; Ruigrok 2008) have also advocated openly emotional journalistic discourses that would lead to repositioning of the author and the reader. These journalisms seek to "capture social complexity in all its richness and nuance, and to celebrate the integrity and cultural authority of the individual reporter" (Pauly 2014: 590) and thus reject the traditional "contrived" display of objectivity. Thus, narrative journalists are not supposed to stay detached; they are invited to view and describe reality through the lens of their feelings, thoughts, and experiences (Harbers and Broersma 2014). In this sense, such emotive practices conflict with the objectivity regime, which is given up for the sake of morality and ethical journalism.

James' colleagues' thoughts proved that the critique of the objectivist notion of professionalism was, indeed, alive and well. Apart from Positivists, who still had the normative studies in their mind, there were more experienced Measurers and, primarily, Franks, whose view that "emotions are one of the facts" (Lotte) best concurred with the opinion that reporters' emotions are a legitimate part of their work. The existence of Measurers and Franks proves that the practice of crisis reporters' emotional management and their experience is shaped not only by the traditional version of journalistic professional ideology but also by its critique, which allows for diverse emotional styles (Peters 2011). Thus, if they stay within the boundaries of quality journalism, crisis reporters can choose the extent to which they let in their "authentic" emotional experience; they have a certain limited freedom in their emotional management (Illouz 2007).

However, it is necessary to stress that rather than following a certain specific stream of attached or literary journalism, the majority of the reporters simply understood emotions as an integral part of the general journalism they performed. Rather than embodying the rise of various "new journalisms," most of the reporters exemplified the increasing normalness of emotion in mainstream news (Pantti 2010; Wahl-Jorgensen 2013). Thus, their views concur, for example, with Glück's reconceptualization of a "good journalist" as one who includes empathy among her professional skills (Glück 2016). Judith articulated this very clearly when she emphasized, "I *use* myself as a person, I *use* empathy, I use my personal skills." Similarly, Glück's interviewees, British and Indian journalists, stressed the importance of empathy and its various dimensions for journalistic storytelling and a successful journalistic career. Their empathy was converted into emotional capital. Such use of one's empathy, transforming personal skills to emotional capital, is one type of journalists' emotional labor, that is, it is immaterial labor that is linked to the precariousness of cultural and information work in general (Hesmondhalgh and Baker 2011).

Combining subjectivity and objectivity, integrating personal and professional identities, may be more typical to topics that alter journalists' perception of their own role (shifting it from purely informational to explanatory, or even educative), such as environmental issues (Tong 2015), children's death (Glück 2016), or terrorism. The case of September 11 provides many examples of shifting norms and practices: "Much reporting after September 11 turned toward a prose of solidarity rather than a prose of information" (Schudson 2011: 49). During and after a terrorist attack, journalistic values and roles can thus differ from impartiality and informing. As Morten Skovsgaard et al. (2013: 38) claim, objectivity is not carved in stone or interpreted uniformly as a norm excluding emotions; rather, "the objectivity norm is open for interpretation …, related to role perception in different journalistic cultures and under different circumstances."

Therefore, crisis circumstances challenge the notion of objectivity as a *cornerstone* of journalistic professionalism. Rather than seeing the more or less detached, neutral version of objectivity as the fixed essence of good journalism, especially after September 11, journalistic professionalism could be defined by journalists' *prudence* (Champy 2009): by their ability to weigh a particular situation in its complexity and make decisions that help them to realize the values and fulfill their roles in the best possible way. In practice, the prudence can mean engaging with the still dominant imperative of objectivity more creatively, embracing "a more diverse and multiperspectival journalism" (Deuze 2019: 132) based on uniqueness of each (crisis) situation and context in general.

Moreover, as some of James' colleagues—Nicolas, Jesse, Giuseppe, Bob, and Lotte—said, the way of using one's emotions in the newsmaking process influences whether one becomes a Cynic, a Stoic, or a Broken ("Everybody knows it's a bad idea to keep it very much for yourself," said Bob), because the freedom of emotional expression shapes the overall experience (Giuseppe).

Professional Ideology and Cynicisms

In turn, the emotional styles are further entangled with professional performance:

> Don't misunderstand me, as if I was just some cynical bastard, thinking technically at such moments [as March 22]—which is not the case, of course. But we have, here in our newsroom—in all the newsrooms—there is an issue of digital versus paper. Which is not so easy to solve, because there's a difference in deadlines and time. So the digital news, you have to have it now and you have to have it first. ... It's even more difficult to do both. To have a digital constant deadline and a classical evening deadline, newspaper deadline. So this is ... a technical problem that we. ... ... Then you have this event, and suddenly. ... ... Because all these issues that were so difficult to tackle on a normal day, they were just solved. And, of course, that's very simple, such an event is easy news. (Jacob)

A certain form of emotional numbness and cynicism, enabling, facilitating or requiring the focus on factual accuracy and technological processing of information, was seen as a personal must, and as a perfect prerequisite for journalistic professionalism (as Josef said, "I have the *advantage* that I am a bit retarded so I always begin to realize it later."). In this sense, the cynical ideology (Sloterdijk 1987) forms a vital part of the journalist's professional ideology. "[T]he ability of [the cynical ideology's] bearers to work—in spite of anything that might happen, and especially, after anything that might happen" (Sloterdijk 1987: 5) perfectly fits into journalists' sensemaking of their professionalism: journalists are "neutral, objective, fair and (thus) credible" and "have a sense of immediacy" (Deuze 2005: 448–449).

On the other hand, as explained above, modern cynicism is an ideology and a social phenomenon from which human aspiration is lacking. The modern cynic is apathetic, refuses to engage with the world, and is resigned to her experience of alienation (Bewes 1997; Navia 1996; Sloterdijk 1987). This position contradicts journalists' professional ideology. Professional journalists "have sense of ethics and legitimacy" and "provide a public service": they "share a sense of 'doing it for the public,' of working as some kind of representative watchdog of the status quo in the name of people" (Deuze 2005: 447–449). Thus, some of James' colleagues understood ideological cynicism as not only a psychological danger similar to other psychological threats but also a threat to professionalism:

The notion of public service journalism means that we never falsely dramatize things. It's about being precise in the description. And at the same time, in the routine we can't—that happens to people as well—slide into a cynical approach, by overlooking things and so on, see? What I've witnessed as well, that people, being burntout, didn't give a damn, a refugee wave didn't motivate them to write a precise headline and they cut the topic dead. (…) So burnout and the related cynicism threaten journalism. (Marek)

Apart from Marek's concern that cynicism goes hand in hand with losing one's motivation to be accurate, cynicism was also dangerous in terms of losing one's ability to empathize and be affected—which is a necessary skill for a good, responsible journalist (Bob, Lilah, Judith; Glück 2016; see the more thorough criticism in the section "Cynics and Kynics: Pissing Against the Idealist Wind"). Becoming too cynical, the critical reporters thought, could mean turning into a vulture.

In short, journalists' professional ideology is self-contradictory, pointing to the already mentioned actor/observer paradox (Andén-Papadopoulos and Pantti 2013; Richards and Rees 2011). On one hand, the ideology requires that journalists accept the position of ideological cynics, stay neutral and detached, and be able to work under any circumstances. On the other hand, the ideology implies their moral and political involvement in the community. Even pointing out the inner inconsistency of journalists' professional ideology, however, does not diminish its strength: "The point is that the embrace, rejection as well as critical reappraisal of objectivity all help to keep it alive as an ideological cornerstone of journalism" (Deuze 2005: 448).

So much for ideologies and journalists' self-definitions. It was almost time to touch ground and James had not yet finished his preparations.

"You Can't Leave Your Journalists Alone with Their Feelings": Organizational Identities
The reporters' emotional experience was also influenced by the technology of power circulating within the media organizations (partly, but not fully overlapping with the power of professional ideology) conducting individual action. To be sure, power, in Foucault's view, is neither owned by nor a base of institutions (such as the media); rather, the latter presuppose, capture, organize, and reproduce it (Foucault 1978). In particular, media organizations reproduced and organized the power over journalists' emotions through the positioning of individuals within the organizational

hierarchy and through official meetings but also through the constantly occurring micro-moments reminding the employees—or the falsely self-employed—of their tasks and responsibilities.

The organizational technologies of power over journalists' emotions were specific and had varying effects in each of the media organizations, since the influence of such technologies always depended on a strategy being pursued by the media and, primarily, on the concrete people who worked in both leading and ordinary positions.

At *VRT* (both the radio station and television channel) and some other media such as *DR*, *I*, *IG*, and in *CR*, the way of working with emotions was allegedly left to the individual reporters. It is necessary to mention that the people James knew at the organizations were established "brands"—strong personalities with established individual agendas and distinct viewpoints familiar to the public:

> If I am shocked because I see something, I wanna say I am shocked. I have seen a lot. You know, the Belgian public knows me a little bit. And I think when I say I've seen so many things, I am shocked by seeing this, it says something to the public. So I think it's ok to say that. (Lotte)

> When I was in Libya, in the first days, I did a lot of reporting on all the casualties that were going on. And I remember that I did an early morning report. And so the first sound you could hear on the radio was the clapping shut of the coffins for all the dead people. You could hear on the radio the flies, flying over the dead bodies. And afterwards we had a discussion at work, and they said, wow, that was very cruel, because you could hear the flies. I said, yeah, but what do you expect, it's Libya, it's August, it's 40 degrees, there is no power, people die. This is what you see! …let them hear how it is. Let them hear how it is. Dead people on the streets in 40 degrees. This is how it sounds. That's the way of emotional reporting. (Jesse)

The organizational identity of experienced parachutists gave them more freedom of emotional expression. On the other hand, the same renowned reporters, often holding the position of opinion-makers, felt intense political pressure "to keep it in the middle" (Sam) in terms of opinions and emotionality. (Sam spoke about campaigns to have him fired; Lotte used to receive a lot of criticism via e-mail and social networking sites.)

The respect for the individual, personalized reporting of well-known correspondents and parachutists was similar at *ČT*. The editors (in chief) did not strongly intervene in the ways reporters chose to manage their emotions and use them in news (Čestmír, Marie), and the reporters felt free to lard reports with their indexical feelings (Vítek). As Marie said, it was because most of the reporters had "encoded" or internalized the work with emotions, in such a way that the editors and editors-in-chief did not need to intervene, except in excessive cases (such as overly political reports or very brutal footage of Daesh).

Nevertheless, at main meetings, the heads of *ČT* news explicitly weighed—and pushed for—visual and informational proportionality, accuracy, and quality of concrete shots and they criticized technological mistakes and so on. This is to say that the leadership was more interested in procedures and technologies of production and sign systems than in emotions. By preferring certain visual and narrative representations over others, the bosses were not only advancing specific crisis visualizations and signification (see McDonald and Lawrence 2004) but also valorizing the crisis (Van Loon 2002).

James minimized the video of Viggo and found a file called "Manual for breaking news" on the desktop. He double-clicked on the icon. It was two pages of rather detailed instructions for the whole *ČT* organization. James read the first few lines (Image 4.4).

Manual for BREAKING NEWS

FLASH NEWS – Broadcasting by a matter of minutes

1) The news is announced by the yellow crawl (responsibility of a graphic editor)
2) The news is announced by the host at the first opportunity (responsibility of the news editor)

   2a) If there is no verified or detailed information, the host, during regular broadcasting, returns to the event verbally and repeats the basic message (responsibility of the head of broadcast)

BREAKING NEWS – Broadcasting by a matter of tens of minutes – host, respondent/s, editor

Image 4.4 *Czech Television*'s manual for breaking news obtained during the fieldwork, Autumn 2015, translated from Czech by the author. Screenshot of the Word document taken by the author

He scrolled through the rest of the file and saw there were only practical and technological guidelines. No mention of emotions whatsoever.

A similar focus on technologies of production, along with analogous internalization of the balance between hard facts and emotion, was apparent at *LS*:

> [You can tell your boss,] I want this story on the top of the page. ... But you never discuss the balance between fact and emotion. Because you know that most of the time it's 90% fact, 10% emotion. That's it. (Nicolas)

However, one of Nicolas' bosses, Louis, did not agree that there is no managerial strategy influencing journalists' emotional work:

> You can't leave your journalists alone with their feelings. I think. It's very important to constantly communicate about the way you are telling the news. I think it's very important. ... it's more a managerial problem. (Louis)

Louis further explained that journalists must be constantly reminded of their audience: who are the readers, what they expect, and that journalists actually write for the readers. Louis' acts of translation of the economic factors of making crisis news into the individual journalistic practices clearly illustrate the entanglement of technologies of power and production (and also technologies of sign systems and the self; Foucault 1988).

The technology of power coming with (from and through) the economic pressure on the media organization was apparent also at *LN*, another commercial newspaper. At first sight, the foreign affairs authors enjoyed considerable freedom, because the owner—Andrej Babiš, the then Czech finance minister and oligarch controlling significant parts of the Czech media, agriculture, and other markets—"doesn't know that foreign affairs exist. He would notice only if Ukrainian rape penetrated the Czech market" (one of the *LN* reporters). Indeed: when James worked for *LN*, he felt as free as a bird in choosing his topics and his writing style, and his adept colleagues enjoyed even more autonomy.

On the other hand, the alpha and omega of all newspaper content is advertisements. The number and length of articles and the layout of each page often had to be adjusted to advertising. It was not unusual for the journalists to re-structure the "World" pages because of modifications in advertising. It sometimes meant significant changes—typically abridging—to the international news section:

We have to re-structure the whole page due to the placement of the advertisement. The girl from Syria is out. It's a pity, Astrid says, but the terror attacks in Thailand are important, because people from Czechia often go there on holiday. (Field notes)

The criteria for keeping or leaving out a topic were international importance, relevance for Czech readers, variety, but primarily the interest of one of the gatekeepers (the bosses/the head of the foreign affairs section) (cf. Harcup and O'Neill 2001).

The economic factors could also be the reason why the superiors criticized articles that were "activist" (see the section "Moral Dilemmas and Guilt"). In short, there was the instruction "to make it balanced." Furthermore, the readers of *LN* expected quality graphics and sensitive work with words and images.

The same was true for another commercial daily, *DM*. Crisis reporting at *DM* combined the emphasis on the individual styles of concrete journalistic personalities with consideration of readers' preferences. This meant that the way of working with one's emotions was partly "a choice you have to make as a journalist" (Sven), but partly something imposed:

[a] difficult question that I need to deal with myself is the balance between the kind of distance that your readers expect from you and also the kind of emotional involvement that the same readers also expect from you. (Jacob)

In practice, the difficult questions and choices often resulted in creative solutions (e.g. illustrations instead of images of victims), and also very careful, sensitive reporting that was close to the notion of peace journalism: a nonviolent approach to cover conflicts, stressing the moderating influence of media during times of conflict (Neumann and Fahmy 2016), similar to the *VRT*'s strategy of "constructiveness" (mentioned in the section "Crisis Is Media-Constructed Is Real").

Despite the specifics of different media organizations, there were some shared ways in which the power circulating within, and organized by, the media influenced the journalists' emotional experience. The power simply pushed the reporters to treat the tragedies and suffering of others as a professional task, to make news, and to make the news fast:

"Why isn't it now? We must do these things immediately, not to wait half an hour!" (Field notes; Čestmír, scolding his subordinates for not having a piece of news ready on a bomb on a Russian aeroplane)

The journalists had to "do the job in any case, whatever happens … it's impossible not to do it" (Matouš); to be at work constantly—"But it's normal. It's a crisis time, so you've got to be there constantly" (Louis); to re-conceive the border between personal and professional time.

In principle, the universal organizational technologies of power over journalists' bodies meant that if rough, raw, genuine, personal emotions did not in any way enhance the news or even had a disturbing potential, then they did not have any place in the workplace during working hours. The emotions had to be policed, disciplined, refined, and polished, which applied also to the freelancers: if they wanted to publish in a particular medium, they needed to accommodate themselves to their established style, or, as Farrukh put it, to "buy their myth."

As described in the previous chapter, the need to constantly handle, postpone, suppress, or utilize one's emotions can result in the development of the Cynic, the Stoic, or the Broken emotional styles (Hochschild 1983; Illouz 2007); or, the Cynics', the Stoics', and the Brokens' emotional styles are formed by the technologies of power circulating within the media organizations (Foucault 1988). This power does not prohibit the use of emotions, reject personal involvement, completely suppress emotional experience, or ban the journalists from feeling compassion for the unlucky. Rather, the power controls, optimizes, orders, and organizes the subjects' emotions (Foucault 1978; Rayner 2001). The (bio-)power brings "life and its mechanisms into the realm of explicit calculations" (Foucault 1978: 143): measures them, objectifies them, and sets them into productive coordination, so that they may operate as one wishes (Rayner 2001).

In other words, the Cynics, the Stoics, and the Brokens are organizational, economic identities: subjects constructed within the relations of work and organization (Du Gay 1996). For Cynics, Stoics, and Brokens, emotions—one of the most intrinsic properties of a living human being (see Illouz 2007; Rosaldo 1984)—have been stripped of their indexicality and the competence to handle them has been translated into professional advancement, that is, social and economic benefits. To be a good, respected, and professional journalist within a media organization simply requires accepting the inherent precariousness related to the emotional labor, turning one's emotions and emotional styles into currency, evaluating and commodifying them (Hochschild 1983; Illouz 2007; Peters 2011).

Yet, the crisis regime did not need to constantly nag the journalists to keep cool. On the contrary, as mentioned above, during crisis times, "Everybody was ready to give a helping hand" (Jacob, speaking about reporting on the terror attacks in Brussels), because everybody had internalized or "encoded" the proper way of handling their emotions (Marie, Nicolas):

> It must be these extraordinary things, and in the moment I feel that the management doesn't need to push the people to make [the news] look better. The people want it themselves. In this sense, Charlie Hebdo was typical. (Viktor)

Technologies of the Self

James got up and went to the toilet. After two minutes of jiggling the handle, he gave up. The more humane flight attendant dashed by, throwing in that "the toilets are out of order." Persuading himself that he did not have to go, James lowered his head and went back to his seat. Luckily, his flight toward the perilous catastrophe was drawing to an end.

He sought comfort in technologies of the self. Foucault defines technologies of the self as a matrix of practical reason

> which permit[s] individuals to effect by their own means or with the help of others a certain number of operations on their own bodies and souls, thoughts, conduct and way of being, so as to transform themselves in order to attain a certain state of happiness, purity, wisdom, perfection, or immortality. (Foucault 1988: 18)

In media organizations, technologies of the self and technologies of power were almost undistinguishable: "under the regime of enterprise, technologies of power … and technologies of the self … are imperceptibly merged" (Du Gay 1996: 137–138). Self-realization, personal responsibility and emotional accountability, self-direction, and self-management become not only economically desirable but also personally attractive. As Eva Illouz (2007: 114) writes, the difficulty of clearly distinguishing between the economic and emotional register of action may mark a new stage of capitalist culture, demanding a united economic-emotional self. The interconnection of professional/organizational and personal, as strictly expressed in Paul Du Gay's statement that "Becoming a better worker is the same thing as becoming a better self" (Du Gay 1996: 137), was illustrated by Vítek's remark that "when a human is a better human, it certainly makes him a better journalist" (see also the section "Parenting"), meaning that psychosocial maturity and holding the correct values is beneficial for professional, organizational identity. In this sense, technologies of the journalistic self are inseparable from organizational power.

In terms of precarity, the technologies of the self carry out the conversion of precarization and exploitation into self-precarization and self-exploitation, so typical for creative professionals (Banks 2007; Lorey 2011). The reporters, with their desire for experience, recognition, and self-realization, adopt the power of their professional ideology and organization and exercise it over their very selves: accepting precarious working conditions as inevitable and unchangeable, obediently taking risks without questioning that it is outsourced to them, and performing potentially harmful emotional labor.

How did the technologies of the self shape the journalists' emotional experience of crisis?

To put it simply, the emotional styles, organizational identities (Du Gay 1996), and economic-emotional selves (Illouz 2007) of the Cynics, the Stoics, and the Brokens were less outcomes of immediate external pressures than outcomes of hard work on their selves: results of "crafting" the experience of involvement, of "finding the right balance of disengagement and nonchalance" (Peters 2011: 303), finding the "right distance" (Bernard 2008; Castra 2004; Molinier 2009). The merging of technologies of power and technologies of the self together with the commodification of emotions means that the line between the media organization and the self becomes blurred. In the end, the journalists feel, perceive, and think largely through the lens of their organizational identity:

> I am there because I am supposed to work there, see? And it determines the experience. (Kryštof)

Looking Through an Ideal Screen
The technologies of the self—the operations effected by the journalists' own means on their own thoughts, bodies, conduct, and ways of being—led to a state in which the journalists looked at crises through the lens of an ideal screen, that is, weighed primarily or exclusively the journalistic potential of the crisis event and its individual aspects:

> When [a crisis happens], I am oblivious to it. Or, I feel what is good for the report and what is not. I draw a line between what to put there and not. (Ester)

Some of James' colleagues kept using the same lens even while *not* at work, like Pavel, who recalled that after the terrorist attacks in Paris in November 2015, he was primarily thinking about how his colleagues "processed" the attacks for broadcasting, how they reacted professionally; how they "worked it out." The tendency to look at things exclusively from the professional and technological perspective was typical for television reporters who, even in the moments of facing suffering and tragedies, considered the future appearance of the crisis event on a screen:

> The person that one is shooting may be in a bad situation, but at the moment of shooting, one thinks of getting good images, and whether the person speaks in an interesting way. (…) There is an element of vulturism in it. (…) So one decides, in a split second, should I shoot it or not? … Because it's terribly illustrative of what happens there. But from the humane perspective, it's debatable. (Matouš)

Again, not only the perception but also the rational considerations were directly and explicitly driven by the logic of the media organizations, such as accepted journalistic codes and the reporters' notion of professionalism and ethics: what the television "can" and "is allowed to" show the viewer. One day, for example, Ester was working on a report on the Syrian war, using images of people tortured to death, when she told James:

> I look at it and don't think in the way 'Jesus Christ, it's a human being with a smashed skull,' but I tell to myself, 'I won't use this one, because it's too much—I need a picture in which he is broken, but less broken.' (Ester)

There was often an aestheticizing tone to these thorough considerations. Especially the heads and editors-in-chief, when they gathered at meetings, regularly spoke about "beautiful" or "nice" pictures of conflict, terrorism, refugees' suffering, and pietistic acts, thus perceiving the world through the lens of an ideal screen (Sontag 2003; see the section of the same name):

> According to Martin, by now the memorials, flowers and candles are boring. … Then, Martin suggests making a report about immediate police interventions: "I saw pictures from *Time*, nice footage, how the bullets spark, nice shots, so if something as pretty would come off.…" He stresses the close ups, the colourfulness; the visual is obviously important. (Field notes)

Martin encourages all to "try to make it like a crime story, put many live cameras there, stuff it there, I really liked it." (Field notes)

The aestheticizing mode of editors' thinking through crises—that is, considering the aesthetic aspects and thus their economic value, turning them into spectacle which was so harshly criticized by Farrukh or Bob—corresponded with framing processes: in this case pasting terrorism into a slightly fictional crime frame or defining the Paris attacks as a crime. As previous research has indicated, Norwegian coverage of September 11 resembled crime news as well (Falkheimer and Olsson 2015; McDonald and Lawrence 2004). A temperament of aestheticism, sometimes verging on nihilism, is one way modern cynicism can appear (Bewes 1997).

Seeing crisis events exclusively, mainly or partly through the lens of the reporters' profession was not limited to witnessing from a distance. Jesse, being asked about the attacks in his own country, gave a smile of apology and said that on March 22 he was in Egypt:

> Q: And how did it feel to be far from here?
> Jesse: As a journalist, it was very frustrating. … Because you wanna be where the news is. Especially as a conflict reporter. I always go to the places where things happen. (…) Yes, of course, as a journalist, you think, oh God, I should be in Brussels.

Jesse's narration well illustrates the inseparability of the media organization from the journalistic self (Du Gay 1996; Illouz 2007; Van Zoonen 1998).

Information and Linguistics

Apart from the focus on the visual and aesthetic, adopting the technological lens manifested itself in the reporters' and managers' immersion in the factual and technological/linguistic details of (reporting on) crises.

First, the reporters and editors expressed a strong commitment to informing the audience accurately (i.e. transmitting to the public only information verified by multiple credible sources with good reputations), and quickly, as these qualities formed their professional ideology (Deuze 2005):

> A reporter, Ella, and two editors (Marie and Václav), discuss where the fence that the story is supposed to report on is: "It is on the Macedonian-Greek border!" "No, on the Serbian-Hungarian border!" "No, on the Macedonian-

Greek border," Ella says. She had written the headline and Václav changed it. Marie supports Ella and says a screen should be made, depicting graphically when and where the anti-immigration fences have been built. She is waving her arms in the air: "And they built it first here, then here, then here." (Field notes)

Second, all the little aspects of the tragic events were being constantly picked over and dissected from the technological and linguistic points of view. How to name the act of destroying people's lives? Is "killing," "murdering," or "executing" the most suitable word? (In journalistic parlance, the police "kill" terrorists, and terrorists "murder" people—but terrorists certainly do not "execute," although they might make it seem that way.) How should the Daesh be referred to? Is this or that not too detailed and unnecessarily explicit? Should the photo of Aylan be broadcasted? ("This is what we really discussed for an hour," Čestmír said.) Are the shootings not wrongly mixed-up? Who should be invited to speak about the issue in the studio? Can the reporter on the spot manage to send the report in time?

Not only were the discussions on the factual, technological, and aesthetic aspects of reporting often mutually interlinked, like in the debate about the location of fences, but they were also often interwoven with a political dimension (see Ben-Yehuda et al. 2013; Neumann and Fahmy 2016; Van Der Meer et al. 2016).

James was becoming more and more impatient. He had scratched the last few letters of the draft of his future report, and wanted—needed—to land. He thoughtlessly, automatically clicked on another random mark of the video, and let Viggo speak. "Yes, there is a human crisis, because in today's world we can contemplate the death or the torture of a human being with the feeling of indifference. Friendly concern, scientific interest, or simple passivity." But how could James care about the suffering of others with such a job to be done at San Lorenzo and such a state of his urinary bladder? He unwittingly, anxiously looked back.

Looking back at cynical ideology (see the sections "Cynics and Kynics: Pissing Against the Idealist Wind"), the professional concentration on the aesthetic, linguistic, and technological aspects of a crisis—instead of its tragedy—seemed a case in point. But besides being an expression of the modern-cynical inauthenticity and detachment from the world, the focus on factual, technological, and aesthetic details of crises could be seen as a manifestation of a kynical commitment to truth-telling, that is, an emotionally charged sense of social and political responsibility (see the section "Professional Ideology and Cynicisms").

Metaphor of Emotional Robots

Getting ready to step onto the uncertain terrain of San Lorenzo, James was looking at the catastrophe more and more through the lens of *The Mo*. Like his colleagues, who deliberately plugged their mindful bodies into the technology of newsmaking, accepted the technological perspective, and let the environment permeate their emotions, thoughts, and feelings, up to the point that these became technologized (see Hansen 2006).

James very often noticed the inanimate ways in which his colleagues discursively constructed their own identities. They used to speak about "switching" between different types of subjectivities, such as the European and the crisis one, the personal and professional one, the normal-times one and the crisis-times one, the authentic one and the theatrical one, and so on:

> My tactic is always to *switch off* in the head. And it's not about being cynical, it's more a defence mechanism in my head. I go somewhere, I report on it, I go back, and I'm in another *room of my head*. (Carl)

> In the given situation, in the given culture, in what was happening there, it just worked like this. There, one simply *switches to another mode* and tries to immerse oneself in things that are important. (Čestmír)

> I think I am quite able to switch. ... To *make a switch in my head*. Because you just have to see what your job is. (Lotte)

> I just *run in the 'affair' mode*. (Olga)

> You just *switch yourself to the mode 'theatre' and run*. (Viktor)

James also noticed that the reporters sometimes perceived the practice of switching between the different "modes" and "regimes," "turning on the professional emotions" (Marie; see Hochschild 1983), or "recharging the batteries" as more difficult than simply being in the crisis environment:

> I don't have the enthusiasm, I just don't feel like doing something else again, because today I had to shift gears and change between three topics which were all enjoyable but it was during one single day. See? So *this* is demanding. I mean, to recharge the batteries. (Vítek)

Such a discursive construction of the reporters' identities is not profession-specific; indeed, it is very similar to the practice of "going into robot" that Arlie Hochschild (1983: 129) noticed among flight attendants. The robotic metaphor falls into the historically deep (empiricist) and common ontological human-machine metaphor (Lakoff and Johnson 2003; see Scheper-Hughes and Lock 1987). As George Lakoff and Mark Johnson (2003) argue, a metaphor is not only a matter of language; on the contrary, the whole human conceptual system is metaphorically defined and structured. *Speaking* of oneself as a rechargeable and switch-off device, the authors postulate, goes hand in hand with *conceiving* of oneself as a segment of a gear train or a machine. Since the metaphor is systematic and coherent, it sets aside the reporters' disposition to get genuinely involved (Peters 2011) that is inconsistent with the human-machine concept.

James glanced at his favorite flight attendant at the nose and felt a wave of fellow feeling.

He recalled a few moments when the technologization of emotions was reduced to absurdity. This happened whenever the reporters thought and spoke of precisely delimited parts of their selves as of machines dissociated from other parts of their selves that were endowed with intentions and authority:

> I wanted to throw up, or wanted to cry and go away and I just didn't want to be there. And I really had to pull myself together and say, Lotte, you cannot do this now, *switch your button*, and you just have to work now. (Lotte)

> I am a journalist, but on the other hand, often *I switch the button off*. (Jesse)

> The human *mind is* so clever! *It builds* a wall, or something. (Diego)

Sometimes, James' colleagues even spoke of themselves as particular types of machines and robots, for example Jesse, who identified journalists' sight with frames, or Čestmír, who explained the reporters' role by likening it to a "flow-through heater":

> You can see like a city which is half ruined, and then you see like a ruined city. But even then, I can still frame the picture, and know, like, this is what happens. And this is what has happened. You frame it and you start reporting on it. (Jesse)

> Well, 'flow-through heater' is a stupid expression, but simply, simply. ... One absorbs, absorbs a ... A ... An emotion, and tries to hand it over again. (Čestmír)

Contrarily, some reporters pointed out the danger and flaws of perceiving oneself in his/her wholeness as a machine and stressed the right balance between a technological and a humane approach to their work:

> If you're just trying to be a machine, follow the reader, it's also very strange. But you don't react in a humane way. (Sven)

> I think journalists should not be machines, but they should still report on the facts. (Jesse)

Similarly to handling their emotions on the output, the ability to achieve harmony between the machine and the humane sides of the self is something that the crisis reporters developed over time. Consider Lotte's above-mentioned experience of reporting on September 11: she was working the whole day "on automatic pilot" on the facts and images: "And you see people jumping from the World Trade Centre, but you don't realize it." According to her, not realizing it was an effect of "some kind of safety button in [her] head." But "shutting one's emotions out" cannot be practiced forever—so she learned to "let in some emotion" even while covering a crisis.

The reporters' embodiment of and plugging into the newsmaking machine that expressed itself in the ontological metaphor was thus perfectly consistent with emotional self-management: handling, suspending one's indexical emotions, disembedding them from particular actions and relationships, and substituting them in accordance with standardized speech and text patterns (Illouz 2007). What the journalists would have spontaneously felt was, within the complex of technologies of production, sign systems, power, and the self, replaced by what they were supposed to perform (cf. Hochschild 1983). The replacement, in turn, destroyed the experience of involvement (see Peters 2011): "I can play, I think I can play very good. But I must be very disconnected with this world," said Sam.

A sudden noise disturbed James' thoughts. He took his headphones off and listened to the metallic voice emanating from the speakers. "We will be landing in five minutes," the voice announced. "Please, remain fastened until the end of the flight." James was relieved, and even agog. By stealth, something or someone switched his journalist's button on.

An Overview

James, while preparing for getting off the airplane and collecting all his devices and belongings, clearly realized that what co-shaped his colleagues' emotional styles was not only the crisis context but also the newsmaking machine, the complex of things, processes, powers, words, and actions that constituted making news.

The socio-material (Orlikowski 2007) technologies of crisis news production affected reporters' emotions in a wide variety of ways. The technologies increased the pressure on accuracy, principles, speed, precision; investment of one's personal time; danger and risk, and thus acted like an agent of precarity.

They allowed the reporters to mediate their authentic experience of the on-site presence in unprecedented ways. They could keep the journalists distant; make them cover as much as possible; allow/push them to approach the crisis scene from unprecedentedly close range, and thus place them into the scene's focal point. At the same time, the technologies were able to help the journalists overcome the stress by bringing their organizational identity (Weick 1995) to the fore.

The technologies of sign systems gave rise to Positivists, reviving and strengthening (Wiik 2015) the traditional positivist-realist version of objectivity-as-a-norm, valuing detachment, complete neutrality, and impartiality (Carpentier and Trioen 2010; Schudson 2001), arguing that crisis news should be emotionless; Measurers, carefully measuring out the "right dose" of emotions in the news; and Franks, claiming that indexical emotions are one of the facts of the story, inherent to the crisis event. Despite the variety of attitudes toward the emotionality of crisis reporting, all the groups allegedly tried to avoid melodrama and utilitarian use of emotion words. In contrast, describing one's "genuine" internal states was typically seen as professionally acceptable/profitable, morally committed, and psychologically helpful.

The way of embedding emotions in news and, in turn, experiencing crisis events, was also co- shaped by technologies of power, particularly the journalistic professional ideology and diverse media-specific managerial practices. The technologies of power merged with technologies of the self, such as self-inducing a needed mood and adopting the organizational/professional lens (Du Gay 1996). As a result, what the journalists would have spontaneously felt was replaced by what they were supposed to perform (cf. Hochschild 1983). This replacement, in turn, weakened the experience of involvement (see Peters 2011).

James felt a sudden increase in air pressure. The negative pressure gave his ears a shock. The airplane was about to land. He closed "The Human Crisis" and snapped his laptop shut.

References

Adam, B. (2003). Reflexive Modernization Temporalized. *Theory, Culture and Society, 20*(2), 59–78.
Altamirano, M. (2014). Three Concepts for Crossing the Nature-artifice Divide: Technology, Milieu, and Machine. *Foucault Studies, 17*, 11–35.
Altheide, D. (2006). *Terrorism and the Politics of Fear*. Oxford: AltaMira Press.
Andén-Papadopoulos, K., & Pantti, M. (2013). Re-imagining Crisis Reporting: Professional Ideology of Journalists and Citizen Eyewitness Images. *Journalism, 14*(7), 960–977.
Banks, M. (2007). *The Politics of Cultural Work*. New York: Palgrave Macmillan.
Beck, U. (1992). *Risk Society: Towards a New Modernity*. London: SAGE.
Beckett, C., & Deuze, M. (2016). On the Role of Emotion in the Future of Journalism. *Social Media + Society, 2016*(3), 1–6.
Behrent, M. C. (2013). Foucault and Technology. *History and Technology, 29*(1), 54–104.
Ben-Yehuda, H., et al. (2013). When Media and World Politics Meet: Crisis Press Coverage in the Arab–Israel and East–West Conflicts. *Media, War and Conflict, 6*(1), 71–92.
Bernard, J. (2008). Bonne distance et empathie dans le travail émotionnel des pompes funèbres: L'analyse des interactions en milieu professionnel. *Journal des Anthropologues, 114–115*, 109–128.
Berti, C. (2016, March 23). Attentats de Bruxelles: Ce n'est pas la fin, c'est le début. *Le Soir*. Retrieved from http://www.lesoir.be/archive/recup/1159646/article/debats/editos/2016-03-23/attentats-bruxelles-ce-n-est-pas-fin-c-est-debut
Bewes, T. (1997). *Cynicism and Postmodernity*. London: Verso.
Boltanski, L. (1999). *Distant Suffering: Morality, Media and Politics*. Cambridge: Cambridge University Press.
Camus, A. (2016, April 4). Albert Camus' Historic Lecture, "The Human Crisis," Performed by Actor Viggo Mortensen. *Open Culture*. Retrieved from http://www.openculture.com/2016/04/albert-camus-historic-lecture-the-human-crisis-performed-by-actor-viggo-mortensen.html.
Carpentier, N., & Trioen, M. (2010). The Particularity of Objectivity: A Post-structuralist and Psychoanalytical Reading of the Gap Between Objectivity-as-a-value and Objectivity-as-a- practice in the 2003 Iraqi War Coverage. *Journalism, 11*(3), 311–328.
Castra, M. (2004). Faire face à la mort: Réguler la "bonne distance" soignants-malades en unité de soins palliatifs. *Travail et Emploi, 97*, 53–64.

Champy, F. (2009). *La Sociologie des Professions*. Paris: Presses Universitaires de France.
Creech, B. (2018). Bearing the Cost to Witness: The Political Economy of Risk in Contemporary Conflict and War Reporting. *Media, Culture & Society, 40*(4), 567–583.
Culler, J. (1997). *Literary Theory: A Very Short Introduction*. Oxford: Oxford University Press.
Czarniawska, B. (2011). *Cyberfactories: How News Agencies Produce News*. Northampton: Edward Elgar.
Deleuze, G. (1996). *Foucault*. Praha: Herrmann a synové.
Deleuze, G., & Guattari, F. (1988). *A Thousand Plateaus: Capitalism and Schizophrenia*. London: Continuum.
Deuze, M. (2005). What Is Journalism? Professional Identity and Ideology of Journalists Reconsidered. *Journalism, 6*(4), 442–464.
Deuze, M. (2011). Media Life. *Media, Culture and Society, 33*(1), 137–148.
Deuze, M. (2019). On Creativity. *Journalism, 20*(1), 130–134.
Du Gay, P. (1996). *Consumption and Identity at Work*. London: SAGE.
Falkheimer, J., & Olsson, E. K. (2015). Depoliticizing Terror: The News Framing of the Terrorist Attacks in Norway, 22 July 2011. *Media, War and Conflict, 8*(1), 70–85.
Festinger, L. (1957). *A Theory of Cognitive Dissonance*. Stanford: Stanford University Press.
Foucault, M. (1978). *The History of Sexuality: Volume I*. New York: Pantheon Books.
Foucault, M. (1988). Technologies of the Self. In L. H. Martin, H. Gutman, & P. H. Hutton (Eds.), *Technologies of the Self: A Seminar with Michel Foucault* (pp. 16–49). London: Tavistock Publications.
Foucault, M. (2005). *The Hermeneutics of the Subject: Lectures at the College de France, 1981–82*. New York: Palgrave Macmillan.
Giddens, A. (1991). *Modernity and Self-Identity: Self and Society in the Late Modern Age*. Cambridge: Polity Press.
Glück, A. (2016). What Makes a Good Journalist? *Journalism Studies, 17*(7), 893–903.
Greene, R. W. (2012). Lessons from the YMCA: The Material Rhetoric of Criticism, Rhetorical Interpretation and Pastoral Power. In J. Packer & S. B. Crofts Wiley (Eds.), *Communication Matters: Materialist Approaches to Media, Mobility, and Networks* (pp. 219–230). London: Routledge.
Hansen, M. (2006). Media Theory. *Theory, Culture and Society, 23*(2–3), 297–306.
Harbers, F., & Broersma, M. (2014). Between Engagement and Ironic Ambiguity: Mediating Subjectivity in Narrative Journalism. *Journalism, 15*(5), 639–654.
Harcup, T., & O'Neill, D. (2001). What Is News? Galtung and Ruge Revisited. *Journalism Studies, 2*(2), 261–280.
Hay, J. (2012). The Birth of the "Neoliberal" City and Its Media. In J. Packer & S. B. Crofts Wiley (Eds.), *Communication Matters: Materialist Approaches to Media, Mobility, and Networks* (pp. 121–140). London: Routledge.

Heidegger, M. (1977). *The Question Concerning Technology and Other Essays.* New York: Harper and Row.
Hesmondhalgh, D., & Baker, S. (2011). *Creative Labour: Media Work in Three Cultural Industries.* London: Routledge.
Hochschild, A. R. (1983). *The Managed Heart.* Berkeley: University of California Press.
Høiby, M. H., & Ottosen, R. (2015). *Journalism Under Pressure: A Mapping of Editorial Policies for Journalists Covering Conflict.* Oslo: Høgskolen i Oslo og Akershus.
Illouz, E. (2007). *Cold Intimacies: The Making of Emotional Capitalism.* Cambridge: Polity Press.
Lakoff, G., & Johnson, M. (2003). *Metaphors We Live By.* Chicago: The Chicago University Press.
Latour, B. (2005). *Reassembling the Social: An Introduction to Actor-Network-Theory.* Oxford: Oxford University Press.
Lievrouw, L. A. (2014). Materiality and Media in Communication and Technology Studies: An Unfinished Project. In T. Gillespie et al. (Eds.), *Media Technologies: Essays on Communication, Materiality and Society* (pp. 21–52). Cambridge: The MIT Press.
Lorey, I. (2011). Virtuosos of Freedom: On the Implosion of Political Virtuosity and Productive Labour. In G. Raunig, G. Ray, & U. Wuggenig (Eds.), *Critique of Creativity: Precarity, Subjectivity and Resistance in the 'Creative Industries'.* London: MayFly.
Lull, J. (2007). *Culture-on-Demand: Communication in a Crisis World.* Oxford: Blackwell Publishing.
Massumi, B. (1995). The Autonomy of Affect. *Cultural Critique, 31,* 83–109.
McDonald, I. R., & Lawrence, R. G. (2004). Filling the 24×7 News Hole: Television News Coverage Following September 11. *American Behavioral Scientist, 48*(3), 327–340.
Moeller, S. D. (1999). *Compassion Fatigue: How the Media Sell Disease, Famine, War and Death.* London: Routledge.
Molinier, P. (2009). Temps professionnel et temps personnel des travailleuses du care: Perméabilité ou clivage? Les aléas de la "bonne distance". *Temporalités, 9,* 1–14.
Navia, L. E. (1996). *Classical Cynicism: A Critical Study.* London: Greenwood Press.
Neumann, R., & Fahmy, S. (2016). Measuring Journalistic Peace/War Performance: An Exploratory Study of Crisis Reporters' Attitudes and Perceptions. *International Communication Gazette, 78*(3), 223–246.
Nord, L. W., & Strömbäck, J. (2003). Making Sense of Different Types of Crises: A Study of the Swedish Media Coverage of the Terror Attacks Against the United States and the U.S. Attacks in Afghanistan. *Press/Politics, 8*(4), 54–75.
Nord, L. W., & Strömbäck, J. (2006). Reporting More, Informing Less: A Comparison of the Swedish Media Coverage of September 11 and the Wars in Afghanistan and Iraq. *Journalism, 7*(1), 85–110.

Olsson, E. K., & Nord, L. W. (2015). Paving the Way for Crisis Exploitation: The Role of Journalistic Styles and Standards. *Journalism, 16*(3), 341–358.
Orlikowski, W. J. (2007). Sociomaterial Practices: Exploring Technology at Work. *Organization Studies, 28*(9), 1435–1448.
Packer, J., & Crofts Wiley, S. B. (2012). Introduction: The Materiality of Communication. In J. Packer & S. B. Crofts Wiley (Eds.), *Communication Matters: Materialist Approaches to Media, Mobility, and Networks* (pp. 3–16). London: Routledge.
Pang, A. (2013). Social Media Hype in Times of Crises: Nature Characteristics and Impact on Organizations. *Asia Pacific Media Educator, 23*(2), 309–336.
Pantti, M. (2010). The Value of Emotion: An Examination of Television Journalists' Notions on Emotionality. *European Journal of Communication, 25*, 168–181. https://doi.org/10.1177/0267323110363653.
Parikka, J. (2010). *Insect Media: An Archaeology of Animals and Technology*. Minneapolis: University of Minnesota Press.
Pauly, J. J. (2014). The New Journalism and the Struggle for Interpretation. *Journalism, 15*(5), 589–604.
Pedelty, M. (1995). *War Stories: The Culture of Foreign Correspondents*. London: Routledge.
Peters, C. (2011). Emotion Aside or Emotional Side? Crafting an 'Experience of Involvement' in the News. *Journalism, 12*(3), 297–316.
Plaisance, P. L., & Skewes, E. A. (2003). Personal and Professional Dimensions of News Work: Exploring the Link Between Journalists' Values and Roles. *Journalism and Mass Communication Quarterly, 80*(4), 833–848.
Post, S. (2015). Scientific Objectivity in Journalism? How Journalists and Academics Define Objectivity, Assess Its Attainability, and Rate Its Desirability. *Journalism, 16*(6), 730–749.
Rayner, T. (2001). Biopower and Technology: Foucault and Heidegger's Way of Thinking. *Contretemps, 2*, 142–156.
Richards, B., & Rees, G. (2011). The Management of Emotion in British Journalism. *Media, Culture and Society, 33*(6), 851–867.
Rosaldo, M. Z. (1984). Towards an Anthropology of Self and Feeling. In R. A. Schweder & R. A. LeVine (Eds.), *Culture Theory: Essays on Mind, Self and Emotions* (pp. 137–157). Cambridge: Cambridge University Press.
Ruigrok, N. (2008). Journalism of Attachment and Objectivity: Dutch Journalists and the Bosnian War. *Media, War & Conflict, 1*(3), 293–313.
Scheer, M. (2012). Are Emotions a Kind of Practice (And Is That What Makes Them Have a History)? A Bourdieuian Approach to Understanding Emotion. *History and Theory, 51*, 193–220.
Scheper-Hughes, N., & Lock, M. (1987). The Mindful Body: A Prolegomenon to Future Work in Medical Anthropology. *Medical Anthropology Quarterly, 1*(1), 6–41.
Schudson, M. (2001). The Objectivity Norm in American Journalism. *Journalism, 2*(2), 149–170.

Schudson, M. (2011). What's Unusual About Covering Politics as Usual. In B. Zelizer & S. Allan (Eds.), *Journalism After September 11* (2nd ed., pp. 44–54). London: Routledge.
Skovsgaard, M., et al. (2013). A Reality Check: How Journalists' Role Perceptions Impact Their Implementation of the Objectivity Norm. *Journalism, 14*(1), 22–42.
Sloterdijk, P. (1987). *Critique of Cynical Reason*. Minneapolis: University of Minnesota Press.
Sontag, S. (1977). *On Photography*. London: Penguin Books.
Sontag, S. (2003). *Regarding the Pain of Others*. New York: Picador.
Sorribes, C. P., & Rovira, S. C. (2011). Journalistic Practice in Risk and Crisis Situations: Significant Examples from Spain. *Journalism, 12*(8), 1052–1066.
Steensen, S. (2017). Subjectivity as a Journalistic Ideal. In B. Kjos Fonn et al. (Eds.), *Putting a Face on It: Individual Exposure and Subjectivity in Journalism* (pp. 25–47). Oslo: Cappelen Damm Akademisk.
Tong, J. (2015). Being Objective with a Personal Perspective: How Environmental Journalists at Two Chinese Newspapers Articulate and Practice Objectivity. *Science Communication, 37*(6), 747–768.
Tumber, H. (2011). Reporting Under Fire: The Physical Safety and Emotional Welfare of Journalists. In B. Zelizer & S. Allan (Eds.), *Journalism After September 11* (2nd ed., pp. 319–334). London: Routledge.
Usher, N. (2019). Journalism's Biggest Challenge? Journalists. *Journalism, 20*(1), 140–143.
Van Der Meer, TGLA. et al. (2016). Disrupting Gatekeeping Practices: Journalists' Source Selection in Times of Crisis. *Journalism*. Epub ahead of print 16 May 2016. https://doi.org/10.1177/1464884916648095.
Van Loon, J. (2002). *Risk and Technological Culture: Towards a Sociology of Virulence*. London: Routledge.
Van Zoonen, L. (1998). A Professional, Unreliable, Heroic Marionette (M/F): Structure, Agency and Subjectivity in Contemporary Journalisms. *European Journal of Cultural Studies, 1*(1), 123–143.
Vos, T. P. (2011). 'Homo Journalisticus': Journalism Education's Role in Articulating the Objectivity Norm. *Journalism, 13*(4), 435–449. https://doi.org/10.1177/1464884911431374.
Wahl-Jorgensen, K. (2013). The Strategic Ritual of Emotionality: A Case Study of Pulitzer Prize- winning Articles. *Journalism, 14*(1), 129–145.
Wahl-Jorgensen, K. (2016). Emotion and Journalism. In T., Witschge (Ed.), *The SAGE Handbook of Digital Journalism*. London: SAGE Publications(pp. 128–143). Epub ahead of print. Retrieved from http://orca.cf.ac.uk/87552/.
Weick, K. E. (1995). *Sensemaking in Organizations*. London: SAGE.
Wiik, J. (2015). Internal Boundaries: The Stratification of the Journalistic Collective. In M. Carlson & S. C. Lewis (Eds.), *Boundaries of Journalism: Professionalism, Practices and Participation* (pp. 118–133). London: Routledge.
Williams, R. (1974). *Television: Technology and Cultural Form*. London: Fontana.

Open Access This chapter is licensed under the terms of the Creative Commons Attribution 4.0 International License (http://creativecommons.org/licenses/by/4.0/), which permits use, sharing, adaptation, distribution and reproduction in any medium or format, as long as you give appropriate credit to the original author(s) and the source, provide a link to the Creative Commons licence and indicate if changes were made.

The images or other third party material in this chapter are included in the chapter's Creative Commons licence, unless indicated otherwise in a credit line to the material. If material is not included in the chapter's Creative Commons licence and your intended use is not permitted by statutory regulation or exceeds the permitted use, you will need to obtain permission directly from the copyright holder.

CHAPTER 5

Emotions, Technology, and Crisis Reconsidered: Ending

James set foot on the steps by the airplane back door and looked around. The land, up to the horizon, was unimaginably paralyzed by ice-nine. James saw the frozen remains of life (Image 5.1).

He had heard it sometimes happens before one dies. First the most recent and then more distant memories flashed through his head.

Long Story Short

Technology

It followed from James' conversations and experience that journalists' emotions were co-shaped by technology, a concept intrinsic to modern Western culture (e.g. Beck 1992; Foucault 1978; Heidegger 1977; Van Loon 2002; Williams 1974). In particular, the journalists' emotions were constitutively entangled (Orlikowski 2007) with the newsmaking machine: the complex of technologies of the self, technologies of power, technologies of sign systems, and technologies of production (Foucault 1988).

The technologies of the economic-emotional self, guiding individuals to perform forms of self-direction and self-management which result in both an economically desirable and personally attractive self (Illouz 2007), led the journalists to perceive and think through the organizational perspective. The emotional styles/organizational identities (Du Gay 1996) of the Cynics, the Stoics, and the Brokens are thus outcomes of work on the

Image 5.1 A frozen city. Drawing by Peter Van Goethem, 2017. Courtesy of the artist

journalists' selves: results of "crafting" the experience of involvement, of "finding the right balance of disengagement and nonchalance" (Peters 2011: 303), and of finding the "right distance" (Bernard 2008; Castra 2004; Molinier 2009).

The practice of crafting a proper economic-emotional self is hardly distinguishable from the technologies of power: journalists' professional ideology and power circulating within specific media organizations. Furthermore, the practical performance of professional ideology is inextricably linked to views about how emotions should (not) appear in news:

the technologies of sign systems. While the traditional, positivist-realist journalistic ideology does not allow for journalists' emotions, the prevalence of Measurers and Franks proves that crisis reporters' practices of emotional management and their experience are shaped not only by the ideology but also by its critiques, which makes diverse emotional styles possible (Peters 2011). In turn, the reporters' subjectivity, including empathy, becomes central to their professional performance (Glück 2016; Steensen 2017). On the other hand, the freedom of emotional management is limited. If crisis reporters want to stay within the boundaries of quality journalism, they must exercise self-restraint and include their "authentic" emotional experience in the news only in a functional, understated way. (Yet, even the use of this limited freedom can help one not to break down and become a Stoic instead.) All things considered, the value of emotionless objectivity is not carved in stone or interpreted uniformly but rather is open for interpretation and related to particular circumstances (Skovsgaard et al. 2013). *Crisis* circumstances challenge the notion of objectivity as a *cornerstone* of journalistic professionalism.

The possible rethinking of journalists' professional ideology vis-à-vis crisis circumstances is thus intertwined also with the particularity of technologies of production in a crisis and in individual crises. Crisis circumstances inevitably alter journalists' practices and routines that are constitutively entangled with things (Orlikowski 2007). Rather than working as intermediaries, things and material technologies act as mediators with various shades of influence "between full causality and sheer inexistence" (Latour 2005: 72) on human action and emotion.

All these aspects together—all the technologies or matrices of practical reason telling people how successful professionals should conduct and operate their bodies, souls, and thoughts (Du Gay 1996; Foucault 1988)—construct the forms of subjectivity that are most appropriate to the practice of crisis reporting.

Emotions

To make a long story short, the typical emotional path is started upon with expectations and professional aspirations—in the case of James' colleagues usually with "idealist-activist" aspiration (see Urbániková 2015) and the mythic notion of becoming a renegade war correspondent (Pedelty 1995). However, the newsroom routine is often frustrating, heavy, tiring, and boring at the same time. Unexpected and surprising negative events enliven the routine and resolve some newsroom problems but also trigger emotional shocks (Dubberley et al. 2015). Speaking about post-traumatic stress *disorder*, depression, early waking *syndrome*, and other forms of mental ill-health (e.g. Aoki et al. 2012; Feinstein et al. 2015; Reinardy 2011; Richards and Rees 2011), triggered by exposure to violent content, reproduces the tendency to see *social* and *systemic* problems as individual and biographical (Beck and Beck-Gernsheim 2001; Scheper-Hughes and Lock 1987). The analysis shows exactly the opposite: what shapes crisis reporters' emotional culture and emotional styles are the intrinsic features of their job: the newsmaking technology and the crisis circumstances. Furthermore, it is precisely the act of individualization of crises, perceiving the emotional responses to social crises as an individual problem and subject to individual coping strategies, which turns reporters' emotions into a *sociological* problem.

Direct or vicarious on-site presence, facing risk and empathizing with the Others who suffer in parts of the world sharply contrasting with Europe, bring about states and feelings of sadness, indignation, pity, revulsion, consternation, anger, fear, stress, tension, guilt, absurdity, compassion, horror, and tiredness (cf. Dubberley et al. 2015; Hight and Smyth 2003; Pedelty 1995). All these emotional states make the professional paradox of acting and observing (Richards and Rees 2011) more pressing. Eventually, the continuous oscillation between boredom and emotional jolts may lead to cynicism and compassion fatigue (Moeller 1999)—emotional states that threaten not only the journalists' well-being but also their personal integrity and the quality of their journalism.

Crisis

Getting to the cynical standstill is facilitated by routinization of crises. In the minds of the journalists, crisis became a norm and the absurd turned into routine (see Koselleck 2006; Pedelty 1995; Zelizer and Allan 2011). The journalists saw crisis as a ubiquitous, all-encompassing phenomenon; crisis was defined by its inflation, generalized character (Vincze 2014; Wagner 1994), by its polyphony and multi-level scope. To James' colleagues, "crisis" could mean anything—and meant everything. An inside-the-media crisis (Olsson and Nord 2015), usually organizational, technological, professional, or personnel situation not far from a breakdown. At the same time, it meant an outside-the-media temporary or continuous major negative event with wide impact on society. Crisis even meant the very essence of the current phase of modernity with its global risks and insecurities, biographized by individuals and manifesting in peoples' everyday lives (Beck 1992; Beck and Beck-Gernsheim 2001; Giddens 1991). For crisis was delimited by the suffering of individuals coming largely from areas that contrasted with the journalists' own worlds but also by the journalists' own trauma. Crisis was also understood as both the real and the media-constructed (Beck 1992; Van Loon 2002). All these meanings of "crisis" were interconnected, resonated, or interfered with each other, dragging the journalists into a mental state of continuous awareness of existential problems, death, suffering, catastrophes, and, perhaps most importantly, the world's absurd inequalities and uncanny differences.

Their lived experience proves that while mediating between and existing within the incommensurable worlds, they are actors too—even more inevitably when they find themselves in the middle of events. The notion of their "dual state" is thus based on the false assumption that journalists are, on grounds of their professional authority (which is, in turn, based on the objectivistic illusion of Truth), able to step out from the world—albeit only with one foot—and to look at events from above—even though only with one eye. James' colleagues, however, actively lived inside crises: they were witnesses, victims, and political actors (Ben-Yehuda et al. 2013; Van Der Meer et al. 2016).

Those who did not break down thus became to some extent cynical or stoic, the difference being that for Stoics, maintaining professional principles, such as following the facts, was vital (Becker 1998; Sellars 2006).

This was the account reconstructed in dialogue with James' memories.

EMOTIONS, TECHNOLOGY, AND CRISIS RECONSIDERED

And the account shed new light—sometimes reaffirming, sometimes further complicating—on the once-provisionally defined concepts of technology, crisis, and emotions.

Emotions

Most obviously, it had become even clearer that emotions are not merely innate, biophysiological phenomena (Thoits 1989). Even emotions once considered "basic," "primary," and culturally universal (see Ekman 1999; Ekman and Cordaro 2011), such as fear, anger, disgust, relief, and amusement, are historically and cross-culturally variable based on situational causes, experience, meaning, display, and regulation (Thoits 1989). Paul Ekman himself later in life reconsidered his initial claim about cultural universality: even the basic emotions "differ in their appraisal, antecedent events, probable behavioral response, physiology and other characteristics" (Ekman 1999: 45). Indeed, the fear, anger, disgust, relief, amusement, and other emotions felt by James' colleagues not only emerged from the context of crisis reporting, but their experiencing, meaning, display, and regulation also varied based on their constitutive entanglement with the newsmaking machine. Most importantly, the journalists' emotions also yielded to the individualist and/or macho myths still surrounding crisis reporting. The very fact that many journalists considered their work-related emotions an intimate, personal problem, even a taboo, even though "subjective experiences and emotional beliefs are both socially acquired and socially structured" (Thoits 1989: 319), adds one more dimension to the social character and sociological relevance of emotions, laying bare the process of individualization and biographization of risks and crises (Beck and Beck-Gernsheim 2001; Giddens 1991).

Technology

Second, the analysis illustrates a line of continuity between the Foucauldian notion of technologies of (bio-)power, defined above as the power that brings "life and its mechanisms into the realm of explicit calculations" (Foucault 1978: 143), measures them, objectifies them, and sets them into productive coordination, so that they may operate as one wishes, and the equally influential Heideggerian notion of technology. For Martin Heidegger (1977), technology means revealing and enframing. It "reveals the Earth, man himself" (Inwood 1999: 211), molding and fulfilling our purposes, revealing us and everything in nature as standing-reserve. It is also a way of enframing and ordering beings, a ceaseless objectification, qualification, quantification, and systematization of the world reducing it to the level of stock (Rayner 2001). Technology transforms human beings and culture into a stockpile. According to Timothy Rayner (2001), the concepts intersect in important aspects: they both conceive reality (the whole of nature in Heidegger's case and the human population for Foucault) as a field of resource; both regard the objectification-commodification of reality as mediated by technology, driven by the vision of situating all forms of life within a domain of technical manipulation; both pursue setting all natural "material," that is, life, in order. In other words, both concepts pursue the overall management of life. The emotional management (Hochschild 1983; Illouz 2007) that James' colleagues exercised, making their emotions more closely harnessed to instrumental action and economic rationality, is an example of these intersections. In line with the application of Foucault to labor process theory (see Knights and Willmott 1989), Eva Illouz (2007) and Peter Fleming and André Spicer (2003) understand "colonizing" the identities of workers and their emotions as a mark of the latest phase of capitalism and its managerial logic, in which

> corporate power and worker subjectivity intersect within social relations of organizational domination. (…) What we take to be our most intimate and personal habits and dispositions cannot be separated from the political economy of the post-industrial labour process and late capitalism. (Fleming and Spicer 2003: 158)

Thinking of this absolute rationalism embracing human subjectivity and emotions, James, while descending the last few back door steps, recalled the "human crisis" that Viggo Mortensen, on behalf of Albert Camus, spoke about (Camus 2016).

Crisis

Third, is not this what crisis means above all? Camus, speaking of "the human crisis," equates the results of absolute rationalism to those of nihilism. Similarly, for Heidegger, nihilism is synonymous with the inherently modern all-encompassing technological enframing, leading to the forgetting of being as such (Rayner 2001).

More specifically, the empirical data show the way in which the technology of crisis reporting and journalists' professional ideology partly overlap with ideological cynicism: journalists need to be able to work despite anything that might happen (Sloterdijk 1987), which also means staying at least partly detached under any circumstances and being able to work without delay (Deuze 2005). This requires a certain limited variety of emotional postures—including, by the way, the cynical one. In this sense, the newsmaking technology turns humans into human resources (see Heidegger 1977; Rayner 2001). In order to be respected professionals, it is favorable that the journalists turn their once-indexical emotions into a stockpile and merge their emotional and economical selves (Illouz 2007).

In terms of media professionals' precarity, the crisis reporters' (self-) precarization—regardless of whether they were formally employed or worked as freelancers—thus consisted not only of the physical and psychological risks they faced at work but also of the often thought-through translation of their emotions into resources and, in turn, into forms of capital. For Heidegger and Camus, this alone would be a sufficient symptom of the "human crisis" and a "forgetting of being as such" (Rayner 2001).

James still needed to descend a step deeper, though. For the absolute rationalism expanded from journalism's ideology to the realm of media representations, marking another aspect of the human crisis. "There is a human crisis, because in today's world we can contemplate the death or the torture of a human being with the feeling of indifference. Friendly concern, scientific interest, or simple passivity," Viggo echoed in James' head. The ideological cynicism (Sloterdijk 1987) resided precisely in this apathy and refusal to engage with the world (Bewes 1997). Particularly the focus on the technological, aesthetic, and linguistic details of others' suffering, driven by economic rationality, in short, its spectacularization (Boltanski 1999; see also Debord 2005) or valorization (Van Loon 2002), keeps not only journalists but also audiences detached and disconnected from the world, since the escalation and intensification of mediated violence and horror leads to compassion fatigue (Moeller 1999). Consequently, audiences are unable to meet the essentially humane moral commitment to take action—albeit in a form of "mere" committed speech—when witnessing others' suffering. In this context, Luc Boltanski (1999: xvi; see also from p. 147 on) speaks about a

> contemporary crisis of pity which is characterised, precisely, by a loss of confidence in the effectiveness of committed speech, by a focus on the media and the 'spectacle' effects they produce, by a temptation to fall back on the community, and finally, and most profoundly, by a scepticism with regard to any form of political action orientated towards a horizon of moral ideals.

In other words, the increase in the quantity and intensity of the spectacles of suffering brings about uncertainties about the suffering and its representation. These uncertainties, in turn, dissolve the moral commitment and lead to a crisis of humanitarianism.

"Crisis" can thus also mean the irresistible spreading of ideological cynicism.

(Extra) Media Action?

Cynicism was a phenomenon that did not yield to James' embryonic cynicism. As has been said, he maintained and even believed in some humane and journalistic principles and ideals. "Compared with previous ages control of emotions in experiencing nature, as that of nature itself, has grown. Involvement has lessened, but it has not disappeared," Norbert Elias wrote in 1956 (Elias 1956: 228). In the sea of cynicism, James, feeling some vague responsibility, still hoped to see a few islands of possible engagement and spontaneity. Corresponding to the two areas of the "human crisis," these islands appeared in three realms: media practices and representations, media organizations, and non-media global actors.

First, as argued in the sections on journalists' professional ideology, focusing on technological, aesthetic, linguistic details, or speed is not necessarily a sign of an ideologically cynical attitude. Such a focus can be a manifestation of the journalists' professional sense of accuracy, immediacy, validity, and thus the commitment to stick to the public service ideal (Deuze 2005). Be they public service, commercial, or independent, media professionals and organizations can thus actively question the traditional professional ideology as a whole and strengthen and build on this non-cynical part of their ideology by insisting on: providing public service (i.e. active collecting and dissemination of information in the name of people and public service principles), fairness and honesty (i.e. processual objectivity rather than the neutral and detached version of objectivity), autonomy and independence (in their everyday practices and journalistic routines), accuracy rather than precedence, and ethics (Deuze 2005).

However, such a deliberate abandonment of media practices connected to ideological, modern cynicism does not mean that journalists should forsake the irony, mockery, and satire of classical kynicism. On the contrary: this challenging "pissing against the idealist wind" (Sloterdijk 1987: 103) with its truth-telling and care of oneself (Foucault 2005), and especially with its intellectual rebelliousness against existing beliefs and practices, is compatible with certain parts of the journalists' professional ideology.

More generally, such a critical reappraisal of journalists' professional ideology means accepting *prudence*—the ability to weigh a particular situation in its complexity and make decisions that help the journalists to meet the values and fulfill their roles in the best possible way (Champy 2009)—as a defining feature of professionalism. In practice, prudent crisis reporting would entail sensitivity to the particular objectivity-as-a-practice

(Carpentier and Trioen 2010) and using emotionality in a nonviolent, moderating, peaceful way. In this sense, prudent crisis reporting would be close to Johan Galtung's notion of peace journalism: "journalism of attachment" to all victims that "tries to depolarise by showing the black and white of all sides, and to de-escalate by highlighting peace and conflict resolution as much as violence" (Galtung and Fischer 2013: 99; see also Neumann and Fahmy 2016 and Ruigrok 2008).

Galtung and Fischer (2013) suggest that empathy and creativity are required of peace journalists; Glück (2016) extends the ability to empathize to all good journalists. Similarly, Boltanski (1999) claims that the media, to avoid spectacularization of suffering and reproducing the crisis of pity, can take action through a form of effective speech, consisting not only of hard facts but also of description of the journalist's internal states (such as indignation). Boltanski further suggests that a possible way to simultaneously tell the facts about suffering and to show how one has been affected by it is to nourish the imagination by denunciation, sentiment, and aesthetics. The most suitable form for feeding the imagination is, according to the author, narrativized reality or realist fiction: "These forms actually seemed to be especially suitable for the description of affective states which do not normally figure in juridical, economic or political documents" (Boltanski 1999: 54). Narrativized reality, not surprisingly, lies at the core of narrative journalism which, as Eric Neveu (2014) believes, could be a decent future for the profession.

Prudent crisis reporting could thus also mean including some principles of literary or narrative journalism into everyday journalistic performance: employing more authentic and openly emotional journalistic discourses, using the—often already available—freedom of emotional expression, creativity and the lens of one's feelings, thoughts and experiences (Harbers and Broersma 2014; Pauly 2014). Such journalism would not only better capture the richness of social complexity but also lead to more critical and ethical engagement with the suffering of Others.

The point, however, is by no means to advocate the egocentricism of the Western visitors to crisis zones that several James' colleagues so harshly criticized. The point is to encourage media professionals, once they witness things that appear unthinkable and unreasonable within their privileged bubble, to act as full-blown *mediators* between the contrasting worlds. Nikki Usher (2019: 142) perfectly encapsulates the role that journalists' open emotionality can play when she asks: "Can journalists stop talking about themselves? Probably not. But perhaps they need to do a better job showing why they—elite national journalists—matter."

Second, the privilege of Western crisis reporters does not exclude their precarity. In fact, the "privilege" to witness how the planet turns, to be there when history unfolds, their interest, and involvement form its core. Getting stories, they take risks. Face to face with the world's absurd contrasts and the Others' tragedies, they need to perform tough emotional labor. In the worst-case scenario, they end up broken: overworked, burnt out, and cynical. Their privilege thus creates a potentially destructive cocktail of good and bad work processes (Hesmondhalgh and Baker 2011).

Therefore, the cynical crisis, manifesting itself by turning journalists into human resources, is to be fought in the newsrooms and corridors of media organizations. After September 11, Howard Tumber wrote that "It is imperative that measures are taken worldwide to improve the safety, security, and psychological welfare of journalists and the prosecution rates of those responsible for the killing of journalists. Without such actions, we are all vulnerable to the spin and propaganda of governments, military, warlords, and the operations of international crime" (Tumber 2011: 333). There are also sufficient legal arguments (see the section "Coping Strategies") that media organizations should attempt to prevent work-related health problems, which result, in some cases, in cynicism.

"I personally find it a disaster, the way in the big newsroom we do not pay attention to the risks associated with crisis," Nicolas said, criticizing his employer. Media organizations should help journalists to deal with difficult emotions. Similarly to breaking news manuals, media organizations should "get a range of measures ready, which, however, must be applied with regard to the individuality of each reporter" (Šimon). Raising awareness of potential mental health problems may be a good beginning (Aoki et al. 2012); at least some emotional and psychological training both in newsrooms and journalism schools could reduce the emotional shocks. As Nicolas suggested, helping journalism students to understand their possible future problems and raising awareness by the cooperation with NGOs, universities, and media houses can prepare their brighter future. In addition, the newsrooms should, according to Nicolas, draw on the knowledge of such trauma more by formally employing senior reporters for on-the-spot reporters' support and supervision:

> to have at least, let's say, what I call 'a control tower.' So when you're in a war zone, or in a crisis zone, somebody that you can call and say, Nicolas, I got into a problem, what would you do if you were me? ... Making sure that you have somebody experienced, staying at the newsroom, accessible ... who would give you advice. (Nicolas)

The problem with such prevention, supportive, and also therapeutic tools (see the section "Coping Strategies") may be that, if isolated, they can be further criticized for producing forms of subjectivity ideal for crisis circumstances, that is, adapting individuals for the continuous state of crisis. Therefore, without keeping the supportive and therapeutic mechanisms de-individualized by questioning what the journalists can see (or saw) and can do (or did), without making relevant the crisis itself and the journalists' position within the crisis, the therapy, prevention, and support are primarily simply further technologies of governmentality (see Väliaho 2014).

Furthermore, in accordance with the above-suggested questioning of the traditional professional ideology, strengthening of its non-cynical parts, and including narrative journalism into everyday journalistic performance, Sven proposed that media organizations can help to reduce journalists' work-related stress by encouraging them to focus on positive (not only negative) events and constructive solutions to social problems and by advancing new, creative media genres and formats that help journalists to express their on-the-spot experience in its complexity. These approaches that understand objectivity as an ethical practice rather than an objectivistic norm, not only help to de-escalate conflicts, bridge the gap between here and there, but also make journalists' work-related emotional experience sustainable.

Third, the ideological cynicism is, as some of the reporters suggested, nourished by the exploitative logic of the media industry. The logic determines the conditions under which the crisis news is produced, that is, outsources the risks to individuals, and is kept alive by the graded levels of risk that the different groups of individuals involved in crisis reporting face. Risk, as Creech (2018: 578) points out, thus "takes on a particularly economic tenor, echoing the increasing precarity of all news labor."

Therefore, a way to tackle the ideological cynicism could be bridging the contrasting worlds not only by narrative approaches but also by "recasting witnessing not just as a moral imperative, but one that also comes with costs that are distributed unequally" (ibid.: 579), and eventually, by evening up the precarity of employed international correspondents, freelancers and local journalists, fixers and stringers. This requires decoupling the work of crisis journalism from its solely market-oriented understanding, decoupling the risk of individual bodily harm from economic logic, and re-centering it within the realms of policy and politics. However, it takes including a wider variety of actors than just news organizations, such as national governments and global NGOs. The latter have already done good job of making the risk, precarity, and their unequal distribution more visible, and of interconnecting the journalists' global community.

James stepped on the ground. He felt tingling in his feet. An amber gleam in Sophie Schlesinger's eyes pierced the dimness of the airfield when she glanced back at him from a clunker, stopped in front of the arrivals hall. "Comin' with us?" she called airily.

References

Aoki, Y., et al. (2012). Mental Illness Among Journalists: A Systematic Review. *International Journal of Social Psychiatry, 59*(4), 377–390.
Beck, U. (1992). *Risk Society: Towards a New Modernity.* London: SAGE.
Beck, U., & Beck-Gernsheim, E. (2001). *Individualization: Institutionalized Individualism and Its Social and Political Consequences.* London: SAGE.
Becker, L. A. (1998). *A New Stoicism.* Princeton: Princeton University Press.
Ben-Yehuda, H., et al. (2013). When Media and World Politics Meet: Crisis Press Coverage in the Arab–Israel and East–West Conflicts. *Media, War and Conflict, 6*(1), 71–92.
Bernard, J. (2008). Bonne distance et empathie dans le travail émotionnel des pompes funèbres: L'analyse des interactions en milieu professionnel. *Journal des Anthropologues, 114–115,* 109–128.
Bewes, T. (1997). *Cynicism and Postmodernity.* London: Verso.
Boltanski, L. (1999). *Distant Suffering: Morality, Media and Politics.* Cambridge: Cambridge University Press.
Camus, A. (2016, April 4). Albert Camus' Historic Lecture, "The Human Crisis," performed by actor Viggo Mortensen. *Open Culture.* Retrieved from http://www.openculture.com/2016/04/albert-camus-historic-lecture-the-human-crisis-performed-by-actor-viggo-mortensen.html.
Carpentier, N., & Trioen, M. (2010). The Particularity of Objectivity: A Post-structuralist and Psychoanalytical Reading of the Gap Between Objectivity-as-a-value and Objectivity-as-a- practice in the 2003 Iraqi War Coverage. *Journalism, 11*(3), 311–328.
Castra, M. (2004). Faire face à la mort: Réguler la "bonne distance" soignants-malades en unité de soins palliatifs. *Travail et Emploi, 97,* 53–64.
Champy, F. (2009). *La Sociologie des Professions.* Paris: Presses Universitaires de France.
Creech, B. (2018). Bearing the Cost to Witness: The Political Economy of Risk in Contemporary Conflict and War Reporting. *Media, Culture & Society, 40*(4), 567–583.

Debord, G. (2005). *Society of the Spectacle*. London: Rebel Press.
Deuze, M. (2005). What Is Journalism? Professional Identity and Ideology of Journalists Reconsidered. *Journalism*, 6(4), 442–464.
Du Gay, P. (1996). *Consumption and Identity at Work*. London: SAGE.
Dubberley, S. et al. (2015). *Making Secondary Trauma a Primary Issue: A Study of Eyewitness Media and Vicarious Trauma on the Digital Frontline*. Eyewitness Media Hub. Retrieved from http://eyewitnessmediahub.com/research/vicarious-trauma.
Ekman, P. (1999). Basic Emotions. In T. Dalgleish & M. Power (Eds.), *Handbook of Cognition and Emotion* (pp. 45–60). New York: John Wiley and Sons.
Ekman, P., & Cordaro, D. (2011). What Is Meant by Calling Emotions Basic. *Emotion Review*, 3(4), 364–370.
Elias, N. (1956). Problems of Involvement and Detachment. *The British Journal of Sociology*, 7(3), 226–252.
Feinstein, A., et al. (2015). Witnessing Images of Extreme Violence: A Psychological Study of Journalists in the Newsroom. *Journal of the Royal Society of Medicine*, 6(2), 1–7.
Fleming, P., & Spicer, A. (2003). Working at a Cynical Distance: Implications for Power, Subjectivity and Resistance. *Organization*, 10(1), 157–179.
Foucault, M. (1978). *The History of Sexuality: Volume I*. New York: Pantheon Books.
Foucault, M. (1988). Technologies of the Self. In L. H. Martin, H. Gutman, & P. H. Hutton (Eds.), *Technologies of the Self: A Seminar with Michel Foucault* (pp. 16–49). London: Tavistock Publications.
Foucault, M. (2005). *The Hermeneutics of the Subject: Lectures at the College de France, 1981–82*. New York: Palgrave Macmillan.
Galtung, J., & Fischer, D. (2013). *Johan Galtung: Pioneer of Peace Research*. Berlin: Springer-Verlag.
Giddens, A. (1991). *Modernity and Self-Identity: Self and Society in the Late Modern Age*. Cambridge: Polity Press.
Glück, A. (2016). What Makes a Good Journalist? *Journalism Studies*, 17(7), 893–903.
Harbers, F., & Broersma, M. (2014). Between Engagement and Ironic Ambiguity: Mediating Subjectivity in Narrative Journalism. *Journalism*, 15(5), 639–654.
Heidegger, M. (1977). *The Question Concerning Technology and Other Essays*. New York: Harper and Row.
Hesmondhalgh, D., & Baker, S. (2011). *Creative Labour: Media Work in Three Cultural Industries*. London: Routledge.
Hight, J., & Smyth, F. (2003). *Tragedies and Journalists: A Guide for More Effective Coverage*. Dart Center for Journalism and Trauma. Retrieved from http://dartcenter.org/sites/default/files/en_tnj_0.pdf.
Hochschild, A. R. (1983). *The Managed Heart*. Berkeley: University of California Press.

Illouz, E. (2007). *Cold Intimacies: The Making of Emotional Capitalism*. Cambridge: Polity Press.
Inwood, M. (1999). *A Heidegger Dictionary*. Oxford: Blackwell Publishing.
Knights, D., & Willmott, H. (1989). Power and Subjectivity at Work: From Degradation to Subjugation in Social Relations. *Sociology, 23*(4), 535–558.
Koselleck, R. (2006). Crisis. *Journal of the History of Ideas, 67*(2), 357–400.
Latour, B. (2005). *Reassembling the Social: An Introduction to Actor-Network-Theory*. Oxford: Oxford University Press.
Moeller, S. D. (1999). *Compassion Fatigue: How the Media Sell Disease, Famine, War and Death*. London: Routledge.
Molinier, P. (2009). Temps professionnel et temps personnel des travailleuses du care: Perméabilité ou clivage? Les aléas de la "bonne distance". *Temporalités, 9*, 1–14.
Neumann, R., & Fahmy, S. (2016). Measuring Journalistic Peace/War Performance: An Exploratory Study of Crisis Reporters' Attitudes and Perceptions. *International Communication Gazette, 78*(3), 223–246.
Neveu, E. (2014). Revisiting Narrative Journalism as One of the Futures of Journalism. *Journalism Studies, 15*(5), 533–542.
Olsson, E. K., & Nord, L. W. (2015). Paving the Way for Crisis Exploitation: The Role of Journalistic Styles and Standards. *Journalism, 16*(3), 341–358.
Orlikowski, W. J. (2007). Sociomaterial Practices: Exploring Technology at Work. *Organization Studies, 28*(9), 1435–1448.
Pauly, J. J. (2014). The New Journalism and the Struggle for Interpretation. *Journalism, 15*(5), 589–604.
Pedelty, M. (1995). *War Stories: The Culture of Foreign Correspondents*. London: Routledge.
Peters, C. (2011). Emotion Aside or Emotional Side? Crafting an 'Experience of Involvement' in the News. *Journalism, 12*(3), 297–316.
Rayner, T. (2001). Biopower and Technology: Foucault and Heidegger's Way of Thinking. *Contretemps, 2*, 142–156.
Reinardy, S. (2011). Newspaper Journalism in Crisis: Burnout on the Rise, Eroding Young Journalists' Career Commitment. *Journalism, 12*(1), 33–50.
Richards, B., & Rees, G. (2011). The Management of Emotion in British Journalism. *Media, Culture and Society, 33*(6), 851–867.
Ruigrok, N. (2008). Journalism of Attachment and Objectivity: Dutch Journalists and the Bosnian War. *Media, War & Conflict, 1*(3), 293–313.
Scheper-Hughes, N., & Lock, M. (1987). The Mindful Body: A Prolegomenon to Future Work in Medical Anthropology. *Medical Anthropology Quarterly, 1*(1), 6–41.
Sellars, J. (2006). *Stoicism*. London: Routledge.
Skovsgaard, M., et al. (2013). A Reality Check: How Journalists' Role Perceptions Impact Their Implementation of the Objectivity Norm. *Journalism, 14*(1), 22–42.

Sloterdijk, P. (1987). *Critique of Cynical Reason*. Minneapolis: University of Minnesota Press.
Steensen, S. (2017). Subjectivity as a Journalistic Ideal. In B. Kjos Fonn et al. (Eds.), *Putting a Face on It: Individual Exposure and Subjectivity in Journalism* (pp. 25–47). Oslo: Cappelen Damm Akademisk.
Thoits, P. A. (1989). The Sociology of Emotions. *Annual Review of Sociology*, 15, 317–342.
Tumber, H. (2011). Reporting Under Fire: The Physical Safety and Emotional Welfare of Journalists. In B. Zelizer & S. Allan (Eds.), *Journalism After September 11* (2nd ed., pp. 319–334). London: Routledge.
Urbániková, M. (2015). *Českí študenti žurnalistiky v medzinárodnej perspektíve: hodnoty a postoje nastupujúcej žurnalistickej generácie*. PhD Thesis, Masaryk University, Czech Republic.
Usher, N. (2019). Journalism's Biggest Challenge? Journalists. *Journalism*, 20(1), 140–143.
Väliaho, P. (2014). *Biopolitical Screens: Image, Power and the Neoliberal Brain*. Cambridge: The MIT Press.
Van Der Meer, TGLA. et al. (2016). Disrupting Gatekeeping Practices: Journalists' Source Selection in Times of Crisis. *Journalism*. Epub ahead of print 16 May 2016. https://doi.org/10.1177/1464884916648095.
Van Loon, J. (2002). *Risk and Technological Culture: Towards a Sociology of Virulence*. London: Routledge.
Vincze, H. O. (2014). 'The Crisis' as a Journalistic Frame in Romanian News Media. *European Journal of Communication*, 29(5), 567–582.
Wagner, P. (1994). *A Sociology of Modernity: Liberty and Discipline*. London: Routledge.
Williams, R. (1974). *Television: Technology and Cultural Form*. London: Fontana.
Zelizer, B., & Allan, S. (Eds.). (2011). *Journalism After September 11* (2nd ed.). London: Routledge.

Open Access This chapter is licensed under the terms of the Creative Commons Attribution 4.0 International License (http://creativecommons.org/licenses/by/4.0/), which permits use, sharing, adaptation, distribution and reproduction in any medium or format, as long as you give appropriate credit to the original author(s) and the source, provide a link to the Creative Commons licence and indicate if changes were made.

The images or other third party material in this chapter are included in the chapter's Creative Commons licence, unless indicated otherwise in a credit line to the material. If material is not included in the chapter's Creative Commons licence and your intended use is not permitted by statutory regulation or exceeds the permitted use, you will need to obtain permission directly from the copyright holder.

CHAPTER 6

Creative Nonfiction and the Research Method

CREATIVE NONFICTION

This is a research monograph which takes the form of a novel. This novel is filled with ethnographic data reconstructed in accordance with social-scientific research principles.

The method of writing which brings together empirical material and fiction has been named "creative nonfiction" (Caulley 2008). It grew of "the new journalism" (see Pauly 2014) that emerged in the 1960s and 1970s. Other authors claim that the methods of "experimental writing" emerged from feminist and postmodernist criticisms of earlier qualitative research reporting as "deliberate attempts to reposition the author and the reader" (Ezzy 2002: 151). Be that as it may, the principle of creative nonfiction resides in combining the most reliable information with an imaginative and narrative approach.

The model has spread in reporting qualitative research, particularly since the 1990s among those who wanted to exercise the sociological imagination in a vivid yet empirically grounded way. As argued by major literary theorists (e.g. Genette 1990; Schaeffer 2014), there are numerous borrowings, exchanges, and intersections between fictional and factual narratives:

> If one took into consideration actual practice, one would have to admit that there exists neither pure fiction nor history so rigorous as to abstain from all 'plotting' and all novelistic devices whatsoever, and therefore that the two domains are neither so far apart nor so homogeneous as they might appear. (Genette 1990: 772)

© The Author(s) 2019
J. Kotišová, *Crisis Reporters, Emotions, and Technology*,
https://doi.org/10.1007/978-3-030-21428-9_6

Within the realms of sociology and anthropology, intimate links between the disciplines and literature and the enriching potential of artistic inspiration have been recognized, for example, by Zygmunt Bauman and Clifford Geertz:

> we have to come as close as the true poets do to the yet-hidden human possibilities; and for that reason we must need to crush the walls of the obvious and self-evident, of that prevailing ideological fashion of the day whose commonality is taken for the proof of its sense. Demolishing such walls is as much the sociologist's as it is the poet's calling, and for the same reason: they lie about human potential while barring the disclosure of their own bluff. (Bauman 2000: 79–80)

> It is not clear just what 'faction,' imaginative writing about real people in real places at real times, exactly comes to beyond a clever coinage, but anthropology is going to have to find out if it is to continue as an intellectual force in contemporary culture—if its mule condition (trumpeted scientific mother's brother, disowned literary father) is not to lead to mule sterility. (Geertz 1988: 141)

According to Douglas Ezzy, utilization of the links between fiction and fact "does not lead to relativist scepticism but to a more sophisticated approach to social research" (Ezzy 2002: 149). Such "a science that is aesthetic, moral, ethical, moving, rich, and metaphoric as well as avant-garde, transgressing, and multivocal" (Richardson 1997: 16; quoted in Ezzy 2002: 149), however, poses some challenges both to the author and to the reader.

In particular, the research monograph taking the form of a novel based on ethnographic data combines factual and fictional narrative: "[F]actual narrative and fictional narrative behave differently towards the story which they 'report' by the mere fact of this story's (supposedly) being in one case 'truthful' (as Lucian put it), in the other case fictional, that is, invented by someone. ... What counts here is the official status of the text and its reading horizon" (Genette 1990: 756–757). Using terms borrowed from literary theory, the discourse of the book combines fictional and factual parts of a plot (that, if taken chronologically, would be quite clearly divided by the first few lines of "An Introduction to Crisis Reporting: Setting Out": James' recollections are usually real, while his present situation is fictitious) (Culler 1997). The combination of fact and fiction in one discourse thus makes it complicated to determine the "reading horizon."

What follows therefore can be read as a guide for the reader who is uncertain about the reading horizon.

The Factual in the Fictional in the Factual Narrative

On the one hand, if we consider only the ethnographic data and the reality of the research monograph (i.e. leaving aside James' own story), the narrative is factual. One thing that distinguishes factual and fictional narratives is the relationship between the author, narrator, and character (Genette 1990). In the research monograph, the author is identical to the narrator (me), while the main character is someone else (James):

$$\text{Author} = \text{narrator} \neq \text{character}$$

This is to say that I, as the author, seriously adhere to the story, for which I assume responsibility (Genette 1990). It is precisely this unity of author and narrator that defines factual narrative; "this is so whatever the tone, truthful or otherwise, of the syuzhet or, if you prefer, whatever the status, fictional or otherwise, of the fabula" (Genette 1990: 766–767).

Furthermore, the journalists' (again, leaving aside James and Sophie Schlesinger) stories are referential and advance claims of referential truthfulness (Schaeffer 2014). Regardless of its creativity, even creative nonfiction can and must remain true to the validity and integrity of the information it contains. (In principle, one could even insist that thorough anonymization does not deform reality less than adding an explicitly fictional character; see Gutkind 1997.) "For the qualitative researcher writing creative nonfiction, the result is only as rigorous as the rigor of the research and the data on which the writing is based" (Caulley 2008: 445).

In this sense, this book is a kind of "historical narrative" (Genette 1990). The factual plane of the work consists of the factuality of, first, the research monograph written by a researcher adhering to principles of ethnographic research, and, second, the ethnographic data reconstructed in the way explained below.

On the other hand, between the ethnographic data and the reality of the research monograph, there is the imaginary story of James who, while enacting his own story, tells/recalls the story of his colleagues based on their own narratives:

$$\text{Author} \neq \text{narrator} \neq \text{character}$$

The presence of a metadiegetic narrative—a secondary narrative, or a story told, dreamt, or imagined by a character—is a plausible indication of fictionality. In this sense, the narrative is a "heterodiegetic fiction" (Genette 1990). The fictional plane is delimited by the story of James, Fred, Sophie Schlesinger, the flight attendants, the other passengers, the catastrophe, San Lorenzo, and ice-nine (which does not mean, of course, that the characters and the scene do not have any model in reality; quite the opposite—see later in this chapter).

While we tend to define factual and fictional narratives as a pair of opposites, their pure forms are only to be found in a test tube, so that one cannot set one in opposition to the other (Genette 1990; Schaeffer 2014; see above). This, of course, means neither suggesting that fact itself is a mode of fiction, as some have done, nor ruling out ontological realism. The fact that discourse and narrative are constructions does not necessarily mean that fact is fiction or the constructed nature of narratives does not make them fictional (Schaeffer 2014).

Where the Fictional Narrative Is Not an End in Itself

Consequently, while the distinction between facts, lies, half-truths, and inventions matters, the fictional and factual genres are permeable, and this book—its argument and conclusions as presented in the "Emotions, Technology, and Crisis Reconsidered: Ending"—attempts to profit precisely from the intersections of the factual and fictional narratives. There are various types of intersections: mainly those that happen in James' head and those that happen in the story—at the airport or in the airplane. Taken together, they have five main functions: illustrative, allegorical, organizing, effective, and self-reflexive. The following subsections present examples of the intersections and arguments why these intersections are functional—and thus why the fictional narrative is *not* an end in itself.

Illustrative: Form Is Content
What used to be called content and form/expression/representational scheme has been recognized as entwined (see Rorty 1979). What would once have been called the "form" of the book bears some of its arguments in two respects.

First, the data illustrate that the traditional journalistic objectivity-as-a-norm (Carpentier and Trioen 2010), including the commitment to detachment, neutrality, and impartiality (Deuze 2005), is neither feasible nor desirable. Likewise, the nature of the form challenges the established traditional positivist-realist approach to objectivity, which "argues that research reports should present objective facts, established by scientific methodology, and that values should be left out of the report" (Ezzy 2002: 148). The kind of writing employed in this book, as an "emergent method," questions such an understanding of research accounts and explores the borders of knowledge (Hesse-Biber and Leavy 2008: 12).

The particular tactic of unifying the form and content is based on the assumption that there are some parallels between social-scientific and journalistic norms; for example, both journalists and academics think objectivity is attainable and desirable (although each of the groups defines it slightly differently; Post 2015). By writing in both fictional and factual genres, I attempt to stress that journalism, like science, cannot and need not mirror hard facts in an objective, non-committed, detached, factual, neutral, impartial manner. Journalism, like science, necessarily involves subjectivity, commitment, emotional engagement, values, and preconceptions. As Sam would say, journalists have to stick to the facts, and/but as Franks would say, emotion is one of the facts. Clifford Geertz and Gérard Genette would talk in a similar manner about science:

> The pretense of looking at the world directly, as though through a one-way screen, seeing others as they really are when only God is looking, is indeed quite widespread. But that is itself a rhetorical strategy, a mode of persuasion. (Geertz 1988: 141)

> this 'objective' kind of narrative seems to me as typically fictional as the other 'subjective' kind, and together these two symmetrical forms of focalization characterize fictional narrative, as opposed to the ordinary attitude of factual narrative, ... 'omniscient' narrative is even less verisimilar than the other two types, logically speaking. (Genette 1990: 762–763)

Thus, by adding the fictional level, I attempt to emphasize that the detached, aperspectival notion of objectivity is not plausible and disturb the notion in practice by stressing an individual perspective (that of James). Journalists, like scientists, necessarily speak from a certain perspective (which should not lead us astray into ontological relativism; Fay 1996).

Second, the form is the content by *illustrating* the account reconstructed based on the ethnographic data. In other words, the fictional narrative serves as an allegory of the real journalists' emotional development under crisis circumstances. This function deserves to be further expanded upon and explained.

Allegorical: Thicker Than Thick
The whole fictional narrative is an allegory consisting of several metaphors[1]: for example, the catastrophe at San Lorenzo, ice-nine, freezing, James, and the journey. The time has come to take the metaphors down. To explain them bluntly:

- The fictional narrative alludes to Kurt Vonnegut's dystopic novel *Cat's Cradle*, first published in 1963 (Vonnegut 2011).
- As in *Cat's Cradle*, San Lorenzo refers to a fictional Caribbean island; the ice-nine, developed by the Manhattan Project, stands for a solid structure of water that, when contacting liquid water, turns its molecules into molecules of ice-nine (the ice-nine kills instantly when brought into contact with soft tissues); the catastrophe then expands globally by freezing the world's oceans, which Vonnegut uses as a plot device.
- The process of freezing is a metaphor of one of the ideal-typical emotional developments of journalists, the process of becoming cynical.
- The development itself is represented by the metaphor of a journey—namely, the flight.

As a whole, James' journey, his mental states, starting with not-so-unpleasant excitement, shivers, curiosity, and pop-up personal memories, and ending with the hectic drafting of a report, immersion in technological details, and working on suppression of his physiological needs, his goal—arriving at a frozen island hit by the worst of crises—his admiration for his role model, and so on, all together form an allegory of the interviewees' retrospective reconstructions of their emotional development. (The soundness of the allegory was "validated" by Sven, who, after reading James' story, said that 20 years ago he was exactly like James, and

---

[1] The difference between the two poetic devices being that while metaphor is a single figure of speech that translates meaning between two particular things, suggesting their non-literal similarity, allegory is extensive and coherent and works at the level of the whole story or text (Mirvaldová 1972).

started to recall specific moments: e.g. traveling by car across Kosovo with other journalists reporting on the Kosovo War.)

There are many less substantial and partial metaphors, as well. In particular, what happens in the fictional story is very often a metaphor of developments of the factual study. Let me cite an example:

> He heard the robotic flight attendant's voice emanating from speakers, and took off his headphones. "... and the number is constantly growing," she just said, most probably informing the passengers of the latest developments at San Lorenzo. The audience reacted by deafening silence. The voice was waiting for questions. No questions were coming. Was it anxiety, or apathy (Van Loon 2002)? Probably both, James thought. It took less than half of a second, and the same flight attendant suddenly emerged from behind, imperceptibly singing a joyful tune with a hint of melancholy and striding towards the nose. Someone cut through the silence with a question. James rather aimed his attention back to the technologies.

This unfolds when the data illustrate the magical, surreal character of crisis reporters' experience (shaped, among other things, by technology), particularly the multiplication of their selves (i.e. the fact that they simultaneously exist physically and on screens, here and there, in Europe and in conflict zones). Similarly, the flight attendant's voice is still waiting for passengers' questions while her body marches around. Furthermore, the piece of text implicitly reflects upon the possible dealing with existential questions and ontological insecurity triggered by the sense of the surreal. The metaphor thus enables me to suggest the unspoken and to address diverse issues in one single image.

The fictional part of the narrative thus allows me to allegorically express complex meanings, tensions, and alternate viewpoints. As Milan Kundera (1988) wrote in *The Art of the Novel*, complexity is the novel's spirit; the novel says to the readers that things are more complex than the readers think they are. In addition, it "offers a method for following and actively pursuing our 'hunches' in order to see where they take us" (Hesse-Biber and Leavy 2008: 4–5).

Who Is James?

In this context, the metaphor of James holds a special position. On the one hand—and most of all—he is an ideal-typical figure and his personality traits are borrowed from the real-world interviewees, although his character is rather a personification of a subset of the interviewees' younger, less experienced, child-free selves (see Sven's reaction to James above). He is an idealist—his criticism and his insistence on certain principles echo some of the reporters' thoughts. At the same time, he cannot deny that the catastrophe, together with the mythic haze of crisis reporting, arouses him. Consider the following excerpt:

> Going to San Lorenzo, he said to himself aloud. It immediately occurred to him that he must have seemed ridiculous to the young woman that was still two steps behind him. Everyone here was going either to San Lorenzo, or to one of the neighbouring islands that were expected to be contaminated by the ice-nine very soon—long before their arrival. For a second, the nervousness he experienced was bodily again. He shivered, felt the urge to erupt into laughter, and jump, pull a face or cry.

Only after James had "wised up" to the not-so-exceptional nature of his experience was he able to suppress his bodily movements and uncontrolled manifestations of nervousness. Thus, the excerpt also illustrates the normalization of crisis (Pedelty 1995). Later, he would get tougher, like the interviewees did, especially if he were to have children:

> The birth of my first child was an absolutely essential moment that formed me as a journalist. Because it, at the best moment, kicked my ass and shot me down from the … bumptious journalistic cynicism of a young journalistic nitwit. (Vítek)

This makes James' initial mind-set and the way he comes out a metaphor for the typical path journalists follow during the emotional development and a core of the allegory as a whole.

Moreover, James' gendered experience and minimalist, unpromising love life points the way toward telling a typical personal story about the interviewees, whose work, gender, need for independence, ways of being in a relationship and family life often significantly interfered with each other. The reporters' stories were sometimes too intimate and/or unrelated to the main research questions to be included in the main research storyline but seemed tightly interwoven with and important for understanding the crisis reporters' emotional culture; therefore, I decided to burden James with them.

On the other hand, James' character concerns the focalization of the narrative, that is, the questions of who sees and who speaks (Culler 1997). While James is not identical to the author and the narrator, he is a bearer of the data: his thoughts and memories present my own thoughts, field notes, and excerpts from interviews. In other words, I follow James' recollections and construct a story based on and in dialogue with his previous experience; thus, with James we share the point of view from which a story is being told, and the fictional and the factual narratives meet in these (his/mine) collected memories (i.e. in the empirical material). The fictionality is delimited by the author's—my—direct access to James' consciousness (Genette 1990), while the factuality resides in the identity of the author and narrator and in the realness of the interviewees.

In addition, James' figure allows the expression of more than only my own position. For instance, his harshness and mockery illustrate the intellectual posture of a classical kynic (Navia 1996), so they relate to the illustrative function of the factional narrative.

Organizing: Meaningful Complexity
The fictional level of James' journey has also an organizing function. While the metaphor(s) I use allow the expression of complex meanings in a dense way, the order of the narrative—its chronology and linearity (Genette 1990)—creates a storyline that is more or less easy to follow. As Ezzy writes,

> The task of writing is to reconstruct this multifaceted, multidimensional ball of information into a linear story with a beginning, middle and end. The written report cuts a single line, or thread, through the complex ball of understanding. The best writing achieves this task of providing a well-written story while retaining a sense of the complexity and nuance suggested by the image of the ball of understanding. (Ezzy 2002: 139)

James' retrospective of his previous experience thus enables me to organize the story of the ethnographic data into a meaningful discourse and impose a linear order on the data and related literature (see Culler 1997). Although a particular order is not, in principle, specific to either fictional or factual narratives (Genette 1990), James' story helps to stress the tale-like character of ethnographic writing (Ezzy 2002) and, through the use of metaphors, retain the sense of complexity.

Effective: Less Boredom, More Engagement
A well-organized narrative is also potentially more reader-friendly. The same applies to using the fictional narrative in general: writing in the style of creative nonfiction makes research reports less boring (Caulley 2008). In particular, realistic details further conjure emotions and images in readers.

In turn, the creative style potentially makes the research accounts more read and those who read them more engaged. According to Asleigh Watson,

> novel writing presents sociologists with a process and medium through which they can expand their work for a more public, engaging, affective, and panoramic sociology. ... Sociological novels work to bring the local and global into dialogue, and may help achieve the scope and panoramic depth that sociology requires. (Watson 2016: 431)

Watson argues that interlocutor engagement and knowledge exchange are some of the key strengths of creative nonfiction. Indeed, when I asked the interviewees to comment on the draft version (see later in this chapter) and pointed out the "experimental" nature of the text, some of them expressed interest in the way it was written that, allegedly, increased their desire to read it. As researchers from the Dart Centre have illustrated, raising awareness of psychosocial risks itself can make a difference:

> Situations in which staff are exposed to unexpected, disturbing content sometimes result from a lack of organisational awareness about the traumatic impact of content in general and/or from shoddy and inappropriate workflows. ... This [has] a more traumatic impact upon them as opposed to when they [are] warned in advance, for example, that they would be viewing a massacre. (Dubberley et al. 2015: 22)

In short, if the journalists are more interested in the research due to the fictional narrative, the word can spread slightly further and better raise awareness of psychosocial risks among journalists and newsroom and media managers. In Bauman's words, the awareness itself and seeing alternatives can be deployed "in the fight against the social sources of all, even the most individual and private, unhappinesses" (Bauman 2000: 89).

Such an aspiration also raises the question of engagement. The research is engaged. With Boltanski (1999; see the section "Moral Dilemmas and Guilt"), I consider it impossible to see journalists' work-related troubles without taking action, if only in the form of committed speech. (This is related to the illustrative function: the book also argues that journalists should not be directly or indirectly asked to sacrifice their humaneness.) Together with Bauman, who writes that "A non-committal sociology is an impossibility" (Bauman 2000: 89), I can see only one way of doing sociology.

6 CREATIVE NONFICTION AND THE RESEARCH METHOD   199

Self-Reflexive: Some Intimate Excerpts
Last but not least, the fictional narrative is infused with moments that have a self-reflexive meaning and function, albeit they often give only a hint that needs to be further explained. Most importantly:

> a. James looked out the window. In the distance, he saw the last passengers of a just-landed flight striding into the airport building. A tall, slim man was leading two little children by the hands. Nostalgia for his father overwhelmed him—his childish sense of humor, silent conspiratorial bursts of laughter, his huge warm, dry, lined palms that he used to put on anthills when James was a little boy; ants would climb up his hands—the swarming astonished James; and his habit of shaking the walnut tree in the garden, so that James could pick up the nuts. It was more than a year since his father passed away.
>
> Losing him led James into an even greater need for independence. And, here he was: ready to make good use of it. Although the pain was still stabbing.

The scene refers to a particular moment when my personal life became directly entangled with the research process. While I was conducting participant observation at *ČT* in December 2015, my own father had a sudden, very serious, life-threatening health problem. He found himself in "crisis"—in the initial meaning of the word—together with the whole family. For several very intense days and long anxious weeks and even months, we did not know if he would survive. The event affected the fieldwork in at least two ways: not only was I unable to work for some time but also asking my interviewees about the meaning of crisis became very hard and painful. At the same time, the situation revealed the humaneness and empathy of some of the research participants and inevitably and irretrievably changed my researcher's image. For example, I remember calling Čestmír, crying, telling him about my father, canceling an interview, and postponing the field work. After I became able to work again, he was very helpful and our interaction became more personal.

> b. While putting his worn carry-on suitcase into overhead storage, James saw her face. The young woman who had always been two steps behind him was now sitting right in front of him. No doubt it was her. Sophie Schlesinger, the crisis reporter. He saw her yesterday on TV while watching the first flashes on the San Lorenzo catastrophe.

(...) She was always equipped with thorough knowledge of the context. Taken together, it gave the impression that she was gifted by some preternatural capabilities.

In fact, it was she who inspired James not only to become a journalist, but, which is crucial, to try to do his best. But most importantly—and this was something that James did not realize—her somewhat moral and responsible approach to the profession was what kept alive James' hope for the existence of some basic values and principles. And now, she was sitting here, toughing it out.

The character of Sophie Schlesinger is modeled on a combination of Sophie Thunus, my colleague at Centre de recherche et d'interventions sociologiques in Liège, a running partner with whom I shared the office, and Eva Šlesingerová, my Czech supervisor. Meetings with both brilliant women strongly impacted my enthusiasm and curiosity, and their general approach to research—very ethical and dutiful—shaped my own ideals.

c. Y was one of those who stayed in James' life even after they were no longer colleagues. They became friends—or something like that. They once went for a beer after work and ended up talking about French poststructuralists, which apparently happened to create an implicit alliance—even before they knew "it" about each other. In the months and years that followed, they used to meet every now and then, holding existentialist conversations (that proved to be even more binding).

This and other mentions of James' "friends" refer to the inseparability of my own personal and professional contexts. Some of the interviewees turned into friends—mainly Sven, but also Matouš, Tobiáš, Ida, and Pavel, and I stayed in contact with many others. Seen from the opposite perspective, I got to the ethnographic sites and gathered contacts to the reporters through unrelated professional and personal networks (although I never "observed" my previously existing friends; see more on the access to the media organizations below). While friendship in ethnographic enquiry can cause confusion of roles (Hendry 1992), the friendships entangled with the fieldwork I conducted happened to be rather of benefit to the research. For example, they have allowed me to discuss the findings and exchange interpretations and ideas with practical experts in the field.

The following section deals with self-reflection in a more systematic way. For one more story—this time fully factual—needs to be told.

The Research Method

Establishing the Field

This research monograph is based on my Ph.D. research that started in 2014. In early spring 2015, I changed my supervisor and was rethinking the initial research project on media and anomie. The new supervisor, or "consultant," suggested that I could simply go to a newsroom for a few weeks and see what to focus on.

I did so, opportunistically using my previous professional networks as sources for research ideas and data (Riemer 1977). I used to work for *Czech Television* (not in reporting but as PR support for a small unit producing documentaries and experimental TV shows), so I contacted a former colleague, who redirected me further to his superiors. They granted me access to the newsroom of the *Czech TV* web news service.

Czech TV (Česká televize; *ČT*) is a Czech public service broadcaster running six channels, including a 24/7 news channel, and an online news service. It was created in 1992 from its Czechoslovak antecedent and operates in Prague, Brno, Ostrava, and all regions of the country. In the Prague headquarters where I conducted the fieldwork, there are a number of specialized newsrooms. Being funded mainly by television fees (set by an Act of Parliament), it has roughly a 7 billion CZK (roughly 272 million EUR) yearly budget and remains independent of the state budget and the state, although the Czech Television Council that controls the activities of *Czech TV* is elected by the Chamber of Deputies.

The newsroom of the online news service, selected like the other research sites (see below) partly opportunistically, partly based on pragmatic considerations, and partly on the basis of foreshadowed research problems (Hammersley and Atkinson 1995; Riemer 1977), thus became the first site of my ethnographic enquiry. It consisted of about 15 writing journalists (each of them focusing on a certain range of topics), sometimes lacking desks, chairs, computers, screens, and other equipment. It was situated in a high-rise building that forms a part of *ČT* headquarters.

I started to perform what Martyn Hammersley and Paul Atkinson (1995: 1) define liberally as "participating, overtly or covertly, in people's daily lives for an extended period of time, watching what happens, listening to what is said, asking questions," including long-term intellectual, intuitive, physical, emotional, and political immersion (Amit 2000). I used to sit at different spots in the newsroom (depending on the taken desks) and participated in newsmaking. Although the media professionals knew I was a researcher and had been acquainted with the research topic, I was lucky that they treated me like an intern (cf. Czarniawska 2011). They authorized me to prepare online news content and write articles, gave me counsel, and in a few cases even minutely examined my writing attempts.

Embodied in the fieldwork were qualitative interviews ranging from semi-structured to less structured, in-depth, and narrative conversations between a journalist and me in the role of a researcher (Arksey and Knight 1999). During this early research period, I conducted five research interviews and had many smaller talks about making crisis news and using technology.

The data I reconstructed during this early stage of the research were rich and messy, but the phase proved to be essential for constructing the field. As Vered Amit writes,

> the ethnographic field cannot simply exist, awaiting discovery. It has to be laboriously constructed, prised apart from all the other possibilities for contextualization to which its constituent relationships and connections could also be referred. This process of construction is inescapably shaped by the conceptual, professional, financial and relational opportunities and resources accessible to the ethnographer. (Amit 2000: 6)

Indeed, I entered the newsroom with sensitizing preconceptions of "crisis" as an event outside-the-media (Olsson and Nord 2015) and a somewhat vague but rather neo-materialist understanding of "technology." These sensitizing concepts guided my observations and alerted me to some important situations (Bowen 2006). Most importantly, their initial understanding helped me to construct an ever-changing interview guide (Arksey and Knight 1999). However, the sensitizing concepts and the research problem were to be improved and refined, as their survival depended on the data (Bowen 2006). As Hammersley and Atkinson write,

> the nature of the setting may still shape the development of the research questions. This arises because … in ethnographic research the development of research problems is rarely completed before fieldwork begins; indeed, the collection of primary data often plays a key role in that process of development. (Hammersley and Atkinson 1995: 37)

Eventually, while both concepts, "crisis" and "technology," provided a good starting point for building analysis, they survived in a thoroughly redefined way (see the "Ending"). I left the newsroom with a more

Foucauldian understanding of technology, taking into consideration circulating power (Foucault 1988) and a confused view of crisis.

But most importantly, analysis of the early data gave rise to emotions as a third conceptual axis of the research. I was taken by surprise by the blackness of the journalists' humor and by the eagerness the research participants showed when something, no matter how negative, happened. As Viktor said, "Things like floods, I terribly enjoy them. Finally, something is going on! Floods are journalistic Olympics." These contrasting, up-and-down emotional fits seemed significant, theoretically, practically, morally, methodologically resonating (see Tracy 2010), and fascinating.

Thus, the initial phase enabled me to clearly delimit the research problem: technological shaping of journalists' emotional experience in crisis situations. I wanted to know:

1. What does "crisis" in "crisis reporting" mean?

The journalists' experiences and perspectives were primary here: it seemed that by living inside-the-media rather than with the media (Deuze 2011), they also lived inside crises and inside the logic of organizational and psychological needs of crisis moments outside-the-media (Olsson and Nord 2015). Many of them also bore the weight of the immediate crisis of modernity/risk society (Wagner 1994; Beck 1992; Giddens 1991), as they were constantly being reminded of the possibility of mass death and destruction. It seemed that this kind of life and need was crucial for their emotional experience and development.

2. What is crisis reporters' emotional experience?

The experience of life inside a milieu delimited by so many levels of crisis-ness needed to be further explored and described. Thus, I posed the question, what were the journalists' immediate emotional responses and where did they lead in the journalists' own sensemaking, long-term perspective (Weick 1995)?

3. How does technology articulate journalists' emotional experience of crisis?

It was clear from the early data that the journalists' emotional development was influenced not only by the ubiquity of crisis but also by the logic of newsmaking and the journalistic job in general: by routines and devices, work with words and images, existing journalistic norms and organizational practices, and the ways in which the journalists worked on their selves accordingly (Foucault 1988). This made it possible to study their emotional experience as emotional labor (Hochschild 1983).

The core of the interview guide thus revolved around the three concepts (Arksey and Knight 1999); nevertheless, I always adjusted some of the questions based on each individual's specific typical tasks (e.g. regions she covered) and particularities of experience (e.g. an emotionally powerful, life-threatening situation, or reporting on a crisis close to home). Likewise, the observations gradually became more focused. Narrowing the research aim on the way and specifying the interview guide and things to pay attention to during participant observation after entering the first newsroom proved to be vital for meaningful coherence of the study (Tracy 2010). Such "a continuous movement between pre-existing interpretive frameworks, both theoretical and popular, and the data of observation, collected during both intentional observation and everyday life" (Ezzy 2002: 25) then characterized the whole research process.

Immersion in the Research Problem

After spending the first few weeks in the newsroom of the online news service, I knew it would be valuable to come closer to reporters with more hands-on experience. The contacts I had made in the high-rise building helped. I wrote a formal e-mail to the head of news, asking for access to the core *ČT* newsrooms and simultaneously applied for a job with a team of beginning reporters. In two weeks, I received a phone call from the team and permission to start my fieldwork among the novices in November 2015. However, two days after the fieldwork started, I arranged a meeting with the head of the foreign affairs desk and was allowed to sit in the control room next to the primetime news anchors and experienced media professionals working on foreign affairs news. I spent with the (about 20) foreign affairs reporters two almost full-time months (although the incident with my father somewhat shortened the actual period of time). Since I lacked the necessary skills to make reportage, I observed without participating in the newsmaking practices (Hammersley and Atkinson 1995; cf. Czarniawska 2011) but with participating in some meetings (of both the foreign affairs desk and the news in general) and informal moments (coffee and smoking breaks).

6 CREATIVE NONFICTION AND THE RESEARCH METHOD

The fieldwork overlapped with several crisis moments and states: most importantly, the terrorist attacks in Paris in November 2015, the so-called refugee crisis, and the shooting down of a Russian jet fighter by the Turkish army (with unpredictable consequences). These tragic events made me a direct, real-time witness of the journalists' practices of crisis reporting and the newsroom rush, which made the research process opportunistic in yet another sense (Riemer 1977).

I also conducted ten interviews with foreign news reporters, including flying or parachute reporters (Cottle 2009) and foreign correspondents. I sought to interview primarily journalists, reporters, and foreign correspondents who had extensive direct experience with crisis reporting. It was here that the category of "crisis reporter" emerged. The label denotes simply "journalists involved in crisis reporting" (Neumann and Fahmy, 2016: 227) and defines the journalists by what they do without claiming that "crisis reporter" is a pre-established sort of person (Latour 2005) or a standardized professional segment. However, some of the journalists bore traits of Mark Pedelty's "war correspondents": cool renegades living an adventurous, independent, brave life (Pedelty 1995: see pages 24 and from 29 on).

Additionally, I traced everything else that seemed to be important and accessible. Occasionally, I took photos of the site, read relevant documents, such as legal acts and internal guidelines for crisis reporting, and followed the social media accounts of some of the interviewees and other research participants. I also read their stories online and watched their reports on TV (although I did not conduct analysis of media content, as analysis of media representations would not address the research questions).

In late January 2016, not long after the fieldwork in the ČT's control room, I left for Liège, where I planned to conduct interviews.

My ethnographic study was becoming more and more multi-sited, approaching the research problem rather as a European or global phenomenon than as a locally bounded problem. George Marcus explains:

> multi-sited ethnography is an exercise in mapping terrain, its goal is not holistic representation, an ethnographic portrayal of the world system as a totality. Rather, it claims that any ethnography of a cultural formation in the world system is also an ethnography of the system, and therefore cannot be understood only in terms of the conventional single-site mise-en-scene of ethnographic research. ... For ethnographers interested in contemporary local changes in culture and society, single-sited research can no longer be easily located in a world system perspective. (Marcus 1995: 98–99)

This is the case of crisis reporting and the media in general, which is why media studies has become an important arena where this approach has emerged (Marcus 1995). As has been illustrated, the distinctions between global and local, social and individual, here and there, are untenable in crisis reporting. Also the journalists, often traveling or staying abroad, themselves saw their frame of reference rather in the professional ecosystem than in their media organization or nation-state. The multi-sited and multilingual approach to ethnography was thus more suitable than conventional single-sited research.

This particular form of multi-sited ethnography also excluded methodological nationalism (Beck 2007), which equates societies with nation-states and sees them as cornerstones of sociological analysis. Such a methodological habit becomes less appropriate vis-à-vis the cosmopolitan condition, related to, for example, global risks that connect actors across borders. Beck even imagines that

> a cosmopolitan mixture in global sociology could give birth to a cosmopolitan vision for the humanities [that] has a strong standing against the retrogressive idealism of the national perspective in politics, research and theory. (Beck 2007: 289–290)

Following this critique of methodological nationalism, I did not compare between nation-states and national media or journalists *systematically*. Comparison based on nation-state borders is included only in cases where history makes the borders significant for understanding the research problem. Such a selectivity is, I believe, legitimate not only for the sake of methodological cosmopolitanism but also because multi-sited ethnography is marked by inevitable asymmetry in quantity and intensity of data reconstructed by varied fieldwork practices employed at the individual sites (Marcus 1995).

In Belgium, I conducted ten interviews (eight from March 2016 to June 2016, two additional in July 2017) with both Flemish and Walloon journalists from *VRT* (the Flemish public service broadcaster), *De Morgen* (a Flemish progressive newspaper; *DM*), and *Le Soir* (the largest Walloon newspaper; *LS*). Any systematic sampling proved to be impossible; I was not able to make random journalists reply to my requests for an interview, so I initially used my previous personal and professional networks and then continued with purposeful snowball sampling. While the only rationale for snowball sampling is ease or convenience (Ezzy 2002), I eventually happened to interview some of the most prominent and experienced Belgian conflict reporters.

The first interview took place on March 15. A week after that, on the morning of 22 March 2016, three coordinated suicide bombings occurred in Brussels: two at Zaventem Airport and one in central Brussels at the Maalbeek metro station. Thirty-two civilians and three perpetrators were killed, and more than 300 people were injured. The bombings, plotted by a Salafi jihadist militant group known as Daesh or ISIL, constituted the deadliest act of terrorism in Belgium's history.

Even if some Brusselians might have anticipated the atrocities, given that the perpetrators belonged to a terror cell which had been involved in the November 2015 Paris attacks, their first-hand experience deeply shook the city and other parts of Belgium. Many people grieved—the Belgian government declared three days of national mourning—and faced the paralysis of the country's infrastructure. For the first time in their lives, those Belgian reporters who commonly travel to conflict zones and disaster sites were suddenly tasked with reporting on a "combat zone event" that was occurring at the place where they, and their families and friends, lived. The traditional commitment to detachment, impartiality, fairness, and professional distance, concepts used by journalists and academics to revisit and re-legitimize objectivity (Deuze 2005), was challenged. It was no longer possible to be a fly on the wall; the journalists' subjective experiences as witnesses, actors, and even indirect victims merged with their professional tasks (cf. Van Zoonen 1998). Thus—besides preventing me from traveling to Prague to my grandfather's funeral—the tragedy induced me to redesign the interview guide and to pay more attention to journalistic professional ideology and to the journalists' sense of the surreal. The subsequent media hype also led to postponing the interviews, since the journalists were busier than in normal times (McDonald and Lawrence, 2004). We all lived and worked inside the crisis, all the more so that our occupation was concerned with the issue.

By then, the answer to the question about what was social about emotions already seemed clear (see the "Ending"). Diverse pieces of sociological and anthropological research and theory long ago proved that emotions do not belong exclusively to the domain of psychology but are a relevant and researchable theme within sociology and anthropology (e.g. Beatty 2013; Hochschild 1983; Illouz 2007; Lutz and Abu-Lughod 1990; Rosaldo 1984; Scheper-Hughes and Lock 1987), whether concerned with organizations and institutional power structures or the human body and biopower. However, a new question kept arising: how to study emotions? The levels of emotions that sociologists and anthropologists deal with range from emotions expressed in face-to-face bodily and verbal communication to elicitations of unacknowledged individual and collective emotions that play a role in various encounters, from emotions triggered during research interviews to responses to a questionnaire. Emotions can be elicited from written and oral narratives, interviews, observations and participation, emotionally charged visuals, documents, or surveys (Flam and Kleres 2015).

Referring to Arlie Hochschild, Helena Flam (2015) states that it is neither possible nor necessary to make a clear distinction between "authentic" and "surface" emotions. She positions current emotional research in sociology between the purely dramaturgical/ethnomethodological (Garfinkel 1967; Goffman 1967) and psychoanalytical/biologizing/universalistic (e.g. Ekman 1999). As Flam notes, "centuries-long emotions management made it impossible to posit any clear-cut difference between 'authentic,' subjective feelings, and the prescribed" (Flam 2015: 5). Apparently, studying the gap between feelings and displays—the widening of the gap by a specific context and conditions or its intentional elaboration and narrowing, that is, reductions in emotional dissonance, problematizing emotional management, and labor—can reveal much about such major sociological themes as power relations (see Hochschild 1983; Illouz 2007). Yet the basic assumption of emotion-related research remains that "for the most part the observed emotional expressions correspond to specific inner emotional states" (Flam 2015: 8).

This study adopts the shared assumption. By, first, treating verbal and non-verbal expressions as emotion data and, second, taking into account circulating and shared emotions, it fits in between what Flam calls the unorthodox positivist-expressionist dramaturgical approach and the interactionist dramaturgical approach.

Yiannis Gabriel and Eda Ulus (2015) illustrate three different ways of expressing emotions: a person (1) declares that she feels a certain way, (2) acts in a certain way, or (3) tells a story which gives clues about how she may feel. Whether to approach emotions through interviews, that is, as narratives and retrospective sensemaking accounts, or via observations, that is, as bodily practices, is one of the most important and general dilemmas in emotion-related research designs. Although some researchers argue for the latter, reflecting a somewhat Bourdieuian perspective on emotions (Scheer 2012), the narrative approach seems to dominate (see Flam and Kleres 2015). For example, Barbara Czarniawska "plead[s] for studies of the 'rhetoric of emotions,' because this is all there is and this is what needs to be known—i.e. how people speak about their own and others' emotions in different times and places" (Czarniawska 2015: 68). I decided to take the two perspectives as complementary and to combine them within a more comprehensive epistemological framework consisting in observing emotions that the actors explicitly or implicitly express or attribute to each other (Flam 2015).

On one hand, the emotional narratives allowed me to see the reporters' views of their emotional development and past experience. It follows from the research questions that I was interested not only in the immediate emotional practices of crisis reporting and their plugging into the complex of other types of news-production technology but also in a longer biographical process of adjustment to the media life. This process of widening the disruption between feelings and displays by the specific work, working context and conditions, its elaborating and narrowing—that is, managing emotions and performing emotional labor (Hochschild 1983; Illouz 2007) could not be studied without taking a diachronic (retrospective) perspective enabled by interviewing/recalling.

Interviewing the journalists did not give me direct access to their consciousness, but rather to how they made sense of their work-related, technologically co-shaped emotional experience. According to Karl Weick (1995, from p. 17 on), sensemaking is a retrospective, social, ongoing process grounded in identity construction. It is a process enactive of sensible environments, focused on and by extracted clues, and driven by plausibility rather than accuracy. Sensemaking, aptly expressed by the sentence "How can I know what I think, until I see, what I say?" (Weick 1995: 18), means continual redefinition of the puzzle of the sensemaker's self, based on past events:

> experience as we know it exists in the form of distinct events. But the only way we get this impression is by stepping outside the stream of experience and directing attention to it. And it is only possible to direct attention to what exists, that is, what has already passed. (Weick 1995: 25)

Furthermore, as sensemaking is social and enactive of environments, making sense of one's experience is also closely linked to an organization's image. The process thus brings together technologies of the self (Foucault 1988) and the construction of organizational/professional identity (Du Gay 1996), including the reconstruction of the self-myth of "crisis reporter" (Pedelty 1995). By narrating their emotional experience of crisis reporting, the journalists not only made sense of it but also constructed their organizational/professional identities and rendered sensible both their experience and their identities.

On the other hand, observing emotions meant living through the crises together with the reporters, seeing their reactions and indications of their feelings. Here, the practice of "emotional participation" (Bergman-Blix 2015; Wettergren 2015) was very helpful. Emotional participation, that is, critical emotional engagement in the field, enables the researcher's own emotions to be used as both methodological and analytical tools. First, becoming engaged in the emotions that the observed people feel enables the researcher to blend in with the site. Second, the discrepancy between the field participants' habitual emotions and the visiting researcher's nonhabitual emotions serves as an analytical clue. Making use of our own research-related emotions, after all, may appear to be the most open and ethical way of dealing with them. As Benno Gammerl (2015: 153) states, "If emotion is inseparable from cognition, then the researcher's feelings cannot be disconnected from the analytical process." All the more so that the interpretation of emotions depends largely on lay knowledge, only as it plays out against theory and expert knowledge.

In practice, my own non-habitual feelings of surprise and sympathy (see earlier in this chapter) helped me to specify the research problem. Experiencing the same emotionally charged situations as the research participants (particularly the terror attacks in Brussels) allowed me to better understand their frames of mind. Later, being nervous about newsroom deadlines and exhausted by late working hours (see later in this chapter) gave me the opportunity to experience similar bodily feelings as the research participants. Above all, talking about the emotional difficulties, perceived by many of the interviewees as intimate, would have been impossible without some level of closeness and trust.

Being more and more immersed in the field, I became aware of diverse axes of variability of the data. Besides the histories of the national media systems, the journalists' experience depended on media types (TV vs. radio vs. online news), legal status (commercial vs. public service media), types of crises, gender, age, ethnicity,[2] duration of journalistic experience, and so on. Apart from the job, the only thing all the research participants had in common was European nationality. In this sense, the study is Eurocentric and does not take into account experiences of journalists who are at home in conflict zones. This is caused by the opportunistic design (Riemer 1977) and feasibility of fieldwork.

In June 2016, I returned to Prague for several months. After being denied access to *Hospodářské noviny* (*Economic Newspaper*), I again deployed my personal and professional networks to get access to the foreign affairs desk of *Lidové noviny* (*The People's Newspaper*; *LN*), the oldest Czech printed daily. *LN* forms a part of the media house MAFRA, since 2013 a subsidiary of the Agrofert group, owned by the then Czech Minister of Finance and oligarch Andrej Babiš. While it used to be a prestigious paper due to the number of Czech writers, politicians, and philosophers contributing to the content and its focus on foreign affairs and culture, its reputation has been recently modified by the new ownership. In accordance with the general trend in print news, *LN* circulation has significantly decreased during the past two decades; in 2017, the circulation oscillated around 38,000 copies and 200,000 readers per issue.

At *LN*, I spent two full-time months of participant observation, during which I complied with Ezzy's claim that "Qualitative observation, and data analysis, is best done when the observer becomes part of the dance" (Ezzy 2002: xxi). After the first few days of getting the feel of the newsroom and newswork, the foreign affairs reporters loaded work on me. I was allowed to write articles and put forward topics like the others; I even received press credentials (Image 6.1).

We also used to eat together in surrounding restaurants. Over lunches and coffees, I conducted eight interviews (i.e. I interviewed all the journalists in the foreign affairs department and one investigative journalist who covered the terror attacks in Paris in November 2015). Eventually, I stayed and helped in the newsroom a week longer than I had planned, in order to support the foreign affairs desk after its head left for maternity leave. At the end of the participant observation, they insisted on paying me for some of my articles. I was adamant that I did not want any money. They still insisted, their jokey argument being that I could "milk" the owner the oligarch Andrej Babiš—a bit. So I agreed.

---

[2] I use pseudonyms that reflect the media professionals' gender and ethnicity.

Image 6.1 The author's press credentials issued during the fieldwork in *The People's Newspaper*, Autumn 2016. Picture taken by the author

While at *ČT*, I was taking field notes during the observation, and thus was able to describe the field rather thickly even on the fly, in contrast at *LN* I was busy writing stories, so I made only brief notes during working hours (at both *ČT* and *LN*, I was present from about 9.30 or 9.45 a.m. to 6 p.m., including a few weekends), and always wrote everything down in the evening, at night and on "days off."

After returning to Belgium in October 2016, I occasionally turned into a "special correspondent from Brussels" and wrote (paid) reports from the European Council and the Dutch elections. The people at *LN*, having no permanent correspondent in Belgium, were glad that they could publish a report based on on-the-spot experience; I was glad about staying in the field and even merging with it (some of the events I reported lasted until late evening, and so I got acquainted with the stress and rush before deadlines). It was also a unique opportunity to meet other foreign affairs reporters and discuss my research with them. In addition, I liked the idea of working on EU-related media content, which, I think, is underrated in the Czech media. Anytime I traveled back to Prague, I went for lunch with the "colleagues" from *LN* (most of whom, however, do not work there any more at present). Such a "melding of personal and professional roles in ethnographic fieldwork" makes for an experience "which cannot readily or usefully be compartmentalized from other experiences and periods in our lives" (Amit 2000: 7).

Disentanglement

Taken together, the observations and interviews provided a great amount of rich research material.

All the interviews were recorded; each of the interviewees was given a signed informed consent form, stating that by providing the interview, she agrees with its recording and non-commercial usage. Handing the informed consent forms out rather than having them signed by the interviewees and keeping them for myself seemed to be a much better strategy for trust building, which was vital for talking about intimate experiences. The interviewees were also guaranteed the possibility to withdraw from the research project at any time, and by staying in contact with most of them, the consent has been constantly renegotiated (see Sin 2005). Last but not least, the informed consent guaranteed anonymization of the data. First, I withheld only the interviewees' names but systematically kept their affiliations unconcealed. After I was notified by an interviewee and a reviewer of one of my papers that some people might be recognizable, given that the scope of both the media systems is limited, I decided, in the most sensitive cases, to also withhold the affiliations or to unlink the pseudonyms and media organizations by using letters instead of pseudonyms. The interviews were always transcribed (some of them with a help from a Master's degree student in sociology from Masaryk University).

The analytical process was driven by what Corbin and Strauss (2007) call selective and axial (rather than open) coding. As mentioned above, the data collection and analysis were integrated, allowing the analysis "to be shaped by the participants in a more fundamental way than if analysis is left until after the data collection has been finished" (Ezzy 2002: 61). Anytime I had a new transcript or a file of field notes, I added them to Atlas.ti and coded, which allowed me to constantly refine the focus of the research. At the same time, I began with codes derived from the literature but was constantly comparing them against the actual data and revising them, as I believed that "[c]onducting data analysis during data collection results in a more sophisticated and subtle analysis" (Ezzy 2002: 78). The final set of codes was largely asymmetrical and overlapping.

While the emotions narrated in interviews that are subject to sensemaking (Weick 1995) were easy to code, the coding of witnessed emotions was inspired by Julian Bernard's strategy to subjectively interpret others' conduct, verbal and bodily expressions of what we see as a particular emotion (Bernard 2015).

At some point, I decided the study had reached relative saturation (Ezzy 2002), and the analytical process started again. In the end, I regrouped the data based on the relationships of assigned codes to the meaning of "crisis" in "crisis reporting," the emotional experience, and the four levels of technology, in order to let the research findings tell a story (Corbin and Strauss 2007). A few codes were left out as either too detailed or redundant.

To ensure credibility, to enhance procedural and relational ethics (Tracy 2010), and to make the research practice more democratic (Ezzy 2002), I attempted to include the participants in all the phases of the research process. Starting in February 2017, I occasionally sent drafts of (parts of) the study and related articles to those research participants who had told me they were interested or with whom I was in contact. Several times, I received a valuable comment that led to reinterpretation of the data. Finally, in August 2017, I sent the whole draft version without "Ending" to all the interviewees and suggested they read it, to check the interpretations, to comment on anything in the draft, to propose changes, and, primarily, to propose their own vision of the "Ending." (The question that the interviewees saw at the end of the draft instead of a conclusion was "What should happen with James after landing?"). I asked them to send me any comments in late September 2017.

Some of the interviewees wrote me they were interested in the experimental form. Some found the text readable, and even "enlightening." Some acknowledged its accuracy and stressed points and figures that they found particularly familiar (e.g. James, individual jokes, but mainly cynicism as such). Two of them proposed a small shift in interpretation of a specific quote. Only three stuck to the deadline.

Many journalists either wrote me they would not have time to read it or did not reply. They, like James, were busy making news.

Return

The last act of the research process began in autumn 2018, when one of the reviewers of the Ph.D. dissertation-based draft of this book recommended that conducting some interviews with European reporters from countries other than Belgium and Czechia could potentially make the book more relevant for a wider audience.

Conducting an additional 14 interviews between mid-November 2018 and mid-January 2019 with Spanish, Danish, Slovak, Dutch, French, German, Italian, Swedish, and Croatian media professionals (typically print/radio/TV reporters, but also a photographer) specialized in crisis zones or in trauma issues, respectively (Judith, Tim, Finn), did much more than that.

Unlike most of the Belgian and Czech interviewees, many were freelancers or independent media professionals. Finding themselves half outside the system of media organizations, their precarity was generally higher and their criticism of mainstream media practices was scorching. At the same time, the diversity of the societies they came from was reflected in the diversity of their gendered experience. Thus, meeting them (albeit in many cases not in person but via Skype, telephone, or various applications[3]) allowed me to include new issues, reflect upon a greater diversity of hierarchies, and re-write the text accordingly.

Like the previous cohorts, the last group of media professionals got the opportunity to comment on the new draft. This time, I received more reactions. Some of them were signed by "Anthony" or "Gloria" instead of by the real names of my communication partners. None of them suggested any changes.

References

Amit, V. (2000). Introduction: Constructing the Field. In A. Vered (Ed.), *Constructing the Field: Ethnographic Fieldwork in the Contemporary World* (pp. 1–18). London: Routledge.

Arksey, H., & Knight, P. (1999). *Interviewing for Social Scientists: An Introductory Resource with Examples*. London: SAGE.

Bauman, Z. (2000). On Writing: On Writing Sociology. *Theory, Culture and Society, 17*(1), 79–90.

Beatty, A. (2013). Current Emotion Research in Anthropology: Reporting the Field. *Emotion Review, 5*(4), 414–422.

Beck, U. (1992). *Risk Society: Towards a New Modernity*. London: SAGE.

---

[3] Therefore, in most cases of this late phase of the research, the assurance of anonymity and of ethical use of the interviews took place electronically, without using standard consent forms.

Beck, U. (2007). The Cosmopolitan Condition: Why Methodological Nationalism Fails. *Theory, Culture and Society, 24*(7–8), 286–290.
Bergman-Blix, S. (2015). Emotional Insights in the Field. In H. Flam & J. Kleres (Eds.), *Methods of Exploring Emotions* (pp. 125–133). London: Routledge.
Bernard, J. (2015). Funerary Emotions: Categorizing Data from a Fieldwork Diary. In H. Flam & J. Kleres (Eds.), *Methods of Exploring Emotions* (pp. 172–180). London: Routledge.
Boltanski, L. (1999). *Distant Suffering: Morality, Media and Politics*. Cambridge: Cambridge University Press.
Bowen, G. A. (2006). Grounded Theory and Sensitizing Concepts. *International Journal of Qualitative Methods, 5*(3), 1–8.
Carpentier, N., & Trioen, M. (2010). The Particularity of Objectivity: A Poststructuralist and Psychoanalytical Reading of the Gap Between Objectivity-as-a-value and Objectivity-as-a- practice in the 2003 Iraqi War Coverage. *Journalism, 11*(3), 311–328.
Caulley, D. N. (2008). Making Qualitative Research Reports Less Boring: The Techniques of Writing Creative Nonfiction. *Qualitative Inquiry, 14*(3), 424–449.
Corbin, J., & Strauss, A. (2007). *Basics of Qualitative Research: Techniques and Procedures for Developing Grounded Theory*. London: SAGE.
Cottle, S. (2009). *Global Crisis Reporting: Journalism in the Global Age*. Maidenhead: Open University Press.
Culler, J. (1997). *Literary Theory: A Very Short Introduction*. Oxford: Oxford University Press.
Czarniawska, B. (2011). *Cyberfactories: How News Agencies Produce News*. Northampton: Edward Elgar.
Czarniawska, B. (2015). The Rhetoric of Emotions. In H. Flam & J. Kleres (Eds.), *Methods of Exploring Emotions* (pp. 67–78). London: Routledge.
Deuze, M. (2005). What Is Journalism? Professional Identity and Ideology of Journalists Reconsidered. *Journalism, 6*(4), 442–464.
Deuze, M. (2011). Media Life. *Media, Culture and Society, 33*(1), 137–148.
Du Gay, P. (1996). *Consumption and Identity at Work*. London: SAGE.
Dubberley, S. et al. (2015). *Making Secondary Trauma a Primary Issue: A Study of Eyewitness Media and Vicarious Trauma on the Digital Frontline*. Eyewitness Media Hub. Retrieved from http://eyewitnessmediahub.com/research/vicarious-trauma.
Ekman, P. (1999). Basic Emotions. In T. Dalgleish & M. Power (Eds.), *Handbook of Cognition and Emotion* (pp. 45–60). New York: John Wiley and Sons.
Ezzy, D. (2002). *Qualitative Analysis: Practice and Innovation*. London: Routledge.
Fay, B. (1996). *Contemporary Philosophy of Social Science: A Multicultural Approach*. Oxford: Wiley-Blackwell.

Flam, H. (2015). Introduction. In H. Flam & J. Kleres (Eds.), *Methods of Exploring Emotions* (pp. 1–21). London: Routledge.
Flam, H., & Kleres, J. (Eds.). (2015). *Methods of Exploring Emotions*. London: Routledge.
Foucault, M. (1988). Technologies of the Self. In L. H. Martin, H. Gutman, & P. H. Hutton (Eds.), *Technologies of the Self: A Seminar with Michel Foucault* (pp. 16–49). London: Tavistock Publications.
Gabriel, Y., & Ulus, E. (2015). "It's All in the Plot": Narrative Explorations of Work-related Emotions. In H. Flam & J. Kleres (Eds.), *Methods of Exploring Emotions* (pp. 36–45). London: Routledge.
Gammerl, B. (2015). Can You Feel Your Research Results? How to Deal with and Gain Insights from Emotions Generated During Oral History Interviews. In H. Flam & J. Kleres (Eds.), *Methods of Exploring Emotions* (pp. 153–162). London: Routledge.
Garfinkel, H. (1967). *Studies in Ethnomethodology*. Englewood Cliffs, NJ: Prentice-Hall.
Geertz, C. (1988). *Works and Lives: The Anthropologist as Author*. Stanford: Stanford University Press.
Genette, G. (1990). Fictional Narrative, Factual Narrative. *Poetics Today, 11*(4), 755–774.
Giddens, A. (1991). *Modernity and Self-Identity: Self and Society in the Late Modern Age*. Cambridge: Polity Press.
Goffman, E. (1967). *Interaction Ritual*. New York: Pantheon Books.
Gutkind, L. (1997). *The Art of Creative Nonfiction: Writing and Selling the Literature of Reality*. New York: Wiley.
Hammersley, M., & Atkinson, P. (1995). *Ethnography: Principles in Practice*. London: Routledge.
Hendry, J. (1992). The Paradox of Friendship in the Field: Analysis of a Long-Term Anglo-Japanese Relationship. In J. Okely & H. Callaway (Eds.), *Anthropology and Autobiography* (pp. 161–172). London: Routledge.
Hesse-Biber, S. N., & Leavy, P. (Eds.). (2008). *Handbook of Emergent Methods*. New York; London: The Guilford Press.
Hochschild, A. R. (1983). *The Managed Heart*. Berkeley: University of California Press.
Illouz, E. (2007). *Cold Intimacies: The Making of Emotional Capitalism*. Cambridge: Polity Press.
Kundera, M. (1988). *The Art of the Novel*. New York: Grove Press.
Latour, B. (2005). *Reassembling the Social: An Introduction to Actor Network Theory*. Oxford: Oxford University Press.
Lutz, C., & Abu-Lughod, L. (Eds.). (1990). *Language and the Politics of Emotion*. Cambridge: Cambridge University Press.

Marcus, G. E. (1995). Ethnography in/of the World System: The Emergence of Multi-sited Ethnography. *Annual Review of Anthropology, 24*, 95–117.

McDonald, I. R., & Lawrence, R. G. (2004). Filling the 24×7 News Hole: Television News Coverage Following September 11. *American Behavioral Scientist, 48*(3), 327–340.

Mirvaldová, H. (1972). Několik poznámek k rozlišení metafory, alegorie a symbolu. *Slovo a slovesnost, 33*(1), 18–24.

Navia, L. E. (1996). *Classical Cynicism: A Critical Study.* London: Greenwood Press.

Neumann, R., & Fahmy, S. (2016). Measuring Journalistic Peace/war performance: An Exploratory Study of Crisis Reporters' Attitudes and Perceptions. *International Communication Gazette, 78*(3), 223–246.

Olsson, E. K., & Nord, L. W. (2015). Paving the Way for Crisis Exploitation: The Role of Journalistic Styles and Standards. *Journalism, 16*(3), 341–358.

Pauly, J. J. (2014). The New Journalism and the Struggle for Interpretation. *Journalism, 15*(5), 589–604.

Pedelty, M. (1995). *War Stories: The Culture of Foreign Correspondents.* London: Routledge.

Post, S. (2015). Scientific Objectivity in Journalism? How Journalists and Academics Define Objectivity, Assess Its Attainability, and Rate Its Desirability. *Journalism, 16*(6), 730–749.

Richardson, L. (1997). *Fields of Play: Constructing an Academic Life.* New Brunswick: Rutgers University Press.

Riemer, J. W. (1977). Varieties of Opportunistic Research. *Urban Life, 5*(4), 467–477.

Rorty, R. (1979). *Philosophy and the Mirror of Nature.* Princeton: Princeton University Press.

Rosaldo, M. Z. (1984). Towards an Anthropology of Self and Feeling. In R. A. Schweder & R. A. LeVine (Eds.), *Culture Theory: Essays on Mind, Self and Emotions* (pp. 137–157). Cambridge: Cambridge University Press.

Schaeffer, J. M. (2014). Fictional vs. Factual Narration. In P. Hühn et al. (Eds.), *Handbook of Narratology* (pp. 179–196). Berlin: Walter De Gruyter.

Scheer, M. (2012). Are Emotions a Kind of Practice (And Is That What Makes Them Have a History)? A Bourdieuian Approach to Understanding Emotion. *History and Theory, 51*, 193–220.

Scheper-Hughes, N., & Lock, M. (1987). The Mindful Body: A Prolegomenon to Future Work in Medical Anthropology. *Medical Anthropology Quarterly, 1*(1), 6–41.

Sin, C. H. (2005). Seeking Informed Consent: Reflections on Research Practice. *Sociology, 39*(2), 277–294.

Tracy, S. J. (2010). Qualitative Quality: Eight "Big-tent" Criteria for Excellent Qualitative Research. *Qualitative Inquiry, 16*(10), 837–851.

Van Loon, J. (2002). *Risk and Technological Culture: Towards a Sociology of Virulence.* London: Routledge.
Van Zoonen, L. (1998). A Professional, Unreliable, Heroic Marionette (M/F): Structure, Agency and Subjectivity in Contemporary Journalisms. *European Journal of Cultural Studies, 1*(1), 123–143.
Vonnegut, K. (2011). *Cat's Cradle.* London: Penguin Books.
Wagner, P. (1994). *A Sociology of Modernity: Liberty and Discipline.* London: Routledge.
Watson, A. (2016). Directions for Public Sociology: Novel Writing as a Creative Approach. *Cultural Sociology, 10*(4), 431–447.
Weick, K. E. (1995). *Sensemaking in Organizations.* London: SAGE.
Wettergren, Å. (2015). How Do We Know What They Feel? In H. Flam & J. Kleres (Eds.), *Methods of Exploring Emotions* (pp. 115–124). London: Routledge.

Open Access This chapter is licensed under the terms of the Creative Commons Attribution 4.0 International License (http://creativecommons.org/licenses/by/4.0/), which permits use, sharing, adaptation, distribution and reproduction in any medium or format, as long as you give appropriate credit to the original author(s) and the source, provide a link to the Creative Commons licence and indicate if changes were made.

The images or other third party material in this chapter are included in the chapter's Creative Commons licence, unless indicated otherwise in a credit line to the material. If material is not included in the chapter's Creative Commons licence and your intended use is not permitted by statutory regulation or exceeds the permitted use, you will need to obtain permission directly from the copyright holder.

Correction to: Crisis Reporters, Emotions, and Technology

CORRECTION TO:

J. Kotišová, *Crisis Reporters, Emotions, and Technology*,
https://doi.org/10.1007/978-3-030-21428-9

The frontmatter of the book has been revised. The open access funding information in the 'Funding' page xv has been updated to:

This work was supported by the European Regional Development Fund project "Creativity and Adaptability as Conditions of the Success of Europe in an Interrelated World" (reg. no.: CZ.02.1.01/0.0/0.0/16_019/0000734) implemented at Charles University, Faculty of Arts. The project is carried out under the ERDF Call "Excellent Research" and its output is aimed at employees of research organizations and Ph.D. students.

The book is partly based on a Ph.D. dissertation thesis entitled "Freezing: An Ethnography of Crisis Reporters," defended in January 2018 at the University of Liège in Belgium and Masaryk University in Czechia. Some of the data that the book is based on had been published in Journalism and European Journal of Communication as a part of the Ph.D. curriculum.

The updated version of the book can be found at
https://doi.org/10.1007/978-3-030-21428-9

© The Author(s) 2022
J. Kotišová, *Crisis Reporters, Emotions, and Technology*,
https://doi.org/10.1007/978-3-030-21428-9_7

C2

A logo has been added to this page.

 EUROPEAN UNION
European Structural and Investment Funds
Operational Programme Research,
Development and Education

 MINISTRY OF EDUCATION,
YOUTH AND SPORTS

Postscript: Travel Slow and Light

Koen Vidal | foreign affairs | San Lorenzo–Brussels

We arrive at 3 p.m. local time, yet it is dark. The air temperature has fallen to −37 °C. Local authorities estimate that the mysterious substance ice-nine has already caused more than 2000 casualties.

The rattling C-130 aircraft felt like a new phase toward the abnormal. Until a few hours ago, I lived in a peculiar ambiguity. The world I had been moving in was of unbearable normality. The familiar airport of Brussels. The stopover at the equally famous Schiphol-Amsterdam. The long KLM flight to Miami. From Miami to San Lorenzo.

Perhaps the strangest thing was the breezy way the Dutch student sitting next to me told me about the round trip through the States she was starting in Florida. The tax-free shops, the always smiling flight attendants, and the pleasant lightness of the student stand in stark contrast with what I have seen over the last few hours, finding myself at the center of the disaster at San Lorenzo.

New casualties occur every hour.

At least we suppose so. The authorities shroud the catastrophe with an odd silence. Silence which does not allow any questions.

After landing, I register with the American customs authorities who have been instructed to escort journalists to the military zone of the airport. A young soldier with an opaque expression checks my documents and the accreditation signed by my editor-in-chief. Then he allows me into a room where a couple of other journalists are already waiting. Most of them are busy tapping on their laptops.

© The Author(s) 2019
J. Kotišová, *Crisis Reporters, Emotions, and Technology*,
https://doi.org/10.1007/978-3-030-21428-9

To my surprise I notice the familiar face of Jean-Claude. He is busy talking to Sophie Schlesinger whom I met on the C-130.

I met Jean-Claude a couple of years ago in a Brussels hotel where a private meeting was taking place between European businessmen and top people of the regime of Congolese President Joseph Kabundu. Jean-Claude approached me and said he knew me from the little picture that sometimes appears with my articles. He said it was funny that I was at a meeting where journalists were actually not wanted at all. "But I'm also a spy and that makes us colleagues today." He gave me his card on which I read that he was military attaché at the Belgian consulate in Lubumbashi, Congo.

Sophie, Jean-Claude, and I decide to travel together around the eerily distorted island. After being released by the military, we jump into Sophie's dirty aquamarine clunker.

On Our Way

Cruising the disaster zone. Buildings, trees, and plants as if melted away. San Lucho, the island's second city, looks like a painting by Salvador Dali: amorphous buildings, bizarre colors, and no living creatures. The world of my fellow passengers on the plane and the world of San Lucho seem to have nothing in common, as if my final destination was another planet.

Jean-Claude's hearty greeting, shared memories, and stories are warming us and protect us from the freeze outside. Sophie smiles. She tells me she once worked with my editor-in-chief. "But now he apparently leaves the heavy work to young talent," she laughs. She starts an anecdote about how my editor-in-chief, who is known not only for his intellectual genius but also for his legendary clumsiness, twice spilled a glass of wine on the dress of the Congolese president's wife during a reception at the American embassy in Kinshasa. "The second time he even suggested the first lady take off her dress so he could take it to a dry cleaner, but that sounded very stupid of course."

I feel bad to interrupt Sophie, but I need to quickly e-mail the first short article I drafted on the plane to *The Mo*.

When it comes to sending articles, I believe in Murphy's Law: if anything can go wrong, it will. Previous experiences taught me that the closer the deadline, the bigger the statistical chance of an unexpected technical problem. "An article is an article only if it's published in the newspaper," I tell Jean-Claude and Sophie. This time Sophie looks at me with a frown:

"Is that so? Is an article in the newspaper always an article? I don't want to be pedantic, but may I ask what you are going to write about? We just arrived. We haven't talked to doctors, we haven't seen the bodies. The researchers at the Center for Disease Control and Prevention (CDC) in Atlanta just arrived yesterday and are not allowed to talk to journalists."

Indeed. The mist that veils everything is making us confused. All we know are numbers and figures. We did not need to come here for numbers and figures.

I try to convince Sophie on the relevance of my first special report from San Lorenzo. "The New York News already wrote a long article about San Lorenzo and the deadly power of Ice-nine last week." Sophie still looks skeptical. I continue my justification. "And dozens of other media and websites had jumped on the story." Jean-Claude intervenes: "All those articles were based on only one American intelligence report. Or, let me be more precise—and what I'm going to say now is off the record, okay? But the report was compiled by a new task force within the intelligence services. My American colleagues, with whom I have worked for years, were sidelined at the outbreak of the disaster and received no information whatsoever. This task force apparently consists mainly of new, young collaborators, some of whom until recently worked for the Pharma giant Loeb & Kinsey and others worked for LA Analyses, that high-tech company on the West Coast that came into disrepute at the end of last year for complicity in the failed coup in Cameroon. Apparently, they work in a highly secure area where even high-ranking intelligence bosses are denied access."

Sophie Schlesinger has clearly heard this story before, because she is by no means surprised. "In other words," she says, "the official story can be true, but it can also be the winner of the next international book award for science fiction."

The landscape around us speaks for itself, though. Whatever ice-nine is, it is not all right. Being allowed to speak to nobody, it seems that finding out more would take some time. But that means I can't write the spectacular story my foreign editor Fred is begging for. I can hear him already moaning and complaining in my head: "Why do you hesitate on such a mega story? The facts are clear, aren't they? We don't pay you to go to San Lorenzo and then write that nothing has happened! Thousands of people are dying, are you going to deny that?" Yet, I decide to wait with the mega story and instead drop a line to Fred. "The Mo needs to wait. There are no facts to stick to yet."

The problem is that no visitors other than the CDC researchers and the military are allowed to stay for more than three days. State of Emergency, they say. Three days of an uncanny road trip ahead of us.

The internet works fine; one push of the send button and my short message is swiftly sent to the newsroom in Brussels.

Ten minutes later comes a text message from my editor-in-chief. "You're right. We need more facts! I just killed the story. Don't worry about Fred. Good luck, travel slow and light. Greetings to Sophie and Jean-Claude."

Index[1]

A
Abbott, A., 51
Abu-Lughod, L., 207
Adam, B., 125
Affect, 9, 52, 58, 94, 98, 102, 109, 143
Affective turn, 15, 145
Agamben, G., 56
Alcohol, 19, 40, 97, 105, 106
Allan, S., 9, 12, 13, 55, 56, 58, 60, 61, 63, 92, 174
Alsup, J., 48
Altamirano, M., 120, 122
Altheide, D., 5, 9, 135
Amanpour, C., 2, 131
American Cool, 17, 21, 99
Amit, V., 201, 202, 213
Andén-Papadopoulos, K., 4, 5, 13, 15, 15n2, 17, 70, 82, 130, 138, 144, 149
Anderson, B. R., 48
Anxiety, 1, 19, 48, 53, 76, 85, 93, 94, 105, 134, 195

Aoki, Y., 18, 19, 174, 181
Arksey, H., 202, 204
Atkinson, P., 201, 202, 204
Audience, 2, 5, 10, 11, 50, 75, 89, 128, 132, 134, 141, 152, 158, 178, 195, 215
Autopilot, 21, 95

B
Backholm, K., 19, 21, 75, 84
Baker, S., 22, 39, 88, 147, 181
Balčytienė, A., 50
Banks, M., 156
Bauman, Z., 190, 198
BBC, 2, 16, 122, 124
Beatty, A., 207
Beck, U., 20, 52, 53, 56–60, 85, 93, 110, 111, 113, 119, 125, 131, 132, 134, 171, 174–176, 203, 206
Becker, L. A., 104, 175
Beckett, C., 3, 5, 13, 16, 132, 141

---

[1] Note: Page numbers followed by 'n' refer to notes.

INDEX

Beck-Gernsheim, E., 53, 59, 85, 93, 113, 174, 176
Behrent, M. C., 120
Bennett, W. L., 12
Ben-Yehuda, H., 3, 9, 12, 35, 42, 123, 159, 175
Bergman-Blix, S., 210
Bernard, J., 84, 103, 156, 172, 214
Berti, C., 134
Bewes, T., 98–100, 148, 158, 178
Bigo, D., 49
Blaagaard, B. B., 14, 15n2
Bleiker, R., 48
Blumer, H., 6
Boltanski, L., 41, 53, 75, 82, 100, 109, 135, 141, 178, 180, 198
Boredom, 70–72, 74, 76, 92, 112, 174, 197–198
Bowen, G. A., 6, 202
Broersma, M., 146, 180
Buchanan, M. J., 19, 20, 95, 108, 111
Bundy, J., 33

C

Camus, A., 119, 121, 143, 177, 178
Carlson, M., 47, 48
Carpentier, N., 13, 42, 87, 135, 136, 138, 144, 145, 163, 180, 192
Castra, M., 103, 156, 172
Caulley, D. N., 189, 191, 197
Champy, F., 147, 179
Charlie Hebdo, 36, 45, 51, 54, 55, 155
Christians, C. G., 13n1, 16
Clifford, L., 19
CNN, 2, 46, 72, 122, 124, 128
CNN effect, 9
Compassion fatigue, 72, 74, 141, 174, 178
Coombs, T. W., 12, 43

Coping mechanisms/strategies, 6, 19, 95, 105–112, 133, 141, 174
Corbin, J., 213, 214
Cordaro, D., 175
Cottle, S., 3, 9, 10, 12, 44, 59, 60, 78, 109, 205
Coverage, 8–13, 15, 17, 32, 38, 70, 71, 123, 124, 144, 145, 158
Creative nonfiction, 189–215
Creech, B., 88, 88n2, 89, 125, 128, 182
Crisis, viii, 1–22, 29–64, 69–113, 119–164, 171–183, 194–196, 199, 202–205, 207, 214, 215
Crisis reporting, viii, 1–22, 30–63, 79, 90, 92, 99, 107–110, 112, 128, 129, 135, 142, 144, 153, 163, 173, 176, 177, 179, 180, 182, 196, 203, 205, 206, 209, 210, 214
Crofts Wiley, S. B., 4, 7, 120
Culler, J., 136, 190, 196, 197
Cynical ideology, viii, 101, 148, 159
Cynicism, 17, 21, 73, 80, 81, 98–102, 105, 112, 148–149, 158, 174, 177–179, 181, 182, 196, 214
Czarniawska, B., 71, 122, 125, 202, 204, 209

D

Danger, 6, 29, 31, 32, 39, 40, 42, 43, 56, 60, 75, 82, 87–90, 92, 101, 112, 125, 126, 139, 148, 162, 163
De Peuter, G., 39
Debord, G., 178
Deleuze, G., 119, 143
Depression, 9, 19, 75–77, 174
Detachment, 3–5, 13–15, 21, 45, 63, 86, 90–92, 130, 136, 138, 141, 144, 159, 163, 192, 207

Deuze, M., 3, 5, 13, 15n2, 16, 63, 87, 89, 119, 132, 141, 144, 147–149, 158, 177, 179, 192, 203, 207
Doswald-Beck, L., 112
Du Gay, P., 7, 42, 48, 120, 154–156, 158, 163, 171, 173, 210
Dubberley, S., 4, 17, 18n4, 19, 20, 74, 76, 78, 105, 110, 112, 174, 198

E
The Economist, 49
Ekman, P., 175, 208
Elias, N., 15, 98, 179
Emotional labor, viii, 3, 16–22, 42, 103, 120, 135, 143, 147, 154, 156, 181, 204, 209
Emotional management, 102, 103, 146, 173, 177, 208
Emotional style, 16, 17, 21, 74, 93n3, 95, 97, 97n4, 102, 103, 105, 110, 112, 146, 148, 154, 156, 163, 171, 173, 174
Emotions, viii, 1, 6–13, 47, 70, 94–105, 119, 134–143, 171–183, 193
Empathy, 3, 15, 21, 76–79, 81, 92, 94, 112, 146, 147, 173, 180, 199
Engagement, 4, 5, 16, 45, 62, 75, 93, 104, 135, 141, 179, 180, 193, 197–199, 210
Entman, R. M., 11
Ethics, 74, 124, 148, 157, 179, 214
Ethnography, 205, 206
Ezzy, D., 189, 190, 193, 197, 204, 207, 211, 213, 214

F
Faction, 190
Fahmy, S., 5, 9, 110, 153, 159, 180, 205

Falkheimer, J., 3, 11–13, 15, 33, 47, 91, 124, 135, 158
Fay, B., 193
Fear identity, 76, 77
Feinstein, A., 19, 105, 174
Festinger, L., 85, 141
Field, 5, 6, 10, 14, 15, 19, 33, 34, 37, 38, 40, 44, 49, 54, 62, 70–73, 76–78, 84, 92, 93n3, 100–102, 106–109, 124, 127, 128, 131, 133, 144, 153, 157–159, 176, 196, 199–204, 210, 212, 213
Fieldwork, vii, 34, 35, 151, 199–202, 204–206, 211–213
Fischer, D., 180
Fixer, 51, 88, 89, 125, 126, 182
Flam, H., 93, 208, 209
Fleming, P., 100, 177
Foucault, M., 7, 100, 103, 119–121, 134, 143, 144, 149, 152, 154, 155, 171, 173, 176, 179, 203, 204, 210
Franks, 136, 137, 144, 146, 163, 173, 193

G
Gabriel, Y., 208
Galtung, J., 9, 72, 180
Gammerl, B., 210
Garfinkel, H., 208
Geertz, C., 190, 193
Genette, G., 189–193, 197
Giddens, A., 52, 53, 56, 58, 59, 102, 109, 131, 175, 176, 203
Glück, A., 4, 20, 76, 81, 98, 146, 147, 149, 173, 180
Goffman, E., 102, 208
Greene, R. W., 7, 120
The Guardian, 2, 77
Guattari, F., 119

Guilt, 2, 3, 19, 21, 41, 53, 72, 76, 79, 81–87, 92–94, 112, 174
Gutkind, L., 191

H
Hallin, D. C., 9–11, 91, 102
Hammersley, M., 201, 202, 204
Hanitzsch, T., 89
Hansen, M., 4, 119, 160
Harbers, F., 146, 180
Harcup, T., 9, 44, 45, 59, 72, 153
Hay, J., 7, 120
Hayward, M. R., 4
Heaphy, B., 20, 52, 53, 56
Heidegger, M., 119, 171, 176–178
Henckaerts, J. M., 111
Hendry, J., 200
Hesmondhalgh, D., 22, 39, 88, 147, 181
Hesse-Biber, S. N., 193, 195
Hight, J., 4, 17, 20, 76, 105, 174
Hjarvard, S., 9
Hochschild, A. R., 7, 17, 85, 93, 95, 103, 120, 135, 137, 141, 154, 160–163, 177, 204, 207–209
Høiby, M. H., 18, 70, 75, 105, 108, 125, 126
Hopper, K. M., 3, 16, 19–21, 84, 95, 97, 107, 111
Hoskins, A., 5, 9, 12, 91, 110
Hutchison, E., 48
Huxford, J., 3, 16, 19–21, 84, 95, 97, 107, 111

I
Idås, T., 19
Identification, 48, 75–79, 81, 82, 91, 92, 112, 135, 141
Illouz, E., 7, 17, 93, 93n3, 97, 102, 137, 146, 154–156, 158, 162, 171, 177, 207–209

Impartiality, 13, 15, 63, 136, 138, 144, 147, 163, 192, 207
Inside-the-media crisis, 32–43, 63, 123, 174, 203
Interviews, vii, 2, 10, 35, 37, 41, 90, 111, 120, 131, 197, 199, 202, 204–208, 211, 213–215, 215n3
Inwood, M., 176

J
Joelving, F., 2
Johnson, M., 161
Journalism, 3, 30, 54–58, 70, 125, 173, 193
Journalism of attachment, 180
Journalism research, 3, 6
Journalists' professional ideology, viii, 13, 70, 82, 83, 138, 144, 148, 149, 172, 173, 177, 179
Jukes, S., 20, 21, 90, 95

K
Kaleta, O., 56
Keats, P., 19, 20, 95, 108, 111
Kleres, J., 93, 208, 209
Knight, P., 202, 204
Knights, D., 177
Knüpfer, C. B., 11
Koselleck, R., 30, 56, 174
Kotišová, J., 19
Kynicism, 99–101, 105, 112, 179

L
Lakoff, G., 161
Lasch, C., 53
Latour, B., 129, 173, 205
Lawrence, R. G., 7, 11, 15, 47, 56, 73, 123, 124, 151, 158, 207
Leavy, P., 193, 195

INDEX 229

Lewis, S. C., 47, 48
Lievrouw, L. A., 4, 119, 130, 132
Literary journalism, 3, 146
Livingstone, S., 10
Lock, M., 7, 20, 40, 53, 85, 93, 94, 113, 119, 161, 174, 207
Lorey, I., 156
Lull, J., 135
Lupton, D., 60, 61
Lutz, C., 207

M
Marcus, G. E., 205, 206
Marthoz, J. P., 18, 112
Massumi, B., 143
McDonald, I. R., 7, 11, 15, 47, 56, 73, 123, 124, 151, 158, 207
Measurers, 136, 137, 144, 146, 163, 173
Media organizations, vii, 5, 6, 12, 19, 31, 33, 59, 61, 63, 73, 74, 78, 85, 86, 88, 89, 91, 101, 108, 111, 113, 124, 125, 131, 139, 140, 144, 149, 150, 152–158, 172, 179, 181, 182, 200, 206, 213, 215
Mejias, U. A., 91, 92
Mental health, 19, 20, 98, 106, 111, 181
Metaphor, 160–162, 194–197, 194n1
Methodological cosmopolitism, 206
Mirvaldová, H., 194n1
Moeller, S. D., 72, 74, 141, 174, 178
Molinier, P., 103, 156, 172
Moral dilemma, 41, 63, 81–87, 92, 112
Mortensen, V., 119, 121, 143, 177

N
Narrative journalism, 139, 180, 182
Natural disaster, 4, 9, 11, 17, 20, 22, 43, 52, 69, 77, 80, 108

Navia, L. E., 99, 100, 102, 148, 197
Neumann, R., 4, 9, 110, 153, 159, 180, 205
Neveu, E., 180
New Journalism, 139, 146, 189
Newsmaking, 6, 8, 13, 20, 21, 32, 99, 102, 110, 121–163, 171, 174, 176, 177, 201, 204
News production, 7, 87, 105, 122, 123, 127–129, 131, 163, 209
News values, 9, 11, 44
Newswork, 4, 7, 16, 33, 59, 85, 87, 89, 93, 125, 128, 211
New York Times, 92
NGO, 89, 181, 183
Nord, L. W., 5, 11, 12, 14, 15, 32, 33, 44, 72–74, 95, 123, 124, 126, 127, 144, 145, 174, 202, 203

O
Objectivity, 4, 5, 8, 13–17, 20, 21, 62, 135, 138, 139, 141, 144–147, 149, 173, 179, 182, 193, 207
Observation, 32, 72, 202, 204, 208, 211–213
O'Loughlin, B., 5, 9, 12, 91, 110
'Olsson, E. K., 3, 11–15, 32, 33, 47, 91, 123, 124, 126, 135, 158, 174, 202, 203
O'Neill, D., 9, 44, 45, 59, 72, 153
Organizational identity, 131, 149–156, 163, 171
Orlikowski, W. J., 7, 119, 120, 122, 131, 163, 171, 173
Örnebring, H., 50, 71
Ottosen, R., 18, 70, 75, 105, 108, 125, 126
Outside-the-media crisis, 32–43, 63, 123, 174, 202, 203

P

Packer, J., 4, 7, 120
Pang, A., 11, 124
Pantti, M., 4, 5, 13, 15, 15n2, 17, 20, 70, 82, 83, 130, 138, 144, 146, 149
Parachute reporter, 22, 71, 125, 129, 205
Parenting, 79–81, 92, 112
Parikka, J., 119
Pauly, J. J., 4, 16, 138, 146, 180, 189
Peace journalism, 153, 180
Pedelty, M., 19, 34, 39, 42, 56, 70, 76, 85, 87, 90, 98, 99, 102, 106, 125, 127, 173, 174, 196, 205, 210
Peters, C., 3, 14–17, 32, 42, 46, 48, 99, 102, 103, 135, 146, 154, 156, 161–163, 172, 173
Plaisance, P. L., 138
Positivists, 136, 141, 144, 146, 163
Post, S., 145, 193
Post-traumatic stress disorder (PSTD), 1–4, 18, 19, 79, 104, 105, 174
Power, viii, 4, 5, 7, 10, 43–45, 62, 92, 109, 112, 129, 130, 143, 144, 149, 150, 153, 154, 156, 163, 172, 176, 177, 203, 208
Precarity, viii, 22, 38, 39, 87–89, 125, 128, 156, 163, 178, 181–183, 215
Precarization, 87, 156, 178
Privilege, 72, 90, 181
Professional boundaries, 48
Professional identity, 16, 48, 80, 102, 112, 145, 147, 210
Professionalism, 4, 8, 13–17, 19, 32, 136, 142, 144, 146–148, 157, 173, 179
PTSD, *see* Post-traumatic stress disorder

R

Rayner, T., 120, 154, 176–178
Rees, G., 5, 15, 19, 21, 105, 129, 145, 149, 174
Reinardy, S., 19, 73, 105, 174
Reuters, 1, 2, 124
Richards, B., 5, 15, 19, 20, 105, 129, 145, 149, 174
Richardson, L., 190
Riemer, J. W., 201, 205, 211
Right distance, 21, 103, 156, 172
Romano, C., 14
Rorty, R., 192
Rosaldo, M. Z., 7, 93, 94, 119, 154, 207
Rosen, J., 14, 80
Rosenkranz, T., 87
Rovira, S. C., 145
Ruge, M. B., 9, 72
Ruigrok, N., 146, 180
Rutten, E., 92

S

Sambrook, R., 4, 20, 105
Schaeffer, J. M., 189, 191, 192
Scheer, M., 7, 93, 94, 119, 209
Scheper-Hughes, N., 7, 20, 40, 53, 85, 93, 94, 113, 119, 174, 207
Schudson, M., 14, 56, 110, 136, 144, 147, 163
Seeger, M. W., 12, 33, 44
Self-precarization, 156, 178
Sellars, J., 103, 105, 175
Sellnow, T. L., 12, 33, 44
Sensemaking, 85, 148, 203, 208–210, 214
Sensitizing concepts, 6, 7, 202
September 11, 12, 14, 42, 54–58, 73, 76, 91, 94, 128, 144, 147, 158, 162, 181
Shaheen, K., 2

INDEX 231

Sin, C. H., 213
Skewes, E. A., 138
Skovsgaard, M., 147, 173
Sloterdijk, P., 100–102, 148, 177–179
Smyth, F., 4, 17, 20, 76, 105, 174
Sontag, S., 75, 129, 157
Sorribes, C. P., 145
Spectacularization, speactacle, 58, 178, 180
Spicer, A., 100, 177
Sreberny, A., 42
Stearns, P., 17
Steensen, S., 142, 173
Stiegler, B., 107
Stoicism, 104
Strauss, A., 213, 214
Stress, vii, 1, 4, 9, 32, 37n2, 38, 39, 41, 43, 45, 53, 76, 96, 112, 126, 131, 138, 146, 163, 174, 182, 193, 197, 212
Strömbäck, J., 5, 11, 12, 33, 44, 72–74, 95, 123, 124, 127, 144, 145

T
Takahashi, B., 32, 42, 46, 48, 63
Tandoc, E. C., 32, 42, 46, 48, 63
Technologies of power, 7, 120, 135, 143–156, 162, 163, 171, 172
Technologies of production, 7, 120–135, 151, 152, 162, 171, 173
Technologies of sign systems, 7, 120, 134–143, 152, 162, 163, 171, 173
Technologies of the self, 7, 95, 120, 135, 155–163, 171, 210
Technology, viii, 6–8, 15n2, 21, 36, 47, 60, 78, 110, 113, 119–163, 171–183, 195, 202, 203, 209, 214

Terror, 9, 22, 34, 36, 37n2, 50–53, 55, 69, 77, 91, 94, 124, 131, 143, 153, 155, 207, 210, 211
Thoits, P. A., 175
Thoresen, S., 37n2
Thorsen, E., 15n2
Tong, J., 110, 147
Touraine, A., 56
Tracy, S. J., 203, 204, 214
Trauma, 3, 17–22, 38, 39, 41, 42, 48, 75, 78, 90, 105–111, 175, 181, 215
Trioen, M., 13, 42, 87, 135, 136, 138, 144, 145, 163, 180
Tuckey, R. M., 4
Tulloch, J., 60, 61
Tumber, H., 4, 5, 9, 16, 19, 46, 48, 50, 81, 145, 181

U
Ulus, E., 208
Urbániková, M., 173
Usher, N., 110, 142, 180

V
Väliaho, P., 20, 182
Valorization, 178
Van Der Meer, TGLA., 3, 7, 9, 35, 42, 123, 124, 135, 159, 175
Van Leuven, S., 3, 11, 33
Van Loon, J., 9, 29, 57, 60, 61, 119, 127, 131, 132, 134, 151, 171, 175, 178, 195
Van Zoonen, L., 16, 48, 80, 145, 158, 207
Vincze, H. O., 6, 30, 174
Vokuev, M. E., 91, 92
Vonnegut, K., 194
Vos, T. P., 14, 144

W
Wagner, P., 30, 52, 56, 58, 174, 203
Wahl-Jorgensen, K., 5, 16, 109, 110, 135, 137, 141, 142, 146
Waisbord, S., 87
Walaski, P., 43
War, 2, 4, 9, 10, 12, 16–18, 20, 22, 37, 38, 42, 43, 46, 48, 52, 53, 55, 56, 58, 60, 69, 73, 76, 77, 80, 84, 89, 91–92, 111, 112, 125, 127, 132, 144, 157, 181
War correspondent, 55, 70, 71, 87, 99, 101, 131, 173, 205
Watson, A., 198

Weick, K. E., 44, 85, 131, 163, 203, 209, 214
Wettergren, Å., 210
Wiik, J., 136, 163
Williams, R., 119, 171
Willmott, H., 177
Witschge, T., 87, 89

Y
Yates, D., 1

Z
Zelizer, B., 9, 12, 13, 55, 56, 63, 92, 174

The manufacturer's authorised representative in the EU is Springer Nature Customer Service Centre GmbH, Europaplatz 3, 69115 Heidelberg, Germany. If you have any concerns regarding our products, please contact ProductSafety@springernature.com

Printed and bound by CPI Group (UK) Ltd, Croydon, CR0 4YY

23/03/2026

02076663-0003